FORM AND FUNCTION

IN CHICANO ENGLISH

Jacob Ornstein-Galicia
EDITOR

NEWBURY HOUSE PUBLISHERS, INC.
Rowley, Massachusetts 01969
ROWLEY • LONDON • TOKYO

1 9 8 4

Library of Congress Cataloging in Publication Data
Main entry under title:

Form and function in Chicano English.

    Bibliography: p.
      1. Mexican Americans--Language--Addresses, essays,
lectures.   2. Mexican Americans--Education--Language
arts--Addresses, essays, lectures.   3. English language
--Dialects--Southwestern States--Addresses, essays,
lectures.   4. Bilingualism--Southwestern States--
Addresses, essays, lectures. I. Ornstein-Galicia,
Jacob, 1915–
PE3102.M4F6 1983   427'.00896872073   83-8094
ISBN 0-88377-295-7

Cover design by Barbara Frake

NEWBURY HOUSE PUBLISHERS, INC.

Language Science
Language Teaching
Language Learning

ROWLEY, MASSACHUSETTS 01969
ROWLEY • LONDON • TOKYO

First printing: February 1984
Printed in the U.S.A.   5   4   3   2   1

CONTENTS

ACKNOWLEDGMENTS

Sincere appreciation is hereby expressed for a grant from the National Endowment for the Humanities, Washington, D.C., of which this book is a partial outcome. May I also recognize the valuable assistance of Dr. Joyce Penfield, Rutgers University. At the University of Texas, El Paso, let me acknowledge material support from the Center for Border and Inter-American Studies, the Vice President for Academic Affairs, and various types of assistance from the Dean of Liberal Arts, the Office of Contracts and Grants, and the Cross-Cultural Southwest Ethnic Study Center. I should include, too, members of the Linguistics Department and Angie Soto, Executive Secretary. Finally, to many who gave suggestions but who are too numerous to mention, my profound thanks, which go in full measure as well to the Staff of Newbury House Publishers, especially in Editorial and Production, who displayed persistence and expertise, as well as helpfulness, in this enterprise.

As they say in the publishing world, it is a long ways to "30."

Jacob L. Ornstein-Galicia
Volume Editor

INTRODUCTION

One of the most neglected areas of the language field
is ethnic varieties of English. At the first conference
on Form and Function in Chicano English, Raven McDavid,
pioneer dialectologist, declared that there was virtually
no full-length study of an ethnic dialect of English, save
for Einar Haugen's *Norwegian Language in America*. Considering the current importance of cultural pluralism, as
opposed to the melting pot ideal, it seems high time to
alter this situation.

Indeed, in the present volume we address precisely
this lacuna. In preparing a volume on Chicano English,
the editor, pursuing a long-time interest in the Hispanic peoples of America, seeks to bring about a better
understanding of the Mexican-American variety of English
spoken with variations by many, if not most, Chicanos in
the Southwest and elsewhere.

An estimated 10 to 12 million people, Mexican-Americans, make up the largest foreign language population
in the United States. Nevertheless, comparing the amount
of sociolinguistic work done on Black English with the
speech of U.S. Hispanics, one finds that the latter trails
woefully behind.

The stimulus for this volume came from a grant received from the National Endowment for the Humanities,
awarded to the University of Texas at El Paso in 1981.
As a result, it became clear that there was need for a
volume that would elucidate the main aspects of form and
function in Chicano English. No such work exists at present. While no pretense is made of in-depth converage of
the entire topic, the present volume consists of essays
by most of the individuals who have been involved in
some kind of Chicano research. It should be of use to
all those interested in language variation, bilingualism,
sociolinguistics, and the speech of minority groups in
general. It goes without saying that it should have
special appeal to Hispanicists and teachers of Hispanics.

The book is divided into five sections which cover,
immodest as this may sound, the highlights of Chicano
English. The first section, The Linguistic Dimension,
both defines and describes what is meant by Chicano
English. The mood is set here by two disciples of
William A. Labov--one of the most outstanding socio-
linguists of the world--John Baugh and Benji Wald.
Baugh, basing himself on the mistakes made by researchers in the early descriptions of Black English, outlines some of the potential problems that may affect
an adequate definition of Chicano English. Significantly,
he stresses the nature of varieties of English under
social pressure as being dynamic and ever-changing as
opposed to static. Wald, in "The Status of Chicano
English as a Dialect of American English," argues

convincingly for the autonomous status of Chicano English
as a dialect with its own norms rather than its being an
imperfect English. Unlike others in this field, he leans
heavily on observation of the speech behavior of monolingual Chicano English speakers of one particular region,
East Los Angeles.

In a seminal essay entitled "The Range of Chicano
English," Gustavo González illustrates that English spoken
by Chicanos is not necessarily homogeneous but rather
ranges from that reflecting a high degree of interference
to that of convergence with Standard English. He offers
a variety of different syntactic structures to stress the
point that Chicano English can refer to a broad range of
structures, stretching from those reflecting a high degree of interference to those almost totally converging
with Standard English.

Quantitative analysis of acoustic data carried out at
the UCLA Phonetics Lab is provided by Manuel Godinez who
compares the vowels of monolingual General California
English speakers with Chicano English speakers. Finally,
in this section, Joyce Penfield presents some new hypotheses and findings about prosody from empirical field
data of natural conversations between Chicano bilinguals
in informal settings. Although recognized as an important, obviously distinguishing, feature among varieties
of English, prosody is a field badly neglected by scholars of ethnic language varieties.

Since there is so much concern nowadays regarding
reading skills and literacy in our schools, readers will
surely welcome the remaining papers which examine the
interplay between vernacular Chicano English and Standard English. First of all, Herrick describes and discusses the reflexes too often neglected in our interplay
of the spoken on the written word. The situation as explicated by Joyce Penfield in "The Vernacular Base of
Literacy Development in Chicano English" is far more
complex than a straight contrastive issue which simplis-
tically draws on two Standard languages since a dialect
is at issue here.

In the second section of the book, The Sociocultural
Dimension, we attempt to look at some of the sociopsychological aspects of bilingual Chicanos. The first
essay by Maryellen García deals with the dynamics of
Chicano communities and should forewarn us against
over-generalizing about them. Next, the dean of research
on Chicano psychology, Manuel Ramirez III, contributes
an essay on "The Chicano Bilingual, Cultural Democracy
and the Multicultural Personality in a Diverse Society."

The third section, Investigating Chicano English,
is concerned with how research on Chicano English has
been done and what should be researched in future
studies. One of the pioneers of American dialectology,
and a senior editor of the Dialect Atlas of the U.S.
and Canada, Raven McDavid, shares with the readers many

of the lessons learned and the challenges remaining in
the field of dialect studies. This is followed by discussions of investigations of Chicano varieties. First,
the Pan American University Project in the Lower Valley
of Texas at Edinburg is described by Jon Amastae. Next,
Jacob Ornstein-Galicia, Betty Lou Dubois, and Bates
Hoffer tell of their work in working with the corpus of
the El Paso sociolinguistic survey. Jacob Ornstein-
Galicia rounds out the section by advocating networking
as a partial solution to the problem of scarcity of researchers in this field and the logic of collaborative
endeavor.

In the brief section entitled Chicano English in the
Mainstream, attempts are made to look realistically at
societal reactions to Chicano English in a variety of
different modes of communication, including literary
and oral media as well as speech. A panel discussion on
"The Right to Have an Accent," coordinated by Joseph
Perozzi, gives the views of several professionals in the
speech field: Joe Martinez, a speech instructor at a
local community college; Gilda Peña, a speech therapist
in the public school system, and Hector Serrano, a
speech and drama instructor and Director of Bilingual
Theater. Turning to primarily the literary media in the
genre of Chicano literature, Fritz Hensey investigates
the use of Chicano English, along with Willard Gingerich
who focuses on some stylistic devices of Chicano writers.

The volume ends with a brief annotated bibliography
of the major writings on Chicano English, prepared by
Allan Metcalf.

Although it would be an exaggeration to say that all
problems have been examined and solved, the scope and
thrust of this book should recommend it to all serious
students of language variation in general and varieties
of English in particular.

SECTION I:
THE LINGUISTIC DIMENSION

1

CHICANO ENGLISH: THE ANGUISH OF DEFINITION

John Baugh
Department of Linguistics
University of Texas at Austin

The Chicano English community is highly diversified, to say nothing of the other varieties of Hispanic English in the United States. Like Black Vernacular English (BVE), Chicano (vernacular) English is a nonstandard dialect, but this is where the similarity ends. Most of my research on English dialects has looked at nonstandard black speech. The research trends and precedents that have been established for BVE can in turn help future studies of Chicano English. At this stage let it suffice to say that Chicano English is a more complex phenomena, in purely linguistic terms, due to the combined population of monolingual Chicano English and bilingual Chicano English speakers. Black English by contrast consists of a spectrum of dialects within a monolingual paradigm.

As we shall see momentarily, this is an intricate phenomena, because of several linguistic and social factors. My title is drawn from the fact that the Chicano English community is dynamic, and it will continue to be so in the face of continued migration from Mexico. Four general topics will illustrate the point: we will first review the history of Chicano English dialect. Next we will turn to the nature of contemporary (i.e., synchronic) linguistic variation, which, again, is more complex than the corresponding variation in BVE. These observations are going to set the stage to consider the dynamic nature

of the Chicano English population, and the added dimension
of group loyalties, which are reinforced by language and
dialect use. In the final analysis we shall observe that
Chomsky's notion of "linguistic competence" must also be
taken into account in any adequate definition.

Those who are familiar with BVE research will observe
that I have retraced the major themes that grew out of the
early sociolinguistic research trends for Black English.
By outlining the same topics for future Chicano English research, we can perhaps avoid some of the mistakes that have
been made in the past. Black English research has given
rise to other productive studies of language around the
world. By comparison, Chicano English research has been
sorely neglected. As with previous research on nonstandard
dialects in the United States, the ultimate practical value
will be felt in pedagogical terms, when more Chicanos have
an opportunity to gain competitive insights from our observations and suggestions. It is my hope that my brief
remarks point out the scope and magnitude of the issue.

THE EVOLUTION OF CHICANO ENGLISH

The majority of the American population has very
little idea of the richness of the Mexican heritage in the
United States. I will not be providing a detailed survey
of that contribution here, but it should be noted that the
major urbanization of the Southwestern United States was
established by Spanish-speaking people, and the names of
several major cities in the Southwest stand as a testa-
ment to that early settlement. Chicano English is therefore quite old when compared to other ethnic varieties of
English that came to the U.S. with the waves of European
immigrants. However, like the blacks, Native Americans,
and Orientals, the actual history of Chicanos, and their
culture, has been distorted through time and reinforced by
stereotypes. García (1981) illustrates the history of
Chicano English in terms of the generation in which a
family came to reside in the United States. Paraphrasing
her observation, there are some Chicanos who do not speak
Spanish. These individuals are typically members of third-
generation families, where their grandparents were among
the first Chicanos to move to the U.S. There are, of
course, many exceptions across each generation; many tend
to be balanced bilinguals, or they may be dominant in
English with some Spanish borrowings. The more recent arrivals, by contrast, shift emphasis in the direction of
Spanish, such that there is a population of first generation arrivals that know little or no English at all.

Concentrating for the moment on English, we would expect to find a continuum, similar to that described by
Bickerton (1973) for varieties of Guyanese English, spanning between nonstandard Chicano English and impeccable
Standard. The variety of Standard English could be influenced by regional or national norms; thus, standard

Chicano English in Texas may sound different from standard
Chicano English in California. Although some have argued
that the history of Black English has also resulted in a
continuum, Chicano English evolves within a stable bilingual situation, whereas BVE has been tied to a pidgin/
creole history. This is due to the fact that black slaves
were separated from others who spoke their native tongue
upon capture, presumably to eliminate communication and
the potential for uprisings. Spanish speakers, on the
other hand, have gained exposure to English in much the
same way as have other non-English immigrants. The native
language, in this case Spanish, is preserved in the barrio
while the younger generations come to learn English through
increased exposure. As an individual, or perhaps a family,
gains wealth and education, there is increased emphasis
on using standard varieties of English.

In this respect the history of Chicano English is like
every other nonstandard variety of English in the United
States. Insiders know that there are negative stereotypes
about their speech outside of their community, and this
results in several responses. Some call for making the
United States a bilingual nation, pointing to the size and
continued growth of the Spanish-speaking population.
Others, with equally good intentions, say that we must
teach English to everyone as soon as possible so that they
can "melt into the pot." If there is a fact that history
has shown us, and that is echoed in the dialect diversity
that exists today, it is that some immigrants have melted
at a faster rate than have others, and this has historically followed strong racial and ethnic boundaries.

The history of Chicano English, then, is highly diversified, where various Chicanos speak more than one style
of English. Up to this point I have not focused on the bilingual dimension, but it is very relevant. This is where
the question of linguistic competence first appears; some
speakers of Spanish will borrow English words, but for my
purpose here I will not include them within the Chicano
English community because of their lack of proficiency.
In the remainder of the paper I will be referring to Chicano English as any variety of English spoken by a Chicano
who can conduct conversations in English exclusively. This
definition will therefore include Chicanos who are not
competent in Spanish, but borrow elements of Spanish in
their English usage. These distinctions will become clear
in the next section where we look at the variable nature
of modern Chicano English.

VARIATION ALONG TWO LINGUISTIC CONTINUA

The main reason why it will be difficult to define
Chicano English, in terms of a traditional fixed definition, lies in the variable nature of the styles of English
and Spanish that are used. The Black English situation

serves, once again, to illustrate the complexity of the task. In Figure 1, we see the entire Black English population. The vernacular community, that is, the most non-standard speakers, are comprised of those black Americans

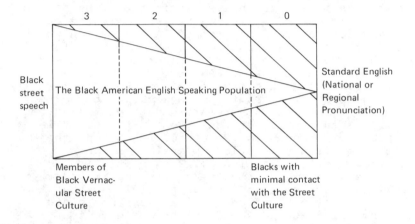

The combination of social domains (that is, Living, Working, and Recreational Situations) where blacks primarily interact with other members of the street culture

FIGURE 1   The Black American English Speech Community

who have minimal contact with whites. They primarily interact with other members of the vernacular black culture in their living, working, and recreational situations. This is represented by the decreasing progression from 3 - to - 0 in Figure 1. Other blacks, included in the right three quadrants of the figure have contacts with nonblacks (primarily whites) in some combination of the preceding social domains. In this case the dialect is distributed along a continuum, although it would be wrong to suggest that all black Americans are part of the same speech community. It would likewise be misleading to suggest that all Chicanos are members of the Chicano English community.

If we extend the same interactional criteria to the Chicano community we get a very different picture due to the vital bilingual influence. While Black English experiences linguistic change within an English grammatical system, the constant influx of monolingual Spanish speakers replenishes a bilingual cycle, the same cycle that has faced every generation of Hispanics to come to the United States. Thus, if a Chicano has limited exposure to non-Chicano English speakers, then it is quite possible,

even likely, that the speaker will need to command fluent
Spanish. There is, nevertheless, a small population that
has limited contact with non-Chicanos, but limited proficiency in Spanish. Figure 2 outlines the bilingual founda-
tions of Chicano English, and, with slight modification,
can be extended to other Hispanic and bilingual communities
in the United States.

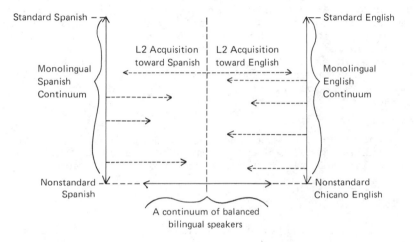

FIGURE 2   Spanish/English Bilingualism in the United States

Here we must contend with two linguistic continua.
Even though our interest is focused on Chicano English, it
does not exist in linguistic isolation. The center line of
Figure 2 represents the balanced bilinguals. These people
are fluent in both languages. Often they are second or
third generation immigrants who have been exposed to Spanish
at an early age. There are thousands of exceptions, however, among the older populations, even first generation
immigrants, who made tremendous personal sacrifices to
learn English. The vertical parameters at the left and
right of the figure correspond to monolingual speakers of
Spanish and English respectively. In both cases speakers
may control more or less standard varieties, that is,
monolinguals and bilinguals alike will control styles of
one or both languages that fall somewhere on the scale
between the standard and nonstandard vernacular. At the
extremes, then, we find the monolinguals, with the center
line representing a continuum of balanced bilinguals. The
limitation in this illustration is that an individual
balanced bilingual may know a nonstandard variety of one
language while controlling a more standard variety of the

other; this will rely very much on personal experience
and several other factors. Generally speaking, we find
that educated speakers tend toward the standard in both
languages, due in large measure to their formal training.
Others, primarily among the less educated populations,
may speak nonstandard varieties of both languages.

Having considered the extremes, including monolinguals
or balanced bilinguals, there are vast numbers of others
who are in the process of learning a second language, be
it English or Spanish, who are not yet balanced bilinguals,
but they are moving in that direction as a result of formal training or increased personal exposure to L2. These
individuals have marginal competence in L2, and they may
produce utterances that are identical, in surface forms,
to that of a balanced bilingual who is "code-switching."
In other words, a balanced bilingual may produce the following sentence:

They can go, y tu tambien, if we have enough money.

However, the same sentence could be produced by an English
speaker with marginal Spanish competence. Similarly, a
balanced bilingual might produce the following sentence:

*Her suegros are from Tennessee y los van a traer
y quieren llevarlos a una corrida de toros.* (Valdés,
1976)

which would more readily be understood by another bilingual
speaker.

The main point that Figure 2 illustrates is the fluid
nature of the bilingual/monolingual exposure that faces
Chicanos. This of course brings the anguish of definition
to mind once again. Peñalosa (1980) provides detailed discussion of Chicano English in his book on Chicano sociolinguistics. He observes a disproportionate amount of research on Spanish, while Chicano English has been neglected by comparison. A critical aspect of any adequate definition must establish the thresholds of fluency that de-
lineate members of the Chicano English community. Scholars
may in turn decide to divide performance ability and per-
ceptive competence, because most people tend to comprehend
L2 long before they become fluent speakers of it.

As Shuy (1980) observed, minority scholars have often
encountered frustrations when they bring their deep personal concerns to social science. In linguistics it has
often been necessary to examine idealized data to develop
formal theories, but the consequence of this tradition is
to examine language as one would a series of still photo-
graphs. The variable nature of Chicano English defies
this kind of idealized categorization. It would be much
more appropriate to think of Chicano English as part of a
linguistic circulatory system. To the best of my knowledge it seems that speakers of Chicano (vernacular) English engage in several different linguistic styles depending on what a given situation calls for. In the case

of balanced bilinguals we might expect code-switching to occur (see Poplack, 1979). On other occasions, the balanced bilingual and monolingual English speakers may style-shift within English exclusively. Thus, when Chicano students attend public schools they may use one style of English with their teachers, and another with their peers on the playground. Similar analogies can be found for the adult populations as well.

Because the Chicano English community includes non-standard vernacular dialects along with Standard English as spoken by Chicanos, we should expect the variation that is presented in Figure 2 to be stable for quite some time. However, if past practice is a fair indication of what we should expect for the future, it will be important to make clear distinctions between the special problems that face speakers of Chicano English; that is, as opposed to the problems of Native American bilinguals, or Black English bidialectals. In the face of shrinking educational budgets there may be a tendency to continue the past practice of simply placing all minorities in the same "language arts" basket; namely, consisting of those populations who do not speak Standard English. As we shall see below, the shared plight of poverty should not imply that various minority groups will be able to use the same language arts strategies to compete on an equal footing with their Standard English counterparts.

DYNAMIC AND FIXED MINORITY POPULATIONS

One need only look at the migratory patterns of minority groups to appreciate their linguistic differences. The Native Americans have seen their mother tongues dwindle, for several well-known historical reasons. Black Americans, on the other hand, are the only American minority where non-English immigrants (i.e., captured slaves) were separated from others who spoke their native African language. This unique linguistic history has given rise to the contemporary bidialectal systems between black street speech (or rural vernacular speech), and more standard varieties of American English. Both of these groups contrast with the situation affecting Chicanos and the varieties of English they speak.

Black speech patterns are changing within an English grammatical system, and there are no longer large numbers of new black minorities, with the possible exception of new Haitians, that will not know some dialect of English as their native language. Hispanics who speak English will encounter a greater range of diversity, because, unlike Native American bilingualism, Spanish is a language with a long-standing written tradition, in the well-known sense of Western culture. And, like all other languages that are spoken in advanced industrial societies, there are some dialects of Spanish that are associated with

poor and/or social elites. Chicano English, then, when
viewed as the varieties of English spoken by Chicanos, regardless of their different linguistic and social experience, is broad indeed.

Another dimension of the Black English situation that
does hold some analogies lies in the need to distinguish
nonstandard varieties of vernacular Chicano English from
the more standard styles of Chicano English, namely, those
that are indistinguishable for Anglo Standard English.
Gonzalez (1974) observes that many middle-class Chicano
families in the U.S. stress the learning of Standard English. However, personal attitudes and spontaneous group
loyalties can be embraced or denied by different ways of
speaking. If the Chicano English situation reflects the
black English pattern, and this should be established em-
pirically, then we would expect individual speakers to
shift their manner of speaking depending on several factors. These factors would include the immediate participants in the speech event, the location of the conversation,
and the topic(s) under discussion. It would be wrong to
suggest that any individual has a fixed style of speech,
and others stratify above or below that particular point.
Rather, different people will control various ranges of
styles; for Chicanos this could include stylistic ranges
in English or English and Spanish, depending on the degree
of bilingual proficiency.

Even when an individiual is a competent bilingual, or
a competent bidialectal, having the ability to use various
styles at will, it is often difficult to predict how speakers will respond to different speaking contexts. This can
be attributed, at least in part, to the competing values
that are conveyed through this spontaneous linguistic selection. For example, imagine a situation where a young
Chicano is talking to his teacher. If some of his friends
walk by, there may be a noticeable shift in the phonology
in the direction of vernacular Chicano English. This type
of shifting conveys group loyalties, and the pride of individuals is often linked closely with their native colloquial dialects. In the following section we conclude our
discussion with the most perplexing definitional problem
of all: How do we establish the factors that influence
dialect loyalties and related linguistic behavior?

DIALECT LOYALTY

Every group that has migrated to the United States
from some foreign land, especially those where English is
not the native language, have experienced a period of
transition. Again, this alludes to the well-known melting
pot myth. The simple fact of the matter is that white immigrants have always melted at a faster rate. Race has always been a larger social barrier than that of a foreign
accent, but a foreign accent or nonstandard dialect can
reinforce social borders, especially when race is a factor.

It is largely for this reason, and the social isolation that has existed among various groups in America, that long standing stereotypes are perpetuated.

The question of dialect loyalty has therefore caused scattered responses, because some members of these groups made every effort to adopt American behavior, including language, as soon as they possibly could. Others, by choice or social exclusion, developed subcultural norms that were shared among intimates of their minority. When poverty and the pervasive lack of educational and economic opportunities are taken into account, those who feel that they are in a "good" social position try to avoid contact with those groups that they feel are less fortunate. The minority group, recognizing these competeing norms, is faced with a paradox. Some have become highly educated, mastering the same norms and behaviors as the social elites. The opposite, of course, holds true for those who reject all things associated with the dominant culture. So, the individual members of the minority group, be they black or brown, may find that their group loyalties are tested as they are judged in two societies.

The competitive nature of American society rewards cultural homogeneity; this is simply a historical fact and is not intended as a value judgment. Nevertheless, when the language of family and friends is linked with a stigmatized dialect, one that is judged negatively by others who are in a relative position of social power, then it is possible for the individual speaker to feel a sense of frustration. This will continue to be the case in the Hispanic community as more and more people come to develop different strategies for their personal survival.

The terms *Uncle Tom* and *Tio Taco* have sprung from the vernacular communities in response to the fact that some members of the racial group have abandoned, or at least are perceived as having abandoned, the masses of less fortunate people who remain in the ghetto/barrio. The fact of the matter is that loyalties are capricious commodities. As Goffman (1959) observes, a single individual may behave in the presence of close friends in ways that are very different from circumstances where there are no friends to judge that behavior. While I have no solution for resolving this paradox, which I consider to be natural, it has a direct impact on Chicano English.

In this paper I have tried to outline some of the considerations that scholars and interested laypersons will want to take into account as studies of Chicano English grow and mature. We have witnessed several major advances in sociolinguistics in the past twenty years, and the number of interested students, educators, and parents has grown tremendously in that time. My main objective has been to outline some of the potential problems that will affect an adequate definition. I base these observations, in part, on mistakes that were made in the early descriptions of Black English; they tended to be quite simplistic, and, by extension, unrealistic. The fact of the matter is that language, to say nothing of languages in change under social pressure, are not static. If I have provided any useful information at all it lies in the recognition that vernacular Chicano English, like other nonstandard dialects of American English, is a dynamic and everchanging linguistic system. Since so much of this research will serve as the foundation of educational and social policies, we must take care not to treat all Chicanos or Hispanics as if they have been stamped out of a single casting. It is my sincere hope that our combined efforts will give rise to precise analyses of these dialects, and that these studies ultimately serve the needs of the entire Chicano population.

REFERENCES

Bickerton, Derek. 1973. "The Nature of a Creole Continuum." *Language* 5(49): 640-669.

Chomsky, Noam. 1965. *Aspects of the Theory of Syntax*. Cambridge, Mass.: M.I.T. Press.

García, Maryellen. 1981. "Spanish-English Bilingualism in the Southwest." In Bruce Cronnell, ed., *The Writing Needs of Linguistically Different Students*. Los Alamitos, Cal.: SWRL Educational Research and Development.

Goffman, Erving. 1959. *The Presentation of Self in Everyday Life*. New York: Doubleday-Anchor Press.

González, Gustavo. 1974. "The Acquisition of Questions in Texas Spanish." In Garland O. Bills, ed., *Southwest Areal Linguistics*. San Diego, Cal.: Institute for Cultural Pluralism, San Diego State University, pp. 251-266.

Peñalosa, Fernando. 1980. *Chicano Sociolinguistics: A Brief Introduction*. Rowley, Mass.: Newbury House.

Poplack, Shana. 1979. "Sometimes I'll Starta Sentence in Spanish Termino en Español: Toward a Typology of Code-Switching." New York: Center for Puerto Rican Studies, City University of New York. Working Paper #4.

Shuy, Roger. 1980. "Foreword." In Fernando Peñalosa, *Chicano Sociolinguistics: A Brief Introduction*. Rowley, Mass.: Newbury House.

Valdés, G. 1976. "Code-Switching Patterns: A Case Study of Spanish/ English Alternation." In G.D. Keller, R.V. Teschner, and S. Viera, eds., *Bilingualism in the Bicentennial and Beyond.* New York: Bilingual Press/Editorial Bilingue, pp. 58–85.

2

THE STATUS OF CHICANO ENGLISH AS A DIALECT OF AMERICAN ENGLISH*

Benji Wald
National Center for Bilingual Research
Los Alamitos, California

The varieties of English spoken by Mexican-Americans throughout the U.S. are referred to collectively as Chicano English. Until recently, the concept of Chicano English had not received much attention in the form of study or analysis. The compendious bibliography of Teschner, Bills, and Craddock (1975) extending to the mid-1970s lists a small number of minor works, mostly from the perspective of error analysis in educational settings, but no major works. To a large extent the reason for this neglect was based on the assumption, ultimately of folk origin, that the English of Mexican-Americans

*The research on which this paper is based is an outgrowth of the assistance through support and encouragement of the Chicano Studies Center of UCLA in 1976, and NIE-funded research at NCBR. Of course, this support does not imply the endorsement by any of these institutions of any ideas and/or conclusions expressed in this paper. I want to specifically acknowledge the assistance and aid of Adelaida del Castillo, Steve Gomez, and Carmen Silva-Corvalan in particular phases of this research. Finally, I would like to acknowledge and thank all participants to the conference at which this paper was first delivered for stimulating discussion and insight into the topic of Chicano English, and congratulate Dr. Jacob Ornstein-Galicia for consolidating and organizing a conference specifically addressed to the issue pursued in this paper.

could be explained entirely in terms of bilingualism,
and the effect of Spanish on the English of individual
speakers. This notion, that the obstacle to the acquisition of Standard English (defined below) is nothing other
than knowledge and use of Spanish, is pervasive in the
bulk of the literature up to the mid-1970s. Thus, for
example, in one of the first anthologies representing a
selection from more than half a century of scholarship
on the language(s) of Mexican-Americans, the editors note
in their introduction:

> For the most part, divergencies from Standard English
> are the result of incomplete learning even in the
> case of those speakers whose English is no longer
> changing. For such speakers their English grammars
> share many rules with their Spanish. . . (Hernández-
> Chavez et al., 1975, p. xii)

An influential piece of evidence in support of this
assumption is Sawyer's much reprinted study of Spanish-
English bilingualism in San Antonio, Texas (Sawyer, 1959).
Sawyer's study, which is based on the pronunciation in the
reading of a word list by seven Spanish-English bilinguals, found that the two U.S.-born speakers with college
education had the least number of phonological features
attributable to Spanish in their speech. Urban dialectologists have criticized studies of this type for their
unrepresentativeness of the population and inadequacy of
methods for eliciting data representative of everyday
speech (cf. Labov, 1972; Wolfram and Fasold, 1974;
Underwood, 1974). Students of bilingual communities have
proposed that members of such communities may develop
their own linguistic norms for vernacular use, as distinct
from the norms of adjacent monolingual communities, and
certainly from the Standard language (cf. Gumperz, 1966;
Ma and Herasimchuk, 1968). Thus, we may find that some
features historically associated with Spanish, or a stage
in the acquisition of English, have become norms of
English for some segments of the Mexican-American
population.

One of the earliest indications of a shift in point
of view, concerning the English of Mexican-Americans as
a distinct entity deserving study in its own right, comes
from a study by Thompson (1974). In sampling census
tracts in Austin, Texas, Thompson reported that language
shift away from Spanish toward English has accompanied
urbanization of Mexican-Americans in that city, so that
speakers born in Austin report less use of Spanish with
children and peers than those born and raised in rural
areas outside Austin. His conclusions, based on self-
report data of language use, are more visionary than
substantive with respect to development of the concept
of Chicano English, but reflect the perspective further
developed in this paper.

. . . since most Mexican-Americans live in urban
centers, if language shift is in progress, it is
urgent that the study of Mexican-American English
as well as Mexican-American Spanish be emphasized.
As the third and fourth generations in the city
come to predominate in Mexican-American neighborhoods, the language problems will not be those of
Spanish interfering or competing with English, but
of a nonstandard dialect of English conflicting with
Standard English. (Thompson, 1974, pp. 77-78)

The term "Chicano English" (note that Thompson used
the term "Mexican-American English" in the above quote)
received increased attention with the publication of
Metcalf's (1978) study using that title. Metcalf's study
indicates very little further development of the research
on Chicano English compared to the perspectives represented in Teschner et al.'s bibliography referred to above.
However, Metcalf's survey includes some brief studies
indicating further attention paid to distinctive features
of the English spoken by monolingual Mexican-Americans,
for whom Spanish transference is not a direct issue (e.g.,
Gingras, 1978). By the time of the appearance of
Peñalosa's (1980) survey of Chicano sociolinguistics, it
was still possible for him to indicate the paucity of
studies addressed to Chicano English.

The most obvious discrepancy in the field of Chicano
sociolinguistics is that between the extensive use
of English in the Chicano community and the paucity
of serious studies concerning varieties of English
used by Chicanos. Thus, while English is the
dominant Chicano language, especially among the youth
(this varies regionally and locally), there are
but a handful of studies of Chicano English, as
contrasted with the dozens of studies of Chicano
Spanish. (Peñalosa, 1980, p. 115)

Thus, while the study of Chicano English has not seen
much substantive growth in the last decade, recognition
of the importance of the concept shows steady increase in
the last few years. Admittedly, more could be said about
the reasons for the growth and limitations on attention
paid to Chicano English until recently. However, at this
point, the main point of this paper will be introduced as
the further development of the concept of Chicano English,
and what is involved in making it a viable concept among
the dialects and varieties of American English.

We will be concerned with Chicano English as a
linguistic entity. As a social entity, it is to be clearly
understood that Chicano English represents the English
spoken by members of the Chicano and/or Mexican-American
community, a complex community consisting of speakers of
a great variety of bilingualism or monolingualism in

English and Spanish, but united by a common ancestry in the Southwestern U.S. and/or Mexico. Given both the diversity and commonalities of the community, the primary question arises: How is this state of affairs reflected linguistically in the English spoken by members of the community?

In the study of the varieties of English spoken by Mexican-Americans, the following questions appear to me to be of primary importance in assessing their statuses among dialects of American English.

1. In any particular Mexican-American community, what is the nature of the English spoken by both *monolinguals* and *bilinguals*?
2. To what extent do Mexican-Americans share English norms *across* different local communities and what are the *reasons* for this?
3. To what extent does contact with speakers of other varieties of English affect the varieties spoken in separate local Chicano communities?

There will be an attempt to substantively illustrate the direction of the answers to these three questions at the end of this paper.

VARIETY IN AMERICAN ENGLISH DIALECTS

To begin with, we must note that dialectological and sociolinguistic research has established that American English consists of a series of dialects, distributed across various geographically local, socioeconomic, and ethnic groups. The Standard is relatively uniform in American English, and differs from the British Standard only minimally in syntax, somewhat more noticeably in lexicon, and most noticeably in phonology. Since, from a linguistic point of view, the Standard is no less a dialect than other varieties of English, I use the term "vernacular" to refer to the dialect of any locally based speech community. In contrast with the Standard, which in principle does not have local connotations, vernaculars are first-learned varieties within a community, and tend to differ most in phonology and lexicon, and to a lesser degree in syntax, from each other and from the Standard. Different dialects of English (including the Standard by the definition above) share many, probably a majority of linguistic features with each other--which gives coherence to the linguistic concept of English, whether American or worldwide. Some vernaculars are closer to the Standard and to each other than others. Thus, the American Standard, which is currently *r*-ful, i.e., *four* instead of *fou'* (with syllable-final *r* either vocalized or not pronounced at all), is less similar in this respect to the vernaculars of most East Coast and Southern communities than to the vernaculars of other areas of the U.S.

Besides local dialects of English, there are features of English which repeat themselves in different local communities, and have been associated with socioeconomic differences within the communities. Thus, in phonology the stop pronunciation "t" and "d" for [θ] and [ð], as in *three* or *this*, "-in" for unstressed word-final *-ing*, as in *talkin(g)* or *somethin(g)*, have been found to be more frequently among lower SES (socioeconomic status) speakers in all studied communities, whether American or British, than among higher SES speakers in the same communities (cf. Labov, 1972; Trudgill, 1974; Wolfram and Fasold, 1974). Similarly, in syntax, frequency of use of multiple negation, as in *I don't want nobody talkin' to nobody about nothin'* has a similar distribution according to SES, independent of locale.

Finally, research beginning in the 1960s has established the existence of ethnic dialects of American English, associated more with the ancestral origin of a group of speakers than with locale or SES, of which Vernacular Black English (VBE) is the most well established. Although there is local variety in VBE, there is great homogeneity across local communities in a number of features, particularly syntactic, which distinguish it from other varieties of English. A prime example is invariant *be*, associated with a durative or habitual meaning, as in *he always be givin' me trouble*, contrasting with *he('s) givin' me trouble right now*.

Thus, it is quite clear that American English dialects differ in features associated with locale, SES, and ethnicity, and, of course, all three at once. The discussion so far is summarized below, followed by three examples:

Standard: a set of norms associated with media and written language.

Vernacular: a set of norms used among *local* members.

SES: sets of norms associated with SES differences *within* and *across* local communities.

Ethnic: sets of norms associated with ethnic differences *across* local communities.

(1) four (Standard) [fɔər]
     (most Eastern and Southern vernaculars) [fɔ(ə)]
(2) Higher SES (more frequent) fricative: this thing
     (standard negation) I didn't see any.
     Lower SES (more frequent) stop: "dis ting" (still dental)
     (multiple negation) I didn't see none.
(3) Ethnic (VBE) He be drivin' that green Riviera.
     (W 19m, SLA)
     (nearest standard or unmarked equivalent) He's the one who drives that green Riviera.

CHICANO ENGLISH

     Chicano varieties of English differ from most
dialects of English by including bilingual as well as
monolingual speakers. Both types of speakers live in the
same communities, and are often members of the same
families. The term "Chicano English" has been used in
various contexts to cover many things, from the English
of monolingual third generation Mexican-Americans to early
stages in the acquisition of English by adult or child
Spanish speakers--what I call the English of *recent
learners*.
     To the extent that all these types of speakers are
living in the same community and/or have frequent contact
by means of English, we can speak of Chicano English as a
community-based variety of English having not only local,
SES, and ethnic dimensions, but also bilingual dimensions.
     Figure 1 schematizes the maximum speaker range
pattern of interaction understood by the term "Chicano
English."

monolingual →——— ← bilingual

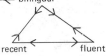

                  recent   fluent

             (long-term or indigenous)

FIGURE 1   Chicano English: Maximum Speaker Range

     Considering the vitality of Spanish in most Chicano
communities, not to deny the extensive use of English,
especially among second generation youth in talking to
each other, the issue of *continuity* of English spoken by
bilingual and monolingual Chicanos is of great interest.
     Because the state and evolution of Chicano English
independent from Spanish is still largely unknown, one
research strategy tends to narrowly base Chicano English
on only monolingual speakers. However, it is an empirical
issue, although not without its analytical problems, to
determine the extent to which the nature of the English of
bilingual Chicano speakers is influenced on an *individual*
level by their Spanish. At the crux of this issue is the
old linguistic issue of *nature* vs. *convention* (cf. Plato,
1963).
     The *nature* position is that, given speakers of Ll
(Spanish), the nature of the English they will speak is
predictable through the interaction of Spanish and
English, *without* consideration of the social context or
the *target* varieties of English to which the speakers
are exposed. In this case, a feature of L2 (English) is
not, strictly speaking, a social *norm*, but an individually
transferred pattern. This position would have to explain

agreement in use among different individuals through
independent creation rather than through mutual influence.
To use a stereotype of Chicano English on the popular
level as well as in the more learned literature, an
extreme form of this position would predict that a
Spanish speaker moving to English from a /ch/-dialect of
Spanish (as opposed to a /sh/-dialect) would inevitably
arrive at the pronunciation *CHoose* for English *shoes*, or
even more interestingly, *naCHion* for *nation* without exposure to such a pronunciation through other speakers.

A *convention* position would have to recognize the
varieties of English, both bilingual and monolingual, the
speaker is exposed to, and admit the possibility that
different conventional strategies for the stages of
acquisition of English may exist in different communities. An extreme form of this position might state that,
regardless of the ultimate origin of the pronunciation
CHoose for *shoes*, the speaker is using it because he or
she has learned it from other English speakers. These two
positions are summarized below.

> *Nature:* There is no social norm. Given source (L1)
> and target (L2) alone, the outcome is predictable,
> e.g., *CHoose* for *shoes* regardless of exposure to
> *CHoose* (for *shoes*).
> *Convention:* There is a social norm. Speaker says
> *CHoose* because she or he has heard others say it.

In the rest of this paper I will take up these
issues, focusing on one variety of Chicano English which
I call East LA English.

EAST LA ENGLISH

East Los Angeles (ELA) is the center of a long-
standing and overwhelmingly Mexican-American community,
and is, by all counts, the largest Chicano community in
the U.S. Because of its dimensions, it is a strategic
site for studying the formation of a distinct dialect of
English, historically based on a Spanish substratum, but
not necessarily currently propelled by it. In the
absence of accurate data, our impression is that both
Spanish and English are widely used in the community.
Spanish is more widely understood than spoken. According
to social rules of language use in the community, Spanish
is not the language of contact among strangers, unless
out of necessity. In some areas we have studied, Spanish
is stigmatized among children and adolescents, and may
be under-reported for use, despite our observations that
those who can use English fluently usually do in preference to Spanish. Nevertheless, the English spoken by
these age groups and others in ELA is distinctive,
although in some respects it superficially resembles the
English of recent learners of Spanish-speaking background.
However, these resemblances are indeed superficial, and it

is easy to distinguish ELA English from the English of
recent learners. Some of the differences will be discussed presently.

In some respects the community resembles the
situation in which a pidgin is said to develop into a
creole; i.e., a new generation is most immediately exposed
to a language (in this case English as L2) which is non-
native to the older generation. Thus, the first variety
of English acquired in ELA must have been learned primarily
from non-native speakers. However, unlike the creolization
situation, most non-native speakers would have been from
the *same* language background (i.e., Spanish), so that
whatever transfers to English from Spanish that arose at
that time were likely to reinforce each other rather than
be leveled out through reduction of heterogeneity. In
addition, native English models from adjacent communities
are accessible both through the Anglo media and through
personal contacts. We have evidence that these indeed
play a role in shaping *some* aspects of the language toward
local Anglo norms, e.g., the stigmatization of palatal
confusion.[1]

ELA English speakers, bilingual as well as
monolingual, lack many of the features that characterize
recent learners of English. This is especially obvious
in phonology; e.g., there is no anaptyctic vowel before
an initial *sC* cluster, although this is commonly observed
among recent learners from Mexico. On the other hand,
syllabification pressures, which may have a Spanish as
well as a nonstandard English source, sometimes lead to
simplification of the initial cluster in spontaneous
speech. This tendency is more common, however, in medial
and especially final position. The examples below illustrate these differences.
(4) *Initial sC anaptyxis* (recent learner)
     a. I e-spend one day, not very muSH. (E 25m, Jalisco
        to LA at 19)
     b. Kathy i-smokes a lot now. (G 20f, Zacatecas to LA
        at 16)
(5) *Initial sC reduction* (ELA English)
     a. You know that movie s'ar . . . (N 19f, ELA)
     b. I know he ain' s'upid . . . (M 16m, CC)
(6) *Final sC reduction* (ELA E)   (N 19f, ELA)
     like in the mornin' I eat uh one sof' boil' egg with
     a toas'_.

Interestingly, our current research indicates that
final cluster reduction in ELA English is distinct from a
similar process among LA Anglo speakers, in that Anglo
speakers rarely reduce final clusters before a pause
(also a feature of the Philadelphia vernacular English
pattern), whereas ELA English very commonly does (as in
the New York City and BE vernaculars cf. Guy, 1976).
Example (7) (Table 1) illustrates this clearly.

(7) Monomorphemic (e.g. toas(t))			-ed (e.g. boil(ed))		
C	P	V	C	P	V
ELA 91%	85%	66%	61%	44%	22%
(11 spkrs)					
WLA 56%	33%	27%	29%	31%	04%
(6 spkrs)					
(N: 290	108	137	101	30	120
221	70	111	75	26	146)

Table 1. Comparison of the mean values of final cluster reduction for
a sample of East LA Chicano speakers and West LA Anglo
speakers. (The environments following the final cluster
are C = consonant, P = pause, V = vowel. The underlining
indicates that P is similar to C among the ELA speakers, but
similar to V among the WLA speakers.)

Concerning variety among Chicano dialects, it is
interesting to note in this context that one older
speaker, who learned English in his teens in Southeast
Texas and has been in ELA for 50 years (since age 21),
has many features of speech that are not found in ELA
English. Among them, he uses anaptyxis both initially as
in:

(8) I don' know how the people can ə-stand it (OS 71m)

and very commonly, internally to avoid a cluster at a
morpheme juncture:

(9) The engine room is the one who keepəs the steam
    goin' . . . He was naməd as the ambāssador to England...

This shows that while anaptyxis distinguishes the
English of recent learners from ELA English, it does not
necessarily distinguish it from *all* dialects of Chicano
English.

Another difference between recent learners of ELA
English speakers is the well-known recent learner
phenomenon of *palatal interchange*. Thus, recent learners
exhibit palatal interchange between Standard and dialectal
English *j* and *y* (one phoneme in Spanish), e.g., pronunciations like *jeer* for *year*, and even *danᵞerous* for
dangerous. But this is not found among English speakers
who grew up in ELA. On the other hand, interchange
between fricative and affricate palatals is commonly
found, although it tends to be stigmatized, in ELA. This
applies to both the pairs *j* and *ž*, and *č* and *š*, so that
on occasion *major* may sound like *measure*.[2]

Example (10) indicates the general difference between
the patterns of palatal interchange of recent learners
and ELA English speakers.

Example (10) indicates the general difference between the patterns of palatal interchange of recent learners and ELA English speakers.

(10)   *recent learner*   *ELA English*

   y ∿ ǰ ∿ ž   y:: j ∿ ž

         č ∿ š   č ∿ š

While the phoneme ž rarely occurs in spontaneous speech, and is largely confined to medial position, we found much interchange of č and š in ELA English, but particularly among bilinguals (cf. Wald, 1979). Detailed analysis revealed that for many speakers CH and SH were distinct phonemes despite the interchange, and that the interchange occurred regardless of the type of Spanish spoken, i.e., whether the Spanish was a /č/ or a /š/ or a mixed dialect. The distinction was demonstrable in that for speakers, a word like *choose* was more often pronounced with CH than a word like *shoes* was, while the reverse was true for *shoes*. Furthermore, speakers were largely unaware of this feature in their own speech, but were aware of the stereotype. This presented a rather unusual case among dialects of English, where two phonemes were distinct but totally overlapping. Since monolingual ELA English speakers showed only residual traces of this feature, we concluded that palatal interchange was not a *stable* dialect feature which would be transmitted to future generations, but rather a communal reflection of a process I have called *unmerger*, by which speakers learn to distinguish two phonemes which occupy the space of a single phoneme in their first language. Whether or not the feature might have become stable in the absence of the heavy stigmatization to which it is subjected remains a matter of conjecture, but one of great importance to the notion of possible linguistic system.

As for the possible routes to unmerger, it is noteworthy that the *medial* palatal interchange found in ELA was not found for the speaker OS, mentioned above in (8). He kept č for CH words but used *sy* or š for SH words both in Spanish and English. The suspicion that Latin cognates common to English and Spanish helped him in this strategy was confirmed by his pronunciation of *prison* as *priSHon*, under the influence of Spanish *prisión*. This possible strategy was not evident in ELA English. OS demonstrates that the type of palatal interchange found commonly in ELA is not inevitable. Thus, there is the possibility of a *conventional* basis for why ELA English speakers follow the route they do.

Of further interest is that č for š was extremely rare in final position in ELA, but was found more strikingly among some Texan Chicano speakers. Again there may be a conventional basis for this difference from ELA English. On the other hand, the kind of speaker mentioned by Edwards and Doviak (1975) for Albuquerque, New Mexico, who varies CH as č, š, but keeps SH intact, was not found in ELA English. But in this case, the prevalence of a /s/-dialect of Spanish is suspected. The reverse case of a woman from Casagrande, Arizona, who kept CH invariant, but varied SH was found in our research. In (11) below, different local types of palatal interchange discussed above are summarized. Further research may confirm that dialect differences both in the Spanish sources and the community conventions for unmerging English phonemes are responsible for these differential patterns.

(11) *Local types of palatal interchange*

	INITIAL (choose:shoes)		MEDIAL (nature:nation)		FINAL (much:mush)	
	CH	SH	CH	SH	CH	SH
ELA	č∿š	š∿č	č∿š	š∿č	č∿š	š (č, *rare*)
OS (cf 8)	č∿š	š∿č	č	š∿š̌(y)	č	š∿s
OA (Az) (Casagrande)	č	č	č	č∿š	-	č∿š
E&D N.M. (Albuquerque)	č∿š	š	č∿š	š	č∿š	š

One distinctive and stable feature of ELA English found throughout the LA area for Mexican-Americans, and claimed to be a hallmark of California Chicano speech, is the pronunciation of *el* as *al*, so that *fell* sounds like *fall* on occasion (cf. Metcalf, 1979, p. 10).[3] Spectrography showed that the vowel is in the *a* rather than the *ae* range (cf. Wald, 1980). This appears to be further development of a feature found less prominently in the Anglo community. Possibly it began as a reinterpretation of the Anglo feature by speakers who restructured English to a 5-vowel system of Spanish. A study of ELA speakers of three generations showed that the bilingual speakers (generation 1 and 2) had total or partial overlap of *e* and *ae*, but assigned *el* as in *belt*, *fell*, *tell* to the *a* range. The younger speaker, who had a clear distinction between *e* and *ae* continued to keep *el* in the *a* range. In (12) below, this feature of EL-retraction (to AL) is summarized for the three speakers.

(12) *El-retraction (as in bell, fell, "LA", etc.)*

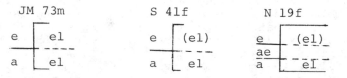

The pervasiveness of this feature among Chicanos in Southern California is an important piece of evidence that there are ethnic features of Chicano English which do not

derive directly from Spanish, but unite various local
Chicano communities.

As a final example, I want to move on to a *syntactic*
feature of ELA English, which illustrates the complexity
of sources and influences on this Chicano English dialect.

MULTIPLE SOURCE NORMS AND SYNTAX

In syntax more often than in phonology, the problem
of multiple possible sources for a feature developed in a
bilingual or formerly bilingual community is evidence.
Among the examples discussed above in phonology, final
cluster reduction is attributable to several sources: a
general trend toward syllable simplification found widely
among languages, the specific Spanish prohibition on
final clusters, and the general nonstandard English
variable associated with SES status and ethnicity (VBE).
Thus, in ELA English, final consonant cluster reduction
is an example of multiple source norm. It has several
possible sources, in both languages.

One common syntactic feature in ELA English is
subject/auxiliary inversion in embedded WH-questions
(hereafter referred to as EQW). Speakers using this
sentence type produce utterances such as:

(13) ... then they asked them where did they live.
     (AR 12m)   T   S

In (13) above, T refers to the tense-marker (past
in did) and S to the subject of the embedded question.
The standard version of the same sentence would be:

(14) ... then they asked them where they lived.
                                  S   T

Note that in the standard version, the subject (S)
precedes the tense-marker (T, past in lived). Both types
are commonly used, even in late preadolescence (ages 10-
12), according to our research.

There are many possible sources for this
construction. It is common in many varieties of nonstandard English. In VBE, where the nonstandard form is
most well developed, it also applies to embedded yes/no
questions, as in:

(15) Hey, tell 'er- ask 'er cn I come over n talk to her.
     (D 18m, SLA)   T S

In ELA English, yes/no questions are always embedded
with if, as in Standard English, even among 10 to 12-year-
olds, e.g.:

(16) we asked him if we could go. (VM 12f)
                  S   T

Beside the nonstandard English source for EQW, and
the Standard English source of the embedded yes/no

question, there is a Spanish source for both constructions, and especially one which differentiates the two
types of embedded questions, e.g.:

(17) EQW   no sé donde se fué su amigo.
                         T   S

    EQ-Y/N   no sé si su amigo ya se fué.
                        S   T

The similarity is that in the Spanish EQW, the tensed
element (which consists of the entire verbal predicate)
precedes the subject, as in the nonstandard English EQW
construction. For the embedded yes/no question the subject tends to precede the tensed element (and accompanying predicate), even though the rules of Spanish word order
allow freedom of subject/predicate positioning for this
construction, just as for independent main clauses.

    There is also a developmental dimension to the EQW
construction (although, interestingly, not for the
embedded yes/no question). Thus, Cazden et al. (1975)
note in their study of Spanish-speaking recent learners
of English, that at first the speakers did not invert
subject and auxiliary (which contains the tensed element)
in either main or embedded questions. However, as inversion developed in main questions, it spread to embedded
clauses for WH-questions (only, as far as the report
specifies).

    Unlike Standard English, Spanish does not distinguish
main and embedded questions for WH-questions (although it
does for yes/no questions). Thus, once speakers had
acquired the auxiliary structure for inversion in main
clauses, the identification of no distinction between WH-
for main and embedded clauses can be transferred from
Spanish.

    Since the model for EQW does exist in nonstandard
English, as well as in Spanish, we cannot easily conclude
that the extension is natural rather than convention
on the basis of development.

    In addition to the factors for convergence on
subj/aux inversion of EQW in ELA English discussed immediately above, there is a functional reinforcement which
may also play a role. This involves the use of the verb
tell for *ask* among both children and adults in ELA.
Either *ask* or *tell* is used to introduce embedded questions
of any type. With embedded yes/no questions it is clear
in either case that the embedding is a question, since
if must introduce a question, e.g.:

(18) So my daughter as'es me if she could stay with
     her friend. (SL 42f)

    So my father wen' n tol' me in a nice way if I
    wanted to get married or go home. (same speaker)

    However, with EQWs, the structure is ambiguous on
the surface without inversion if *tell* is used, since

tell, unlike *ask*, also introduces assertive complements, e.g.:

(19) So she goes to the doctor n the doctor <u>tells</u> her <u>why is she nervous</u>. (SL 42f)

In cases like (19), only the subj/aux inverion (T-S order) signals that the embedded complement is a question, contrast:

(20) ... n the doctor <u>tells</u> her <u>why she's nervous</u>.

(cf. that's <u>why she's nervous</u>.)

In (20) above, there is no signal that the embedded complement is a question rather than an assertion. To the extent that the verb *tell* is used to introduce an interrogative clause, the inversion in the WH-, but not the yes/no, embedded question is necessary to signal the distinction between the two types of complements.

Given these diverse motivations, the use of the inverted EQW is, in itself, neither an indicator of monolingualism or bilingualism, nor of fluency or lack of it in an English vernacular.

CONCLUDING REMARKS

In view of the preceding discussion, we can now offer some preliminary answers to the three questions asked at the beginning of this paper.

1. In ELA there are both differences and similarities in the varieties of English spoken by members of the Chicano community. In the case of CH-SH interchange, we have seen differences across various Mexican-American communities. This may reflect different Spanish bases, different community solutions to unmerger, different individual solutions, or an interaction of any number of these motivations. In East LA, extensive CH-SH interchange is most common among bilinguals. Monolinguals exhibit the feature to a much smaller degree, if at all. On the other hand, subj/aux inversion in EQW and the use of *tell* for *ask* appears to be common to all types of speakers.

2. There are various reasons why features are shared across Chicano communities to the extent that they are. Independent development from a Spanish base, and from pervasive features of neighboring nonstandard English dialects, may both affect development of the ELA English system. Among syntactic norms for which sources in both languages are available, we have discussed final cluster reduction and inversion in EQW. The EL-retraction case has an English base, on which LA area Chicano communities have innovated to a great degree.

3. The influence of neighboring dialects involves comparing Chicano English with neighboring dialects. It is expected that in many ways Chicano English will share many local and SES-associated features with neighboring dialects. Certainly, the retreat of such features as palatal interchange, where the feature is salient and its Spanish origin is stigmatized, owe their origin to neighboring dialects. Continued contact can be shown in the case of shared innovations. Thus, in ELA, the merger of /a/ and /oh/, as in *cot:caught* or *hock:hawk*, shows a similarity to the merger in other LA communities--less often for older than for younger speakers (see Wald, 1980b).

All these features characterize and define variety within Chicano English.

We should not expect to find an inflexible linguistic unity across Chicano Dialects. They will show some differences across locale, SES, and degree of bilingualism. On the other hand, it is not safe to assume that just because particular speakers are bilingual, their English, even if it differs from that of monolingual communities, is a *natural* consequence of their bilingualism. It is evident that *conventional* forces are at work in some Chicano communities, both in providing targets different from those of neighboring and/or superordinate communities, and in providing different routes to those targets.

The existence of English norms shared by both bilinguals and monolinguals in the community, but not found in the same systematic way in neighboring monolingual communities, and the existence of these features across local Chicano communities, will lead to further questions about the pattern and intensity of communicative contact within the overall Chicano community.

Until much more extensive work is done in ELA and other specific Chicano communities throughout the Southwest and other areas where Chicanos are numerous and concentrated, the actual variety and unity of Chicano English will remain problematic, and, it is hoped, programmatic.

NOTES

1. Stigmatization of palatal confusion, especially of CH for SH, as in *CHe* for *SHe*, is the most widely known and used stereotype of a "Mexican accent" in the Southwest. It is shared by all speakers, whether Chicano or not, and provides a source of humor in the community, as well as a basis for teasing.
2. Tensing of *e* before *ž* to approach or achieve identity with *ey*, as in *major*, is characteristic of many monolingual West Coast and Southwestern U.S. dialects of English. It may be representative of a similarly distributed tensing of *e* before voiced

palatals and velars in general, of Southern origin, and including words like *egg*, *leg*, and perhaps also related to the more Midlands and Northern tensing before a velar nasal as in *length* and *Bengal*.

3. Words like *fall* move toward /a/ as a consequence of the merger of /oh/ with /a/, most complete for younger speakers. As noted by Raven McDavid at the presentation of this paper in El Paso, the retraction of *e* before *l* is also known in the Great Lakes area, and a number of other monolingual American dialects. Undoubtedly, the velarization of American /l/ in final position plays a role in this retraction. It is further to be noted, however, that it is characteristic of Northern British (including Scots English, and Northern Irish English) dialects, and of many Northern U.S. dialects, including Detroit and Chicago, to lower stressed short front vowels more generally, of which retraction before /l/ is a specific symptom.

REFERENCES

Bills, Garland D., ed. 1974. *Southwest Areal Linguistics (SWALLOW II)*. San Diego, Cal.: Institute for Cultural Pluralism, San Diego State University.

Cazden, C.B., H. Cancino, E.J. Rosansky, and J.H. Schumann. 1975. *Second Language Acquisition Sequences in Children, and Adolescents and Adults, Final Report*. Washington, D.C.: U.S. Dept. of HEW, NIE Office of Research Grants.

Edwards, A.J., and M.J. Doviak. 1975. "Linguistic Constraints on Variation in Chicano English." Paper presented at the winter meeting of the LSA, December 1975.

Gingras, Rosario C. 1978. "Rule Innovation in Hispanicized English." Paper presented at the annual meeting of the American Dialect Society, Washington, D.C., 1978.

Gumperz, J.J. 1966. "Linguistic Repertoires, Grammars and Second Language Instruction." In *The Sixteenth Annual Round Table on Languages and Linguistics*. Washington, D.C.: Georgetown University Press, pp. 81-91.

Guy, Gregory. 1975. "Variation in the Group and the Individual: The Case of Final Stop Deletion." *Pennsylvania Working Papers in Linguistic Change and Variation*, 1,4. Philadelphia: University of Pennsylvania Press.

Hernández-Chavez, E., A.D. Cohen and A. Beltramo, eds. 1975. *El Lenguaje de los Chicanos: Regional and Social Characteristics Used by Mexican-Americans*. Arlington, Va.: Center for Applied Linguistics.

Labov, William. 1972. *Sociolinguistic Patterns*. Philadelphia: University of Pennsylvania Press.

Ma, Roxanna and Eleanor Herasimchuk. 1968. "Linguistic Dimensions of a Bilingual Community." In Joshua A. Fishman, ed., *Bilingualism in the Barrio. Final Report*. Washington, D.C.: U.S. Dept. of HEW, Office of Education, Bureau of Research, pp. 636-835.

Metcalf, Allan A. 1979. *Chicano English. Language in Education: Theory and Practice*. Arlington, Va.: Center for Applied Linguistics.

Peñalosa, Fernando. 1980. *Chicano Sociolinguistics: A Brief Introduction*. Rowley, Mass.: Newbury House.

Plato. 1963. *Cratylus* (with alternate page translation to English by H.N. Fowler). Loeb Classical Library, No. 167. Cambridge, Mass.: Harvard University Press.

Sawyer, Janet B. 1959. "Spanish-English Bilingualism in San Antonio, Texas." Reprinted in E. Hernández-Chavez et al., 1975, pp. 77-98.

Teschner, R.V., Garland D. Bills and J.R. Craddock. 1975. *Spanish and English of United States Hispanos: A Critical, Annotated Linguistic Bibliography*. Arlington, Va.: Center for Applied Linguistics.

Thompson, Roger W. 1974. "The 1970 U.S. Census and Mexican-American Language Loyalty: A Case Study." In Garland D. Bills, ed., *Southwest Areal Linguistics (SWALLOW II)*. San Diego, Cal.: Institute for Cultural Pluralism, San Diego State University, pp. 65-73.

Trudgill, Peter. 1975. *The Social Differentiation of English in Norwich*. Cambridge: Cambridge University Press.

Underwood, Gary N. 1974. "Needs in Southwest Dialectology." In Garland D. Bills, ed., *Southwest Areal Linguistics (SWALLOW II)*. San Diego, Cal.: Institute for Cultural Pluralism, San Diego State University, pp. 119-144.

Wald, Benji. 1979. "Limitations on the Application of the Variable Rule to Bilingual Phonology: The Case of the Voiceless Palatals in the English of Mexican-Americans in East L.A." Paper presented at NWAVE (New Ways in Analyzing Variation in English) VIII. (To be published in D. Sankoff and H. Cedergren, eds., *Recherches Sociolinguistiques à Montréal*. Edmonton)

_____. 1980a. "Dialect Formation in a Bilingual Community: Preliminary Study of the Evolution of the ELA Vowel System." Paper presented at NWAVE IX, University of Michigan, Ann Arbor.

_____. 1980b. "English in Los Angeles: Searching for a Speech Community." In T. Shopen and J.M. Williams, eds., *Style and Variation in English*. Cambridge, Mass.: Winthrop, pp. 250-272.

Wolfram, Walt A., and Ralph Fasold. 1974. *The Study of Social Dialects in American English*. Englewood Cliffs, N.J.: Prentice-Hall.

3

THE RANGE OF CHICANO ENGLISH

Gustavo González
Graduate School of Education
University of California, Santa Barbara

Any attempt to analyze the syntax of Chicano English in a meaningful way must begin with an examination of the area to be explored. This is a necessary first step because, like so many other things related to the Chicano, the language varieties associated with this population are often shrouded in confusion and misconceptions. Some clarification of just what constitutes Chicano English is thus desirable prior to analysis of any subdivision of it, such as its syntax. In addition to allowing a clearer focus on the topic, it will allow an identification of areas yet to be reached and a tentative set of implications for the education of Chicano children to emerge.

The varieties of English spoken by ethnic groups have been the object of linguistic analysis since the early sixties. Probably the most intensively studied of these has been the English spoken by Blacks. Since the pioneering work by Labov in 1966, numerous articles have appeared analyzing different aspects of this speech variety. One result has been the gradual (though by no means complete) acceptance of Black English as a legitimate dialect of English. The recent (1979) case in Ann Arbor attests to the support that has been found in the courts and to the impact that research on ethnic dialects can have on educational practice. A second result has been the increased interest in studying the speech characteristics of the English spoken by persons from diverse ethnic backgrounds, giving rise to studies on the English of American Indians, the English of Puerto Ricans, and now, the English of Chicanos. These labels have been transformed into Indian English, Puerto Rican English, and Chicano English, respectively.

While this tendency to provide generic labels has made it easier to refer to the varieties of English spoken by the different ethnic groups, it has also helped obscure the diversity of varieties spoken by each of them. The terms imply that the speech referred to is characteristic of *all* speakers who are Indian, or Puerto Rican, or Chicano. Forgotten is the fact that the studies from which the characteristics for each variety were derived were carried out with informants from different age levels and sociocultural backgrounds, by investigators utilizing different approaches (e.g., sociolinguistic, ethnographic). The only commonalities shared by the studies are that the informants came from the ethnic group being examined and that all spoke a variety of English different in some respect from Standard American English.

The great diversity at the core of Chicano English is a reflection of the heterogeneity of the Chicano population, which represents varying degrees of length of residence in the United States. Thus the speakers of Chicano English would include recent immigrants as well as third and fourth generation Chicanos. Linguistically, this heterogeneity is manifested in a range of abilities, from monolingual Spanish at one end of the scale to monolingual English at the other end; that is, a scale ranging from monolingual Spanish speakers struggling with the basic sounds and structures of English to monolingual native-English speakers whose English variety may or may not be discernibly different from Anglo speakers of Standard American English. Peñalosa, in attempting to develop an all-encompassing definition, concludes, "The term Chicano English is ambiguous in that it may refer to all the varieties of English spoken by the Chicano, including varieties indistinguishable from Anglo English, or it may refer to varieties of English spoken only by Chicanos." (1980, p. 115)

The majority of studies to date have chosen as their focus the English of Chicanos whose first language was Spanish and whose English deviates from the Standard American English norm because of influences from Spanish. Examples include Trager-Johnson and Abraham (1973), González (1976), and Cohen (1976). The first two dealt with the English of Chicanos strictly from an interference perspective, while Cohen's study went one step further, attributing some deviations to developmental and dialectal sources. Phonology, morphology, lexicon, and syntax have been examined with mixed results. The area of syntax is a case in point. The following utterances are representative of what is found in the literature:

(1) Because is dirty. (González, 1976)
(2) Because he no want it to be like that. (González, 1976)
(3) He putting he shoes. (González, 1976)
(4) I don't know what's her name. (Cohen, 1976)
(5) How you call these? (Cohen, 1976)

The first example shows possible influence either in the omission of the subject (since in Spanish the overt subject is optional) or in the reduction of the *ts* consonant cluster (*is* for *it's*). In the second sentence the *do* auxiliary, indispensable in the formation of negative utterances in English involving verbs other than *to be*, has been omitted, possibly because of the influence from the parallel Spanish construction. Sentence (3) is an example of a two-word expression in English (*put on*) being rendered as one word. This could be seen as an attempt to parallel Spanish *ponerse*, although it is equally possible that the omission of *on* is part of a more widespread phenomenon involving English prepositions in general. The fourth example involves a realignment in the sequence of elements involved in the formulation of indirect questions. The informant has taken the interrogative structure (*what's her name*) and transferred it, unchanged, to the direct object position. Standard American English requires that the verb be moved to the last position, to form *what her name is*. Example (5) is similar to (2) in that the auxiliary *do*, required in interrogative sentences involving verbs other than *to be*, has been omitted.

Many other examples could be presented. There's the often cited misplacement of the descriptive adjective from pre-noun position as required in English, to post-noun position, as usually the case in Spanish (e.g., *house big* for 'big house'). In the area of morphology, there is the confusion in antecedents (*He have a hammer in her hand*, from González, 1977); subject-verb incongruence (*The father and the little boy is fishing*); and the misformation of verb tenses (*He will caught it*). The last three examples are not as directly attributable to Spanish influence as were the earlier examples and could well be caused by what Richards (1973) has called intralingual interference.

Whether the deviations from Standard American English are due to interference, from Spanish, to interalingual interference, or to developmental considerations, it is clear that the deviations examined above must somehow be accounted for in a description of Chicano English. If Peñalosa's earlier statement regarding the range of Chicano English is true--and I believe it is--the studies conducted to date merely constitute the tip of the iceberg. We have merely analyzed the most obvious, the most easily accessible and noticeable parts of Chicano English, those that are definitely incongruent with Standard American English. This observation applies to phonology,

morphology, syntax, intonation, and lexicon: we have merely
begun to explore the language abilities of the speakers of
Chicano English that are on the non-fluent end of the
spectrum.

Before continuing with our discussion of the different
dimensions and manifestations of Chicano English, we need
to face some difficult questions regarding the status of
Chicano English vis-à-vis Standard American English. To
begin with, is Chicano English to be viewed as a dialect
of English, no better or worse, just different from other
varieties (including Standard American English)? The response to this question is especially critical to, among
other things, educational practices affecting Chicanos. If
Chicano English is granted the status of an accepted dialect of English, educational institutions would be per-
suaded to see its value and would not seek to eradicate
it; that is, the schools would seek to *add* the Standard
variety to the Chicano variety and not replace one with
the other. The development of each would run along separate tracks: Standard English would be taught in the
schools while Chicano English would develop through growing up Chicano or through contact with Chicanos.

A second related question deals with the linguistic aspects of Chicano English, namely: At what point would
Standard English and Chicano English converge completely,
if ever? Stated another way, at what point are fluent
speakers of Chicano English indistinguishable from Standard American English speakers? Is it the nature of Chicano English to more closely approximate Standard English
as its speakers acculturate and subsequently go from being monolingual in Spanish to acquiring complete fluency
in English? Is the label "fluent Chicano English speaker"
synonymous with "fluent speaker of Standard American
English?"

Even if we agree with Sawyer (1969, p. 19) that Chicano English is ". . . simply an imperfect state in the
mastery of English," it would behoove us to look at the
various "imperfect states" that Chicano English goes
through in arriving at Standard American English. There
is a void in the literature regarding the processes involved in the acquisition of Standard English by non-Eng-
lish-fluent Chicano children. What studies do exist of
Chicano children's errors in English (e.g., Cohen, 1976)
are limited to the identification of the deviations and
the listing of possible sources. Unfortunately, no follow-
up studies have been conducted to identify stages and
strategies used in the resolution of a given language difficulty. Serious longitudinal research along these lines
could ultimately uncover a reasonable sequence of English
as a second language for Chicano children whose first
language is Spanish. This, in turn, should prove quite
helpful to teachers of these children in establishing
realistic ESL goals, and in designing relevant instructional programs, curriculum materials, and language

assessment instruments.

If Chicano English is to be considered a dialect of English, it will be necessary to determine what linguistic features are common to all Chicano English speakers. It could well be that certain phonological, morphological, syntactic, lexical, and/or intonational features are shared by all, whereas certain other types of traits are characteristic of subdivisions within the Chicano population. The degree of development of skills in listening, speaking, reading, and writing would be a major factor in categorizing Chicano English speakers in the monolingual Spanish-monolingual English continuum. The result could well be not *one* variety of Chicano English but *several*. Figure 1 illustrates the relationship of the items discussed thus far.

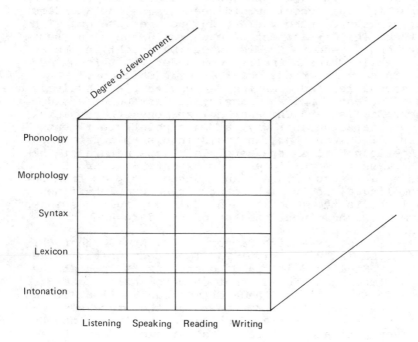

FIGURE 1

Using the three dimensions depicted in Figure 1, it would be possible to arrive at several categories composed of different combinations of language skill (horizontal dimension), language area (vertical dimension), and level of development in the combination of the previous two dimensions. At the monolingual Spanish end of the spectrum, for instance, the degree of development of any horizontal-vertical combination would be very low or nonexistent. At the monolingual English end of the scale, development in

virtually all areas would be at their maximum (with the
possible exception of intonation, one of the last areas
to be mastered, and the use of intonation in written expression, which in English is inapplicable). The intermediate areas of Chicano English, and the areas about
which we know so little, would consist of different
levels of development in the identified skills for the
different areas, in some instances including zero development in a given skill (e.g., writing or reading for
illiterate Chicanos).

Examining the linguistic characteristics of Chicano
English in isolation is only the beginning. In order to
fully appreciate the complexities involved in describing
the language variety and its use, we would need to examine
the use of the variety in different sociocultural contexts common to the Chicano experience. We would need to
ascertain not only which topics, among what participants,
in what settings are appropriate for Chicano English, but
also which linguistic aspects and degree of development
in them would be involved. It is possible that different
configurations of skills, language areas, and level of
development would be appropriate for each different situation.

Limited development of language skills is not a necessary prerequisite to Chicano English; at its most linguistically sophisticated level, Chicano English may represent not just an approximation to (or congruence with)
Standard American English, but conscious or subconscious
knowledge of what distinguishes one variety from the
other and the ability to produce utterances based on this
knowledge. This would be different from speech acts in
which the person's renditions of English sentences were
limited by his or her ability in English. The major difference lies in the reason behind the production of Chicano English utterances: in the first instance, the differences between Chicano English and Standard American
English are *purposely* brought into play; in the second,
the speaker is performing to his/her maximum and is still
unable to produce utterances that are identical to the
supposed target, Standard American English. Needless to
say, a person who is able to produce different approxima-
tions of the standard to fit changing sociolingustic
contexts is at the upper end of our Chicano English scale.

An example will help clarify the difference between
the two. The first involves a Chicano student in an English-
as-a-Second-Language class. The current topic of focus is
the pronunciation of [š], a sound foreign to his Spanish
sound system. The lesson includes the sentence, "She
washes the dishes." The Chicano, having received little
systematic exposure to English, substitutes [č] for [š]
producing [či wačas da dičas], not because he wants to
call attention to his mispronunciation of Standard English
but because this represents the limits of his abilities in
English at this point in time.

For a Chicano on the fluent end of the Chicano English spectrum, the same utterance [či wačas da dičas] may well reflect a more sociolinguistically complex mode of communication. Unlike the earlier situation, the output in this case does not represent the upper limits of the person's abilities in English but the conscious use of a heavily Spanish-influenced variety with certain persons (usually other Chicanos with the same level of command of Chicano English) in certain contexts (usually in informal gatherings at which the participants are reminiscing about their own earlier experiences with learning English). It is a way of poking gentle fun at earlier stages of learning English as a second language. Thus it is not unusual for me to say [tiš] for "teacher" or [bIš] for "beach" when in an informal setting with other Chicanos. This type of interaction has given rise to jokes based on Chicano difficulties with English, such as the one that defines *weiner* as the first one to finish in a Chicano foot race. Interestingly enough, the type of kidding alluded to above seems to occur only with Chicanos from Texas; in my ten years of interaction with California Chicanos, I have yet to witness this type of behavior.

The above is but one example of using a more Spanish-influenced variety of Chicano English to communicate more than would be communicated if the more standard-like variety had been used. The use of the Spanish-influenced variety by persons capable of controlling both signals a special type of relationship, one in which only Chicanos who have experienced the learning of English-as-a-Second Language (and who are now fluent in Standard English) can participate. The above situation also involves only one area of potential Spanish influence, the phonology. It is quite possible for such exchanges to make use of other language aspects, such as the intonation or the syntax. Clearly, much research needs to be done before a complete picture can emerge.

Sociolinguistic consideration aside, it is quite probable that the areas of difference between Standard English and Chicano English are reduced as the Chicano's contact with English increases. Whereas initially there may be differences in syntax, lexicon, intonation, morphology, etc., these may be gradually reduced to intonation and the unusual rendering of certain expressions. Metcalf (1974) makes this observation regarding the intonation of Chicano English:

The most distinctive, persistent, and important characteristic of Chicano English is its intonation. To speakers of other English dialects, the Chicano English speaker often sounds uncertain, wishy-washy and a little crazy--because of intonation patterns that make it seem as if he is asking a question when he should be making a statement, expressing

doubt when he should be certain, and putting stress
on the strangest words for no apparent reason. (p. 55)

Thus, intonation continues to be a problem even among
adults with an otherwise flawless command of Standard
English. It is these speakers who are one step removed
from complete convergence with Standard English speakers
at the oral language level.

The second persistent area is the rendering of certain
expressions. Metcalf (1974, pp. 56-57) classified *wash the
dishes* as Chicano English (compared to *do the dishes*).
Following this example, we posit the following literal
translations as Chicano English:

wash the teeth for *brush the teeth*
make dinner for *fix dinner*

In both cases, the major process operating in a direct
translation (*lavarse* for 'wash'; *hacer/preparar* for 'make')
from Spanish. Relatively speaking, this process is not as
common among the more fluent speakers of Chicano English
as it is for the beginner. But it does persist as an area
of divergence between Chicano English and the Standard.

One of the characteristics of Chicano speech that has
been investigated and written about the most is Spanish-
English code-switching (see, for example, Sánchez, 1972;
Lance, 1969; Valdés-Fallis, 1978; González and Maez, 1980).
In identifying the traits that distinguish Chicano English
from Standard English, should the switching from Spanish
to English (or vice-versa) be among them? Or is code-
switching a separate matter altogether? If code-switching
is considered part of Chicano English, is it a trait of
the lower levels of fluency or the upper levels? Stated
differently, does fluency in Chicano English increase or
decrease a person's ability to code-switch?

The questions are as complex as they are intriguing
and cannot be properly addressed in this paper. The only
aspect that can be addressed is whether code-switching is
a characteristic of Chicano English. It is my view that it
is not, that code-switching is a trait of Chicano *Spanish*.
This reflects what we know about the direction and frequency of code-switching. Our studies and those of others have
have shown that the majority of instances of code-switching among Chicanos proceeds from Spanish to English. That
is, a Chicano who code-switches is much more likely to begin
a sentence in Spanish and finish in English, or inter-
calate an English word into an otherwise completely
Spanish sentence. In addition to this well-documented
tendency, it has been hypothesized (Sánchez, 1972) that
the structure of Spanish determines the type of code-
switch that can happen. This makes the ability to code-
switch a characteristic of the person's Spanish and not
his or her English.

It should be clear from the preceding discussion that
a simple, compact definition of Chicano English is not

possible at present. It should be equally clear that much research remains to be done. We don't yet know enough to ask the right questions. For this reason, it is important to initiate a dialog with other researchers engaged in parallel activities, such as those investigating Black English and Appalachian speech, and with practitioners involved in the education of Chicano children. This latter link will help us apply the results of our research findings to practical situations.

In conclusion, we as linguists, researchers, and educators need to acknowledge the existence of and examine the linguistic and sociocultural characteristics of the full range of Chicano English. We need to go beyond the primitive state of the art in which only the most obvious interference areas from Spanish (low fluency Chicano English) are researched and categorized as Chicano English. Kachru (1977) has observed that ". . . the second-language varieties of English have acquired numerous roles over an extended period--in some cases almost two centuries--and as a result have been embedded in the native sociocultural and linguistic matrix of the area where they are used." (p. 31) It remains to us to decipher the sociocultural and linguistic matrix of Chicano English. The relationship between this variety of English and the English of the schools needs to be established and educational implications beneficial to Chicano children need to be charted. And lastly, longitudinal research on the stages and strategies in acquiring English as a second language is desperately needed to chronicle the process of learning Chicano English. The first step in this direction--acknowledgment of the existence of Chicano English--has been taken.

REFERENCES

Cohen, Andrew D. 1976. "The English and Spanish Grammar of Chicano Primary School Students." In J.D. Bowen and J. Ornstein, eds., *Studies in Southwest Spanish*. Rowley, Mass.: Newbury House, pp. 125-164.

González, Gustavo. 1976. "Some Characteristics of the English Used by Migrant Spanish-Speaking Children in Texas." *Aztlán*, 7(1, Spring): pp. 27-50.

_____ and Lento F. Maez. 1980. "To Switch or Not to Switch: The Role of Code-Switching in the Elementary Bilingual Classroom." In Raymond V. Padilla, ed., *Ethnoperspectives in Bilingual Education Research, Vol. II: Theory in Bilingual Education*. Ypsilanti, Mich.: Eastern Michigan University, pp. 125-135.

Kachru, Braj. 1977. "The New Englishes and Old Models." *English Teaching Forum*, July: pp. 29-35.

Labov, William. 1966. *The Social Stratification of English in New York City*. Urban Language Series, 1. Arlington, Va.: Center for Applied Linguistics.

Lance, Donald M., ed. 1969. *A Brief Study of Spanish-English Bilingualism. Final Report*. Bethesda, Md.: DHEW/EDRS.

Martin Luther King, Jr. Elementary School Children v. *Ann Arbor School District Board*, 473 F. Supp. 1371, 1979.

Metcalf, Allan A. 1974. "The Study (Or, Non-Study) of California Chicano English." In Garland D. Bills, ed., *Southwest Areal Linguistics*. San Diego: Institute for Cultural Pluralism, San Diego State University, pp. 97-106.

Peñalosa, Fernando. 1980. *Chicano Sociolinguistics: A Brief Introduction*. Rowley, Mass.: Newbury House.

Richards, Jack C. 1973. "A Non-Contrastive Approach to Error Analysis." In J. W. Oller and Jack C. Richards, eds., *Focus on the Learner*. Rowley, Mass.: Newbury House, pp. 96-113.

4

CHICANO ENGLISH PHONOLOGY:
NORMS VS. INTERFERENCE PHENOMENA*

Manuel Godinez, Jr.
Phonetics Lab, UCLA

Many linguists looking at Chicano English in the
Southwest have often started from an interference model
and have assumed that members of these communities are
typically bilingual speakers of English and Spanish. However, they have sometimes failed to note that there are
many monolingual English-speaking Chicanos who frequently
exhibit some special linguistic properties. These properties reflect linguistic norms operating within a particular community. Sawyer (1970) in the article "Spanish-English Bilingualism in San Antonio, Texas" states that in
order to merit the term "dialect" a particular variety of
a language should be fairly stable in its structure so
that it can be learned by succeeding generations in each
community. Sawyer (1970) continues saying: "Nothing that
could be called a Mexican-American dialect of English was
found in San Antonio, Texas. The English spoken by the bilingual informants was simply an imperfect state in the
mastery of English." I would like to show briefly in this
study that an interference model does not account for the

*I am indebted to Father Leo Baysinger of Salesian High School,
Brother Eagan Hunter of Notre Dame High School, and to Father John
Venegas and Mr. Trujillo of St. Genevieve High School for making
possible the recordings for this study. This research was supported
by grants from UCLA Chicano Studies Research Center and from the
National Science Foundation to the UCLA Phonetics Laboratory.

entire Chicano linguistic situation. Using comparative
acoustic vowel data from Chicano English and Spanish and
General California English, I will demonstrate that the
regularities within Chicano English represent the linguistic norms for many speakers--at least in East Los Angeles.

Members of a Chicano population of male students at a
local high school in East Los Angeles were interviewed.
From this population a group of Chicano monolingual English speakers and a group of Chicano bilingual English/
Spanish speakers were established. Subjects in both
these Chicano groups were in the eleventh grade, ranged
from 16 to 17 years of age, and were all born and raised
in the East Los Angeles area. For purposes of comparison,
a group representing General American English was established from students at two high schools located in
the San Fernando Valley area of Los Angeles County. These
speakers will be referred to as the "General Californian
English" group. As with the Chicano speakers, the General Californian group were in the eleventh grade, ranged
from 16 to 17 years of age, but were born and raised in
the San Fernando Valley area.

The data summarized here has been detailed in Godinez (1981). In this work, I have already shown that Chicanos who are bilingual speakers of English and Spanish
behave similarly to the monolingual English-speaking Chicanos in East Los Angeles. As a result, I will only refer
here to the data from the Chicano monolinguals and take
this to be representative of both Chicano groups for the
present purposes. Using a typed list, the words: *heed,
hid, head, had, hood,* and *who'd* said in the sentence
frame "Say the word ___ once" were elicited from each of
the subjects. Each of the vowels representing the following vowel phonemes of English were measured: /i/, /ɪ/,
/ɛ/, /ae/, /ʊ/, /u/. Measurements of vowel duration were
made from spectrographs of these recordings. Figure 1
gives the mean duration in milliseconds for each vowel
of each group. The overall mean ($\overline{X}$), the variance (var),
and the standard deviation (sd) of each group are also
given in Figure 1.

The Chicano Spanish data was elicited from the
Chicano bilinguals using the same method as for the
Chicano monolinguals. No significant differences between the Chicano English and General Californian groups
were found using a T-test. An analysis of variance was
also performed on duration measurements which confirmed
the absence of significant difference in duration between the two groups. In contrast to all of these findings, statistically significant differences in the pronunciation or vowel quality of the given vowels were
found between the Chicano English and General Californian English speakers.

Using the same spectrograms used for the duration
measurements, formant values (F1 and F2-F1) were obtained

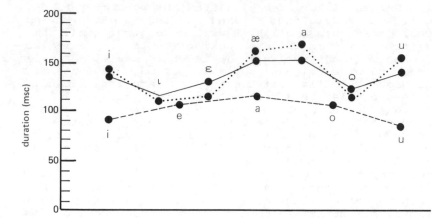

Chicano English

vowel	hid	hɪd	hɛd	hæd	hɑd	hɔd	hud
X̄	135	117	130	152	153	122	139
var	815	828	882	862	986	783	811
sd	30	30	31	31	33	29	29

General Californian English

vowel	hid	hɪd	hɛd	hæd	hɑd	hɔd	hud
X̄	143	112	114	162	168	115	153
var	453	497	225	822	472	719	475
sd	22	23	17	30	51	28	23

Spanish

vowel	piko	peko	pɑko	poko	kuko
X̄	90	109	111	106	84
var	233	403	378	420	469
sd	18	23	22	24	25

FIGURE 1

and a group mean for each of the vowels calculated. Figure 2 and Figure 3 depict this treatment of the data. One
might suggest that these differences are due to interference from Spanish, but Figure 3 shows that the vowels in
Chicano English compared to those in Chicano Spanish are
clearly different.

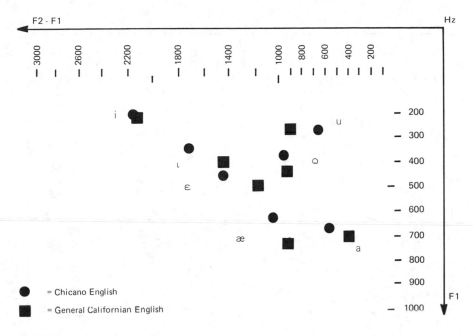

FIGURE 2

Looking at the diphthongs, we find similar results in their quality. Figure 4 reports data elicited from the word *hay* /eɪ/ and Figure 5, the word *high* /haɪ/ for English in the sentence: "Say ___ twice." For Chicano Spanish, the words *seis* /seɪs/ (six) and *hay* /aɪ/ (there is/are) were elicited in the sentences: "Digo ___ dos veces." (I say ___ twice.) and "Decimos ___ dos veces." (We say ___ twice.) Thus Figures 4 and 5 show that Chicano English /eɪ/ is higher and more fronted when compared to Chicano Spanish and General Californian English. We see that Chicano English /aɪ/ likewise differs from the corresponding dipththong of Chicano Spanish and General Californian English. Here /aɪ/ follows a more fronted pathway terminating at a higher point in the formant space than does the /aɪ/ of either Chicano Spanish or General Californian English.

Thus we can conclude that, rather than being primarily determined by interference from Spanish, Chicano English--at least that spoken in East Los Angeles--represents an autonomous social dialect with distinct characteristics passed on by mutual processes of linguistic transmission. The Chicano English situation is a complex one. I have tried to show briefly that certain aspects of this situation can be illuminated through careful quantitative analysis of speech data. The conventions of linguistic norms in line with this type of data have been pointed

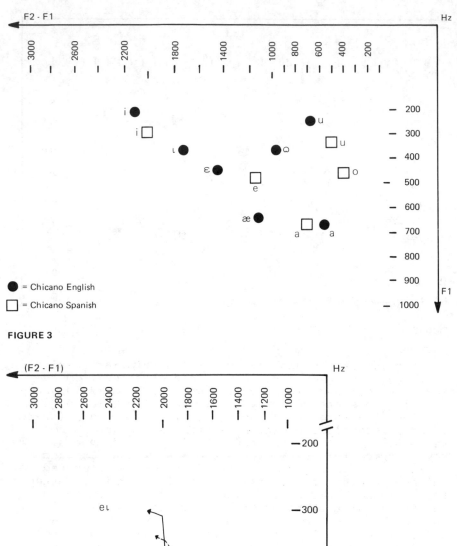

FIGURE 3

FIGURE 4

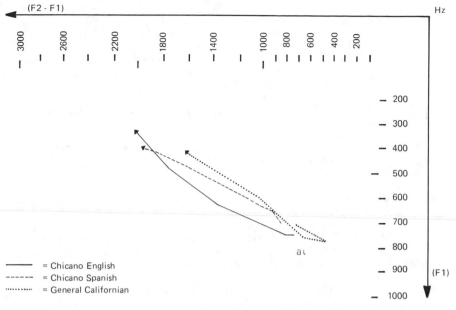

——— = Chicano English
- - - - - = Chicano Spanish
··········· = General Californian

FIGURE 5

out by Trubetzkoy in *Gründzuge der Phonologie* earlier in
the century and are part of language and part of the oral
linguistic character of a language system. As I have already pointed out in "Do Chicanos Speak with a Spanish
Accent?" (Godinez, 1981), we will be able to tackle this
complex situation only if we take a broad linguistic,
socio-historical, and psychological perspective as we
carry out further empirical work in this area. This paper
is intended as a contribution to that endeavor.

REFERENCES

García, Ricardo L. 1974. "Toward a Grammar of Chicano English."
    English Journal, 63(3): 34-38.

Godinez, Manuel. 1981. "Do Chicanos Speak with a Spanish Accent?"
    Paper presented at the Ninth Annual Meeting of the National As-
    sociation of Chicano Studies, April 1981. University of Cali-
    fornia, Riverside.

_____ and Mona Lindau-Webb. 1980. "Reliable Phonetic Differences
    Between Dialects: Chicano and General Californian English."
    Paper presented to the American Dialect Society, July 1980,
    University of New Mexico.

_____ and Ian Maddieson. In press. "Vowel Differences Between
Chicano and General Californian English." *International Journal
of the Sociology of Language.*

Hartford, Beverly S. 1978. "Phonological Differences in the English
of Adolescent Female and Male Mexican-Americans." *International
Journal of the Sociology of Language,* 17: 55-64.

Ladefoged, Peter. 1975. *A Course in Phonetics.* New York: Harcourt
Brace Jovanovich, 1975.

Lisker, Leigh, and Arthur S. Abramson. 1967. "Some Effects of Context on Voice Onset Time in English Stops." *Language and Speech,*
10(1): 1-28.

Lynn, Klonda. 1945. "Bilingualism in the Southwest." *Quarterly Journal of Speech,* 31(2): 175-180.

Macías, Reynaldo F. 1979. "Mexicano/Chicano Sociolinguistic Behavior
and Language Policy in the United States." Ph.D. dissertation,
Georgetown University, Washington, D.C.

Metcalf, Allan A. 1972. "Mexican-American English in Southern California." *Western Review,* 9(1): 13-21.

_____. 1974. "The Study of California Chicano English." *Linguistics,*
128: 53-58.

Ortego, Philip D. 1969. "Some Cultural Implications of a Mexican-
American Border Dialect of American English." *Studies in Linguistics,* 21: 77-84.

Poulter, Virgil L. 1970. "Comparison of Voiceless Stops in the Eng-
list and Spanish of Bilingual Natives of Fort Worth-Dallas." In
Glenn G. Gilbert, ed., *Texas Studies in Bilingualism.* Berlin: de
Gruyter, 43-49.

Sawyer, Janet B. 1970. "Spanish-English Bilingualism in San Antonio,
Texas." In Glenn G. Gilbert, ed., *Texas Studies in Bilingualism.*
Berlin: De Gruyter, pp. 18-41.

Stewart, William A. 1964. "Foreign Language Teaching Methods in
Quasi-Foreign Language Situations." In William A. Stewart, ed.,
Non-Standard Speech and the Teaching of English. Arlington, Va.:
Center for Applied Linguistics, pp. 1-15.

Weinreich, Uriel. 1953. *Languages in Contact.* New York: Linguistic
Circle of New York.

5

PROSODIC PATTERNS: SOME HYPOTHESES AND FINDINGS FROM FIELDWORK

Joyce Penfield
Graduate School of Education
Rutgers University

The purpose of this paper is to describe linguistically some of the prosodic aspects of Chicano English that typify the folk comment often made by Anglo-Americans to the effect that some Chicanos speak in a "sing-song." I maintain in this paper that Chicano English prosody, especially intonation, is a clear marker of ethnic identity for bilingual and monolingual English-speaking Chicanos alike --especially those who have not totally assimilated to Anglo culture. For those in the process of total assimilation, either by choice or force, it is perhaps the last vestige of Chicano identity as far as English speech is concerned. Because Chicano English speakers span a wide geographical area and are represented by an array of different social classes, there is, no doubt, variation in prosodic patterns across the Chicano community. However, many of the prosodic patterns discussed in this paper have been observed, not only in El Paso, Texas, but among monolingual English-speaking Chicano adolescents in East Los Angeles; among bilingual and monolingual Chicanos in San Francisco; and among monolingual English-speaking Anglo children who reside in Chicano neighborhoods in El Paso. Some of the similarities exist probably because only the most frequent and productive patterns which most obviously contrast with Standard Anglo English are described in this paper.

Researchers studying various ethnic groups in the

United States have noted the importance of prosody in
conversational contexts. A few have attempted to describe
prosodic variation. Carlock (1979) noted that prosody was
diagnostic of ethnic group membership in Buffalo, New
York. Non-ethnics were easily able to identify Italian-
American and Polish-American English on the basis of intonation alone. In fact, although they could not analyt-
ically explain how they did this, many non-ethnics were
aware that they made use of intonational cues which Carlock was later able to identify.

Gumperz and Kaltman (1980) studied prosodic differences between Western English conversation and Indian English
(east/Asian). They inferred differences in the use of prosody between these two systems in two dimensions: (1) the
use of prosody in signaling normal information flow; (2)
the use of prosody to signal various kinds of intra- and
intersentential relations like subordination or utterance
finality. In general, they found that, in comparison to
Western English, Indian English bases its prosodic conventions on different syllable-level phonology; a different
level of syntactic breakdown; and different phonological
means for making prosodic distinctions and relations. It
is not surprising that they found breakdowns in natural
conversation between these two groups of speakers because
of differing communicative effect in prosodic cues.

Other researchers have investigated the role of other
prosodic signals at both pragmatic and linguistic levels
in conversation. For Hawaiian English, Vanderslice and
Pierson (1967) examined prominence and duration, among
other things. They found syllables in Hawaiian English to
have equal prominence in terms of loudness and duration.

Theoretical studies of stress in discourse for monolingual English have revealed valuable insights. Bolinger
(1972) noted that stress in English reflects what a speaker feels is important in the sentence; and therefore, he
inferred that stress is determined semantically more than
syntactically. Newman (1979) proved, in an experiment designed to study the role of stress in discourse contexts,
that in English the placement of stress in a sentence affects the listener's expectations as to what can follow.
She suggests that stress may be one of the few cataphoric
devices in discourse. Consequently, she inferred that
those contexts that match expectations that are in turn
generated by stress placement will be comprehended more
rapidly and certainly more clearly than those that would
not be predicted from the stress pattern.

Given the variety of research studies on the various
aspects of prosody which remain as yet scattered throughout the literature, it remains unclear what role prosody
plays in language change, since historical studies rarely
touch on prosody in their research. As far as dialectology
and language contact studies are concerned, all aspects of
prosody may play a crucial role. The permanence of prosodic features, especially intonation, in varieties of

English around the world in such different contact situations suggests an important empirical distinction we need
to pay more attention to than heretofore. To what extent
this apparent permanence resembles the permanence prosody
is suggested to have in brain function also remains to be
studied. For example, Bloomstein (1973), in her intensive
study of phonological implications of aphasic speech,
gives the general impression that in aphasia prosody is
often not disturbed. Those who have observed global apha-
sics also have noted that they tend to keep their intonation patterns when losing most all other linguistic performance abilities. Likewise, language acquisition research
has suggested that children first acquire a comprehension
of intonation before segmentals. Kaplan (1969), who conducted an experimental study on the receptivity of four-
vs. eight-month-old infants to falling declarative statements and rising questions, found an increased heart beat
with the eight-month-old group exposed to Standard English, suggesting that they had acquired a passive comprehension of these intonation patterns. In short, prosody
is probably a permanent and crucial part of language contact which awaits description.

DESIGN OF STUDY

    The data collected in this study consisted of nine
hours of tape-recorded natural, spontaneous conversation
between Mexican-Americans in a variety of rather informal
conversational contexts. It includes two generations of
bilinguals at a family baby shower; discussions on local
television shows with community leaders; and bilingual
adults chatting with bilingual and monolingual English-
speaking Chicano children ages 8 to 12 years. All of the
respondents are native El Pasoans.
    An experimentally designed study was intentionally
avoided because of the nature of the sociolinguistic
situation in which Chicano English usage is embedded.
Observations of interactions in the Chicano community
illustrated the code-switching nature with which Chicano English can be applied by multi-dialectal and bilingual speakers. Adjustments are constantly made vis-
à-vis interlocutors so that conversations with peers
often reflect a relaxed and natural range of dialectal
features which characterize Chicano English. On the
other hand, formal contexts or face-to-face interaction
with Anglos or non-peers may result in a consciously
monitored, virtually dialect-free speech on the part of
bilinguals who are also bidialectal. For the latter
group, at least, an experimentally designed study with
all the proper controls or even direct elicitation
would have completely distorted or masked the data.
    Although the current level of sophistication at-
tained by research on prosody leaves much to be desired,

for Chicano English used by code-switchers the search for
systematic patterns from naturally obtained spontaneous
conversations will have to suffice. The use of technical
equipment is not practical because of the sociolinguistic
situation described above. Spontaneous conversations recorded for this study included background noise, such as
music, telephone rings, multiple conversations, movement
toward and away from the microphone, the crying of babies,
and so on. All of these interruptions ruled out the use
of a machine as prosodic measurement tool.

The intonation patterns generalized in this paper were
found to be the most frequent and productive in the data.
They were also chosen because of their obvious variation
from Standard Anglo English. The latter is being defined
here as that type of English regularly used on nationwide
television and accepted as free of any specific regional
features. It was hypothesized that by defining optimal
prosodic aspects of contrast, some comment could be made
about problems in inter-ethnic communication between Chicano English speakers and Anglos who are not speakers of
Chicano English.

INTONATION: GENERALIZATIONS

Gumperz and Kaltman (1980) distinguish the following
aspects of prosody: (1) intonation, i.e., pitch levels on
individual syllables and their combination into contours;
(2) changes in loudness; (3) stress; (4) variation in both
pitch and loudness; (5) variations in vowel length; (6)
utterance chunking; (7) acceleration and deceleration
within and across utterance chunks; and (8) shifts in overall pitch register. In this paper I am primarily concerned
with intonation and stress. In the tradition of Pike's
(1945) study of intonation in American English, I use
three basic concepts in my description: (1) intonational
contours; (2) changes in pitch; and (3) stress. The intonational contour or rhythm unit will serve as the framework of the analysis, whereas significant changes in pitch
levels within the contours--contour points--will comprise
the basic aspects of the patterns. The same number of
pitch levels as are found in Standard American English are
posited for Chicano English. Whether the distance from one
pitch level to another is the same remains to be determined by more technical equipment at some future date.

Two types of contours are distinguished: final contours, i.e., those which occur near the end of the rhythm
unit and are marked by silence; and pre-contours, i.e.,
those which precede final contours. The points in the contour crucial to the patterns observed are the contour
points, which include rises and falls. Changes in pitch
will be described in terms of (1) the direction and degree of change; and (2) the type of change perceived,
whether a step or a glide. Steps are pitch changes which

are level on each syllable and involve no pitch change,
whereas glides involve a pitch change on a syllable.

Generalization 1. Rising Glides are Used to Highlight or Emphasize Specific Words

Perhaps the most prominent part of Chicano English intonation are rising glides. Unlike Standard Anglo English,
these glides can occur at almost any point in a contour
and on either mono- or polysyllabic words. These glides,
which are usually perceived as a lengthening also, are
used to highlight or emphasize specific words. This is
why they can occur multiply in one sentence or rhythm
unit; in fact, there can be as many as necessary in one
sentence. For example, *rules* and *hair* in (1) and (2).

(1) #₂ Are there any r u l e s for a fair fight? #
     (with pitch markings ³ over rules and ³ over "for a")

(2) #³ You have to cut₂ my h a i r ₂ mom /
     (with pitch markings ³)

Example (1) comes from a discussion about fighting and
(2) is a comment by a son to his mother expressing his
anxiety over others thinking he was a girl because of
his hair length. Both (1) and (2) involve one-syllable
words which would typically occur in Standard American
English on the last stressed monosyllabic word in a
question. The patterns illustrated in (1) and (2) of mid-
sentence rising glides followed by a lower pitch is not
typical of Standard English. Examples (3) and (4) involve two-syllable words which still have the same stress
as Standard English but which remain on the raised pitch
even when unstressed.

(3) # I'm h e a l th y . #   (I never get sick when
     ₂   I'm pregnant.)
     (with pitch marking ³)

(4) # He was c h o k i n g on it. # (Comment about
     ₂   a child chew-
                              ₁   ing a balloon.)
     (with pitch markings ³, 1)

The context of (4) clearly illustrates the need for
emphasis and highlighting by the speaker.
     If Anglos use any prosodic features as diagnostic
tools of ethnic identity, no doubt they make use of
rising glides which occur in pre-contours and mid-sen-
tence position and function to emphasize a point.

Generalization 2. Rising Glides are Maintained at the End of a Declarative Sentence

In line with Generalization 1, rising glides are

maintained in even more unusual environments in contrast
with Anglo English. Even if the rising glide occurs on
the last stressed syllable at the end of a sentence, the
pitch remains up rather than falling as it would typically
do in a declarative statement in Standard English. Example
(5) below illustrates this through a statement made by a
woman when discussing the state she wanted to deliver her
baby in. The statement is really a counter comment she recalled making to her doctor who wanted her to have gas administered prior to delivery.

(5)   #   I   want   to   be   a w a k e   .   #

Of course, in Anglo English finality of a sentence is marked
by a falling glide in such a case. In Example (5), the conversational context from which the statement comes suggests
clearly an emphatic meaning for *awake*, giving the utterance a meaning like: 'I want to be awake when I deliver my
baby, not asleep or drugged.' This example adds weight
again to the argument that rising glides signal emphasis,
contrast, or highlighting in Chicano English.

In short, there are basically two differences between
Standard Anglo English and Chicano English to note here.
Whereas a rising glide can occur syllable-final in Standard English, it would consist of a 3 and rising pitch
which would fade into higher pitches. Example (5) is a 3-
level pitch with no fading into a higher level. Secondly,
such an occurrence in Standard English where pitch 3
occurs sentence final conveys either doubt and surprise or
a question--neither of which were intended by the bi-dia-
lectal, bilingual Chicano English speaker of example (5).

Generalization 3. Sentence Contours Often Begin
                  Above the Normal Pitch of Voice
                  (i.e., Pitch 3)

As has been casually noted by others, there is a
common tendency to begin pre-contours with a pitch above
normal voice, stepping down to pitch 2 at later points in the
the contour as illustrated in (6), (7), and (8). However,
the function is not to highlight or emphasize the pre-
contour, even though in Anglo English this might be the
apparent reason for beginning a pre-contour above normal
pitch level.

(6)   #   All   sports   I   play. #   (Teenager talking
                                             about his interest
                                             in sports.)

(7) # It is a beautiful s t u d i o that's half-way

      built   in   Juarez .   #   (Discussion on T.V.)

(8) #   What a | pretty little girl . # (Mother telling
                                            what people used to
                                            say about her son be-
                                            cause of his long
                                            hair.)

I would suggest that Generalization 3 is responsible for
the interpretations by Anglos of Chicano English speakers
as highly emotional or excited. The use of a high pitch
at pre-contour level, especially over more than one-word
units, would certainly convey this meaning in Anglo
speech, and thus, the Anglo interpretations.

        Generalization 4. Rise-fall Glides Occurring in Sen-
                    tence-final Contours Mark the
                    Stereotypic Chicano "Accent"

        Perhaps the most stereotyped intonation pattern
Chicano English by Anglo Americans is the rise-fall glide
at the ends of sentences. As illustrated in examples (9)
and (10), this glide begins at normal voice level, pitch 2,
rises to pitch 3 on the primary stressed syllable of the
contour and falls either one-half or a full step on the
remaining syllables.

(9) #   To m e / that sounds g o o d. # (Reaction to
                                            a previous sug-
                                            gestion.)

(10) # I don't know what to dr a w . # (Child uncertain
                                            about exactly
                                            what project he
                                            should choose.)

This rise-fall glide is such a stereotypic association
with "Mexican" people that it is not surprising to hear
it at the end of every utterance made by a cartoon character who is characterized as Mexican and named "Speedy
Gonzalez."

        From my observations and the few examples I collect-
ed in the data, I would suggest that the final rise-fall
glide referentially conveys uncertainty or hesitation.
Both (9) and (10) reflect this meaning since in (9) the
speaker was in the process of considering alternatives
to a problem for which she had no definite solution and
in (10) the child was obviously not certain what he
should do. I have equally heard this intonation pattern
at times a speaker had reached a level of toleration to
frustration.

        Generalization 5. Final Endings of Declarative,
                    Neutral Statements Have a One-
                    Pitch Contrast

Contour final endings are extremely complex and involve a variety of different patterns. Those pattern possibilities which we have already discussed have rather non-neutral reference. Generalization 5 refers to neutral declarative statements. Unlike Anglo English which normally makes a 2-pitch contrast to mark finality of a neutral declarative statement, Chicano English makes only a 1-pitch contrast as illustrated finally in examples (11) and (12) which end on pitch 2--the normal pitch of the voice.

(11)   # You can ₂write ₂them . #   (no contrast intended)

(12)   #₂Give her ₂to me . #   (Father at a picnic talking to his wife about their child.)

Quite naturally because finality is necessarily conveyed in Anglo speech by a 2-pitch fall contrast, (11) and (12) tend to be perceived by Anglos as unfinished statements. In Anglo English they would mark non-finality, but in Chicano English they are a productive and common final contour pattern for neutral statements.

STRESS: GENERALIZATIONS

In a few restricted ways stress assignment differs between Chicano and Standard American English. The most common differences are in assignment of major stress on compound nouns and verbs. In Chicano English noun compounds receive their heaviest stress on the second word, whereas in Standard English the reverse is usually true. For example, the term *blackboard* has the heavier stress on the first word in Standard English but on the last word in Chicano English. In some instances, one can find Anglos who use the Chicano English stress pattern, particularly in bilingual communities. It is perhaps this level of prosody which is first and foremost borrowed by Anglos in language contact situations such as those found in multilingual and multi-ethnic communities.

Stress assignment also differs for verb compounds in Chicano English with the heavier stress being placed on the main verb rather than the particle. Therefore, in Chicano English as illustrated in example (13) *sit* would get the heaviest stress.

(13)   # He can't <u>sit</u> up . #

The obvious interpretation of such stress assignment by Anglo English speakers is a contrastive one: 'he can't sit up but he can <u>stand</u> up'. This is not the meaning intended by the Chicano English speaker. A neutral, non-contrastive meaning is conveyed.

IMPLICATIONS FOR INTER-ETHNIC COMMUNICATION

Since prosody is such an ingrained and unconscious linguistic behavior, it follows that communication between different ethnic groups supposedly using the same 'language' but not always the same references for prosodic cues may at points break down. Gumperz and Kaltman (1980) found this to be true in their comparisons of Western and Asian Indian English. Depending upon a particular Anglo's receptive knowledge of Chicano English, similar breakdowns may arise.

Sometime ago in his study of American English intonation from the point of view of Spanish speakers, Pike (1945) suggested that excessive use of one-step rises, especially those going to pitch 3, conveyed overpoliteness in Anglo English. Does this mean that if Chicano English is used to Anglos, it is construed as artificial or insincere politeness because of its typical 1-step rises which are really indicators of emphasis or highlighting?

As we have mentioned, ending a statement on pitch 2 conveys lack of finality or continuation in Anglo English whereas it is often the reverse in Chicano English. It is possible, therefore, to find Anglo speakers waiting for Chicano English speakers to finish a statement that they had in fact already finished. Some Chicanos have noted this. A sort of lack of synchrony in communication which results may cause misunderstandings or awkwardness at least.

As Pike (1945) noted about Standard American English, rising glides denote a lack of confidence. Emphasis and certainty is usually marked by a step up and a glide down in a 2-pitch contrast. We would expect Anglos, therefore, to misconstrue the highlighting of words in Chicano English (carried out by rising glides) to mean lack of confidence or uncertainty. The ironic thing about this is that the more a speaker of Chicano English tries to be emphatic, the more unconfident he or she sounds--given the Standard English system.

CONCLUSION

The evidence suggests that prosody not only marks ethnic membership but, in the case of code-switching Chicanos, it also marks the degree of identification with this membership. It is possible that the more assimilated to Anglo culture and language that one becomes, the less marked their Chicano English prosody is. It would be interesting to ascertain to what degree intonation patterns of Chicano English continue to play a role in conversation as the assimilation to Anglo values increases.

This paper is just the beginning of an attempt to establish those intonational patterns most shared by Chicano English speakers. As suggested previously, there are certainly several varieties of Chicano English and therefore we would expect variation in prosodic patterns as well. To what extent this variation correlates with geographical differences or community boundaries or language development differences, such as code-switching vs. monolingual Chicano English speaking, remains to be determined. We need an analysis of many more informal conversations which are natural and spontaneous, along with the ethnographic and historical-linguistic background of the participants taped, in order to advance in our understanding of prosodic variety in Chicano English, or in fact a description of any aspect of Chicano English.

REFERENCES

Bloomstein, Sheila. 1973. "Some Phonological Implications of Aphasic Speech." In Harold Goodglass and Sheila Bloomstein, eds., *Psycholinguistics and Aphasia*. Baltimore, Md.: Johns Hopkins University Press, pp. 123-137.

Bolinger, Dwight. 1968. "Stress and Information." *American Speech*, 33: 5-20.

_____. 1972. "Accent Is Predictable (If You're a Mind-Reader)." *Language*, 48(3): 633-644.

Bowen, J. Donald. 1956. "A Comparison of the Intonation Patterns of English and Spanish." *Hispania*, 34: 30-35.

Carlock, Beth. 1979. "Prosodic Analysis of Two Varieties of Buffalo English." In Wolfgang Wölck and Paul Garvin, eds., *Fifth LACUS Forum 1978*. Columbia, S.C.: Hornbeam Press, pp. 377-382.

Delattre, P., C. Olsen and E. Poenack. 1962. "A Comparative Study of Declarative Intonation in American English and Spanish." *Hispania*, 45: 233-241.

Durán, Richard. 1981. "Organization of Chicano Children's Narrative Behavior." NIE grant proposal (personal communication)

Gumperz, John. 1981. "Conversational Inference and Classroom Learning." In J. Green and C. Wallat, eds., *Ethnographic Approaches to Face-to-Face Interaction*. Norwood, N.J.: Ablex.

_____ and Hannah Kaltman. 1980. "Prosody, Linguistic Diffusion and Conversational Inference." *Berkeley Language Studies*, 5.

Halliday, M.A.K. 1967. *Intonation and Grammar in British English*. The Hague: Mouton.

Kaplan, Eleanor. 1969. "The Role of Intonation in the Acquisition of Language." Ph.D. dissertation, Cornell University, Ithaca, N.Y.

Laosa, Luis M. 1975. "Bilingualism in Three United States Hispanic Groups: Contextual Use of Language by Children and Adults in Their Families." *Journal of Educational Psychology*, 67(5): 617-621.

Newman, Jean. 1979. "Intonation and Expectation." In Wolfgang Wölck and Paul Garvin, eds., *Fifth LACUS Forum 1978*. Columbia, S.C.: Hornbeam Press.

Pike, Kenneth. 1945. *The Intonation of American English*. Ann Arbor: University of Michigan Press.

Ramirez, Karen. 1975. "Socio-cultural Aspects of the Chicano Dialect." In Garland Bills, ed., *Southwest Areal Linguistics*. San Diego, Calif.: Institute for Cultural Pluralism, San Diego State University.

Register, Norma. 1977. "Some Sound Patterns of Chicano English." *Journal of the Linguistics Association of the Southwest (LASSO)*, 2(3&4): 111-122.

Ryan, Ellen B. and Miguel A. Carranza. 1975. "Ingroup and Outgroup Reactions to Mexican-American Language Varieties." In H. Giles, ed., *Language, Ethnicity, and Intergroup Relations*. London: Academic Press.

Stockwell, Robert, Donald Bowen and I. Silva-Fuenzalida. 1956. "Spanish Juncture and Intonation." *Language*, 34: 641-645.

Vanderslice, Ralph, and Laura Shun Pierson. 1967. "Prosodic Features of Hawaiian English." *The Quarterly Journal of Speech*, 53: 156-166.

6

INTERFERENCE FROM SPANISH PHONOLOGY IN WRITTEN ENGLISH

Earl M. Herrick
English Department
Texas A&I University, Kingsville

When a native speaker of Spanish writes something in English, his or her writing may show several kinds of interference from Spanish. Some of this interference may be orthographical interference, which can be of two different kinds:
1. purely orthographical interference from Spanish into English; and
2. interference in English orthography that comes ultimately from Spanish phonology.

Table 1 has some examples of purely orthographical interference, which occurs because the writer has borrowed some conventions of the Spanish writing system into his or her writing of English. In (1-1), the word *comfort* has been spelled with the letter *N* because Spanish has a spelling convention that a nasal consonant must always be written with the letter *N* if it occurs immediately before any letter except *B* or *P*. In (1-2), (1-3), and (1-4), the words *affection*, *accumulate*, and *appetite* are spelled with a single *F*, *C*, and *P*, respectively, because they are words that have been borrowed into both Spanish and English from Latin, and in Latin they all begin with the prefix *ad*, in which the final consonant has been assimilated to the initial consonant of the stem. The Spanish spelling convention for such words is to spell them with single consonant letters, while the English spelling convention for such words is to spell them with double consonant letters. In (1-5), there is a spelling of the name *Volkswagen* that I

Table 1. Purely orthographical interference from Spanish in English.

	Examples of written English that show interference from Spanish orthography	Correct spellings for the intended English words	Comparable Spanish words or correspondences
(1-1)	confort	comfort	confortable
(1-2)	afection	affection	afición
(1-3)	acumulate	accumulate	acumular
(1-4)	apetite	appetite	apetito
(1-5)	Volkswaguen	Volkswagen	/gen/ ⇄ <GUEN>

once saw on a car inspection sticker that had been filled out by a mechanic in Laredo, Texas. Whether one thinks of this spelling as interference from Spanish into English or into German, it shows that its writer knew the Spanish spelling conventions for words that contain the letter *G*. All of these are examples of purely orthographical interference, and they agree with what we could predict by making a contrastive analysis of the orthographies and the spelling conventions of English and Spanish.[1] Because this kind of orthographical interference arises entirely from the orthographies and spelling conventions of the two languages, it can occur only in English texts that have been written by people who are quite literate in Spanish.

However, the second kind of orthographical interference from Spanish can occur in English texts that have been written by people who are not literate in Spanish. This kind of interference can produce errors which, at first glance, may seem to be bizarre and inexplicable errors in English spelling, grammar, or vocabulary. However, these errors can be explained quite readily if they are seen as the effects of phonological interference from Spanish that has occurred in the phonology of the writer's English idiolect, combined with a reasonable attempt by the writer to spell how he or she thinks the English words are pronounced.

I have often met this second kind of interference in writing done by the students in my freshman classes in English composition.[2] I teach at a university that is located in South Texas, about 100 miles away from the Rio Grande. Many of the students in my composition classes are native speakers of Spanish who have learned rather little about Standard English. Few of them come from the cities along the international border, where they would be in daily contact with the Spanish language as it is used in Mexico. Instead, most of them come from the sparsely settled ranching country which extends for many miles to the north of the Rio Grande. Many of these students come from families that have lived in the same small towns or on the same ranches for more than a century, and they have grown up with little of no exposure to the Standard Spanish language in either its spoken or its written form. They tend to be somewhat literate in Spanish, but they have never had any systematic education in that language, and they feel very uncertain about their abilities to use it correctly. Therefore, when these students write English, their writing does not show the first, purely orthographical, kind of interference from Spanish; they simply are not literate enough in Spanish to make mistakes like that. What their writing in English does show is the second kind of orthographical interference from Spanish: interference in English orthography that comes ultimately from Spanish phonology.

I have met four kinds of this interference: the first comes from confusion between English vowels; the second comes from confusion between English fricative consonants; the third comes from confusion between the English phonemes /č/ and /š/; the fourth happens because of consonant clusters that occur at the ends of English syllables.[3]

Table 2. Phonological interference that produces confusion between English vowels.[4]

	Examples of written English that show interference from Spanish phonology	Correct spellings for the intended English words
(2-1)	just seating down	just sitting down
(2-2)	I have relations leaving close by the campus	... living ...
(2-3)	I use to leave here when I was younger	... live ...
(2-4)	seens were alot of sisters	since we're a lot of sisters
(2-5)	the silence lingers on longer then I would like it to	... than ...

The first of these kinds of interference is illustrated in Table 2. The misspellings shown in examples (2-1) through (2-4) arise from the fact that English has two high, front, unrounded vowel phonemes - [ɪ] and [i:] - while Spanish has only one such phoneme - [i]. Therefore, a person who hears and pronounces English in terms of Spanish phonology will not discern any difference between these two English phonemes. He or she will hear the English words *sitting* and *seating*, in (2-1), as homophones and will pronounce both of them the same way, probably as [sítin]. A person who has this kind of Spanish phonological interference in his or her English will therefore see

no reason why *SEATING* is not a proper spelling[5] for the
English word *sitting*. In (2-2) and (2-3), a person who
does not hear any difference between the English phonemes
[ɪ] and [i:] will regard *LEAVING* as a proper spelling for
the word pronounced [lɪ́vɪŋ] and will regard *LEAVE* as a
proper spelling for the word pronounced [lɪ́v].

Examples (2-1) through (2-3) all contain ordinary
words of written English, and they could therefore be explained as the results of confusion between lexical items,
but I believe they can be explained much more easily as
the results of phonological interference. The example in
(2-4) begins with a string of letters that is not an ordinary word of written English. But the writer's spelling
of English is none too good anyway, and, if she pronounces
this word as [síns], then *SEENS* is probably as good a way
as any to spell it.

Another kind of confusion between English vowels is
shown in (2-5). English has two simple, front, unrounded,
non-high vowel phonemes - [ɛ] and [æ] - while Spanish has
only one such phoneme - [e]. Therefore, a person who
hears English in terms of Spanish phonology will not hear
any difference between these two English phonemes, and he
or she will hear the words *then* and *than* as homophones. A
person who has this kind of phonological interference from
Spanish in his or her idiolect of English will therefore
think it quite reasonable to spell the English words *then*
and *than* in the same way.

Table 3. Phonological interference that produces confusion between
English fricatives.

(3-1)	it was my most priced possession	... prized ...
(3-2)	the baby's hair looks like the fuss on a new tennis ball	... fuzz ...
(3-3)	... race ...	... raise ...
(3-4)	each year many lifes are lost	... lives ...
(3-5)	will safe her for us	... save ...
(3-6)	... ones ...	... once ...
(3-7)	I could go home and convied in my parents	... confide ...

Table 3 has examples of confusion between English
fricative consonants. The distinction between voiced and
voiceless fricatives is phonemic in English, but it is
allophonic in Spanish. Therefore, a person who hears English in terms of Spanish phonology will not be consciously
aware of any difference between homorganic voiced and
voiceless fricatives. The words in examples (3-1) through
(3-5) are spelled with letters ordinarily used for writing
voiceless fricatives; if these words were Spanish, they
would be pronounced with voiceless fricatives, but they

are English words pronounced with voiced fricatives. However, English words are sometimes given spellings that do
not agree with the Spanish allophones that would be pronounced in them. In (3-6) and (3-7), there are words
which are spelled with letters ordinarily used for writing
voiced fricatives, but they are English words pronounced
with voiceless fricatives, and if they were Spanish words
they would also be pronounced with voiceless fricatives.
The writers of these examples seem to have been completely
confused as to what letters should be used for writing
these English fricatives; their confusion can be explained
quite easily as a result of phonological interference from
Spanish, while I think it would be difficult to explain
their confusion in any other way.

Table 4. Phonological interference that produces confusion between
English /č/ and /š/.

| (4-1) | she kept a close wash on me | ... watch ... |
| (4-2) | body chop | body shop |

Table 4 shows a kind of interference that occurs in
Texas, although it possibly does not occur elsewhere. In
the Spanish dialect of northeastern Mexico and the adjoin-
ing region north of the international border, the Spanish
phoneme /č/ is pronounced, in free variation, either as
the affricate [tš] or as the fricative [š] or as anything
in between, such as [ʈš]. In this dialect of Spanish,
therefore, the one phoneme /č/ uses the same sounds as the
two English phonemes /č/ and /š/. In Texas, confusion
between these two English phonemes is a well-known part of
Spanish phonological interference in spoken English, and
Table 4 shows a corresponding confusion as to the spelling
that should be used for words containing these two English
phonemes.[6]

The remaining kind of interference from Spanish phonology in English orthography is phonotactic interference,
which ordinarily results in the shortening of English consonant clusters at the ends of syllables. English has
many syllable-final consonant clusters, which may consist
of two, three, or even four consonants; but Spanish has
only one genuine syllable-final consonant cluster, which
consists of only two consonants and which occurs only in
proper names or in borrowings from Latin. Therefore, a
person who hears and pronounces English in terms of Spanish phonology will presumably not be able to hear or pronounce all of the consonants which make up a consonant
cluster at the end of an English syllable.

When an English consonant cluster at the end of a word
is shortened, the part of it that is lost may or may not
include an entire morpheme. Table 5 has examples in
which entire morphemes are not lost. Sometimes, as in
examples (5-1) through (5-3), the writer uses an actual

Table 5. Phonotactic interference that produces shortened word-final syllables but no loss of inflectional morphemes.

(5-1)	my mine was made up	... mind ...
(5-2)	this pass weekend	... past ...
(5-3)	... worse ...	... worst ...
(5-4)	my Dad has always been strick with his children	... strict ...
(5-5)	this college is convenion for me	... convenient ...
(5-6)	... greatess ...	... greatest ...
(5-7)	this is the closes university to my home town	... the closest university ...
(5-8)	A&I is not the closet college to my home	... the closest college ...

English word that has the single final consonant which he thinks he has heard. Sometimes, as in examples (5-4) through (5-6), the writer constructs a spelling for what he thinks he has heard, and he may show a considerable knowledge of English spelling conventions, even though the result is a string of letters that is not an ordinary word of written English.

This kind of interference can occasionally result in a great deal of confusion. In (5-7) and (5-8), there are two misspellings of the same word which both happen to be actual words of written English. When I first saw these examples, I could not imagine what their writers could possibly mean by *the closes university* or by *the closet college*. Then I realized that both of these spellings were attempts to represent an English word that had been heard in terms of Spanish phonology. Example (5-7) was intended as a spelling for *the* [klóses] *university*, example (5-8) was intended as a spelling for *the* [klóset] *college*, and both of these spellings resulted from attempts to write the English word *closest* without all the sounds of its final consonant cluster.

The same phonotactic restrictions on word-final consonant clusters may also result in the loss of entire morphemes. English has several inflectional morphemes which may be pronounced as single consonants added to the ends of words. One group of these suffixes is pronounced as either [s] or [z]; another group of these suffixes is pronounced as either [t] or [d]. If one of these suffixes is added to a stem that already ends in a consonant, the result is a consonant cluster; and a person who hears English in terms of Spanish phonology will have trouble hearing all of that cluster, especially its last consonant phoneme which constitutes the entire suffix. When such a person writes an English word that has this kind of phonological and grammatical shape, he or she possibly will not

Table 6. Phonotactic interference that produces shortened word-final syllables and loss of inflectional morphemes.

(6-1)	I have many connotation for the word "snake"	... connotations ...
(6-2)	all the doctor and so on would be broke	... doctors ...
(6-3)	his lectures and test were always decorated with big words	... tests ...
(6-4)	Honolulu has many tourist	... tourists ...
(6-5)	... mother ...	... mother's ...
(6-6)	... brother ...	... brother's ...
(6-7)	I am a person that like to live near class	... likes to ...
(6-8)	it show what a person can accomplish	... shows what ...
(6-9)	this is where I live, it close and convenient	... it's close ...
(6-10)	it just that if something happen	... it's just ...
(6-11)	if he can be excuse so that he can go	... excused ...
(6-12)	people get portside mix up with porthole	... mixed up ...
(6-13)	I could have deceive myself	... deceived ...
(6-14)	I had acquire a good background	... acquired ...
(6-15)	cats are suppose to eat mice	... supposed ...
(6-16)	I had been expose to college life	... exposed ...
(6-17)	I use to leave here when I was younger	... used to ...

write its final consonant letter, which would be the only written representation of that suffix, and the suffixed inflectional morpheme will then seem to disappear.

Table 6 has several examples of the disappearance of clitics or inflectional suffixes. Examples (6-1) through (6-4) show the disappearance of the noun-plural suffix pronounced [s] or [z]; (6-5) and (6-6) show the disappearance of the homophonous noun-possessive suffix; (6-7) and (6-8) show the disappearance of the homophonous verbal tense-person-number suffix; and (6-9) and (6-10) show the disappearance of the homophonous contraction of the verb *is*. Examples (6-11) through (6-15) show the disappearance of the verbal past tense or past participle suffixes pronounced [t] or [d].

However, even in normal English pronunciation, the sound of the verbal suffix [t] or [d] tends to be obscured

before the word *to*. Such clusters, which are shown in
examples (6-15) and (6-16), will therefore require different pedagogical treatment. And the word sequence *used
to*, which is shown in (6-17), will require pedagogical
treatment of a still different kind, because it is normally pronounced [yú:stə], as a single phonological word.

Table 7. Loss of inflectional morphemes which form separate
syllables.

(7-1)	one of the finest college of engineering	... colleges ...
(7-2)	one of the difference between the two groups	... differences ...
(7-3)	I went and visit many universities	... visited ...
(7-4)	the school that I attend was neat in appearance	... attended ...

In addition to these simple kinds of interference that
can happen at the ends of syllables, more complicated
kinds of interference can also occur. The phenomenon
shown in Table 7 will require more research before we can
understand why it occurs. The same English inflectional
suffixes that help to form consonant clusters at the ends
of words also have allomorphs that form separate syllables. But, as in the examples in Table 7, these allomorphs of these inflectional suffixes are sometimes not
written, even though they would be separate syllables that
would be pronounceable in terms of Spanish phonology.
Whatever its cause, the omission of these suffixes is not
a result of simple phonological interference.

Table 8. Phonotactic interference that produces shortened
word-medial consonant clusters.

(8-1)	some landlords think that Mexicans accually like to live in slums	... actually ...

An example of phonological interference in a word-
medial consonant cluster is shown in Table 8. In the
English word *actually*, the consonants between the first
two vowels are pronounced [ktš], but Spanish does not have
this word-medial consonant cluster, and the writer of this
example apparently heard only its first consonant.

Table 9. Hypercorrection of consonant clusters.

(9-1)	since the second summer section	... summer session ...
(9-2)	many people do not realized how they are cheated	... realize ...

Table 9 shows examples of hypercorrection, which presumably happens because writers suspect that they are not writing all of the English consonant letters that they should be writing, and so they write extra letters that should not be there.

Table 10. Demonstratives that show two kinds of phonological confusion.

(10-1)	we used one of this to record the movie	... these ...
(10-2)	in both of this cases	... these ...
(10-3)	this table was big enough, but this chairs were too small	... these chairs ...

Table 10 illustrates a problem which arises because both of the English near demonstratives - *this* and *these* - are subject to two kinds of phonological interference that combine to destroy the contrast between them.[7] In (10-1) and (10-2), the word spelled *THIS* is clearly acting as a plural. And the sentence in (10-3) is one that would simply dismay many English teachers. They would see nothing wrong with its first clause, but they would be very unhappy about its second clause. After all (these teachers would think), the student who wrote this sentence knows how to make a demonstrative agree with its head noun, because he did so in the first clause, and he knows that the word *chairs* is plural, because he made the verb agree with it. Why didn't he make the demonstrative in the second clause plural so that it would agree with its head noun *chairs*?

I would suggest that something is actually wrong with both clauses of this sentence, and that both clauses are wrong because of phonological interference from Spanish. The student who wrote this sentence apparently pronounces both the English word *this* and the English word *these* as [dís]. In his or her idiolect, the singular and plural forms of the English near demonstrative are homophones. This idiolect does have distinct singular and plural forms for the far demonstratives; they are pronounced [dát] and [dós] and they are spelled *THAT* and *THOSE*, respectively. But, in this idiolect of English, the near demonstrative, like the definite article, simply does not make a distinction of grammatical number. Therefore, when a student writes something like example (10-3), it will do no good for the teacher to merely insist that the student should have used the plural demonstrative in the second clause. That is just what the student has done because, for him or her, the near singular demonstrative and the near plural demonstrative are both spelled *THIS*.

Now that we have identified and described this kind of orthographical interference in English that comes ultimately from Spanish phonology, what should we do about it?

We must remember that it can easily masquerade as other kinds of linguistic interference and that it can conceal other kinds of interference that occurs along with it. We may therefore have to decide whether a student's errors arise from this kind of interference, or from some other cause, or from several causes at once. But, keeping this possible confusion in mind, there are two things that we can do, one linguistic and one pedagogical.

As linguists, we need to find out just how widespread this kind of interference is. The people among whom I have encountered it may be an unusual group. They belong to a long-settled population which is somewhat bilingual in English and Spanish, but which ordinarily speaks Spanish at home; most of these people have had little experience outside the small communities in which they grew up; they have had some formal education in English; they tend to be somewhat literate in Spanish, but they have had no formal education in it; they live far enough away from Mexico that they lack regular contact with the Standard Spanish language. We should find out whether the same kind of interference occurs in the English that is written by other native speakers of Spanish who have grown up in similar environments. And we should find out whether such interference occurs in English written by native speakers of Spanish who have grown up in other environments.

As teachers of English, we need to educate our fellow teachers so that they will realize what may be going on in their students' minds in order to produce this kind of interference. Many teachers think that a student who repeatedly makes errors like these is just being obstinate or stupid. They will have to learn that, for example, a student who does not hear the difference between the English words *burr* and *burn* can hardly be expected to hear or spell the difference between the words *burns* and *burned*, which end in even larger consonant clusters. Perhaps, with enough practice, a student can learn to hear all the phonemic contrasts of English and can learn to hear all the phonemes in its consonant clusters. If not, he or she may have to learn these words as homophones that have different spellings that are used in different grammatical or lexical environments. But whatever the student does, a teacher who realizes that these seemingly semantic, lexical, or grammatical errors in written English may actually arise from phonological interference in the student's own pronunciation of English will be better prepared to deal with them.

NOTES

1. Contrastive analyses of the phonologies of English and Spanish can be found in Stockwell and Bowen (1965) and in Nash (1977). Nash also contrasts the orthographies of the two languages.
2. Except for (1-5) and (4-2), all of the examples for this paper have been taken from writing done by students at Texas A&I University or by students at high schools in South Texas. The examples which consist of single words without contexts have been taken from some research which Norma Cantú and I did several years ago, and which was reported in Herrick (1977).
3. Except for the third kind of interference, the examples which are given here are merely illustrative, and similar confusion involving other English phonemes can also occur.
4. The headings for the columns in Table 2 also apply to the columns in all of the following tables.
5. Some research will be needed as to whether two written words such as *SEATING* and *SITTING* are used equally often as spellings for both of two spoken words such as [sí:tɪŋ] and [sítɪŋ], or whether there is some preference for one or the other spelling.
6. Example (4-2) is from a hand-lettered sign that I saw on an auto repair shop in downtown Kingsville; it shows that this confusion can operate in the other direction as well.
7. One of these kinds of phonological interference causes both vowels to be pronounced as [i]; the other causes both final consonants to be pronounced as [s].

REFERENCES

Herrick, Earl M. 1977. 'Spanish Interference in the English Written in South Texas High Schools', in Bates Hoffer and Betty Lou Dubois, eds. *Southwest Areal Linguistics Then and Now*. San Antonio, Texas: Trinity University, pp. 162-169.

Nash, Rose. 1977. *Comparing English and Spanish: Patterns in Phonology and Orthography*. New York: Regents Publishing Co.

Stockwell, Robert P., and Bowen, J. Donald. 1965. *The Sounds of English and Spanish*. Chicago: University of Chicago Press.

7

THE VERNACULAR BASE OF LITERACY DEVELOPMENT IN CHICANO ENGLISH

Joyce Penfield
Graduate School of Education
Rutgers University

The sociolinguistic situation in which Mexican-Americans (Chicanos) find themselves in the Southwest is a dynamic and multilinguistically complex one. Although there is some degree of regional variation, bilingualism is the norm. For the most part, Standard English is the dominant language for formal uses, especially written modes of communication, and Spanish occupies the position of a vernacular for informal interaction. This is an over-simplification, however. A Southwest bilingual may display several codes of Spanish and English in his or her repertoire. The term that best illustrates the socio-linguistic situation is "bilingual dialects"--derived from Haugen (1969). Bilingual dialects refer to a linguistic two-dimensionality of function for a dual language community.

The taxonomy given in Figure 1 is a somewhat idealized classification of the linguistic situation. Forming the end points of this continuum are Standard American English and Standard Mexican Spanish, corresponding to the northern dialect. Like other New World varieties, Standard Mexican Spanish developed basically from rustic Spanish speech of the 16th century but has also been influenced considerably through lexical borrowing from Nahuatl and other Indian languages (Ornstein, 1971). A minority of Southwesterners control this variety effectively. Two other dialects of Spanish which can be

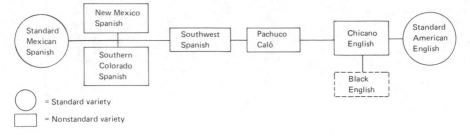

FIGURE 1

distinguished are the Northern New Mexico and Southern
Colorado variety which descended directly from the speech
of the 16th and 17th century Spanish conquistadores as
well as a general Southwest Spanish. The latter, based on
rural Mexican Spanish, is fully a bilingual dialect,
whose norms reflect English contact either in the form of
items in various stages of rephonemicization and semantic
shift or through code-switching.

Pachuco Caló is a specialized jargon or code which
essentially utilizes the syntactic and phonological system of Spanish but creates its own lexical innovations
borrowing from Mexican Spanish, Standard English, Chicano
English, underworld jargon, and the Romany language (Ornstein, 1972). Pachuco Caló enjoys rather wide usage among
younger males throughout the Southwest as a street discourse and for slang effect. Often lexical terms beginning here creep into the Southwest Spanish of other
speakers, so that this street koiné becomes no longer exclusively bound to the lower socioeconomic classes nor
to the delinquents or adolescents. Erroneously, many linguistically naive observers have confused Caló with
Southwest Spanish.

Next along the continuum is the contact vernacular,
Chicano English. Chicano English may be defined as a
variety of English which has originated from contact with
Spanish along with other social and regional dialects of
English, including southern English and Black English. As
more research is carried out on Chicano English in different parts of the Southwest, it becomes clearer that it
is a nonstandard variety of English which displays norms
of its own linguistically, most of which have developed
through contact with other varieties of English. Quite
naturally some of these norms reflect predictable interference between Spanish and English which has developed
diachronically into a community norm. However, other
norms reflect just the opposite, perhaps an attempt to
hypercorrect or display non-interference.

It is important to note the relatively stable nature of bilingualism in the Southwest, reinforced by centuries of co-existence of Anglo and Hispano speech communities and cultures. Such stability is in direct contrast to the dynamic or transitory bilingualism of immigrant groups from Europe who settled in the New World and whose off-spring became monolingual in little more than one generation. Such does not appear to happen in the majority of the Chicano communities in the Southwest. Perhaps this linguistic stability has been aided by the proximity to Mexico and the heavy immigration from Mexico to the U.S. of persons seeking and finding employment both on a short-term basis and as settlers. We must also not forget the ancestral tie between Hispanic families residing in the Southwest and Mexican families reflected in visits to relatives in Mexico or residential movement from one side of the border to the other and sometimes back again. This fluid interchange between Chicanos and Mexicans on both sides of the border acts to counterbalance the heavy English linguistic interference, serving at the same time to prevent the creolization of Spanish and to maintain it essentially as a variety of American Spanish.

Although the situation described above varies more in degree than in substance, El Paso, Texas, which shares the border with its neighboring Mexican city, Juárez, represents the epitomy of the blend between dynamic and stable language contact. Those who have just entered El Paso from different parts of Mexico exert a dynamic influence bringing with them Mexican culture and usually monolingualism in different varieties of Mexican Spanish while those who have lived in El Paso for several generations or more exert a stable influence with their Mexican-American cultural values and both Southwest Spanish and Chicano English or in some cases Standard Anglo English. This stable and dynamic language situation presents problems in literacy development in English which this paper will touch on, since all students involved in my study represent a blend of this stable and dynamic language situation.

LITERACY DEVELOPMENT: LINGUISTIC CONSIDERATIONS

The students referred to in this paper form two major groups in terms of language background. The majority of them have resided in Mexico and received their schooling in Spanish with minimal instruction in English, except for a few students who may have attended binational centers where bilingual education is practiced minimally at the high school level. For the most part, those students meeting the above backgrounds are fairly literate in Spanish and their written English quite naturally reflects predictable interference with English at the syntactic level, while their spoken English reflects a great deal of

phonological interference typical of Spanish speakers
learning English. It is this type of student one expects
to encounter in an English-as-a-second language class.

Occasionally, mingled in this same ESL class are
other students who reflect the dynamics of residential
patterns often typical in border areas. These students
were born in the United States and acquired English through
contact with Black English and Standard English-speaking
monolingual children while usually maintaining some degree of Spanish in the home. Quite typically, these
students may have resided in almost monolingual English-
speaking communities in the U.S. for at least the first
6 or 7 years of their life and then were returned to
monolingual Spanish-speaking communities in various parts
of Mexico to finish their primary and secondary education.
Upon returning to the U.S. to begin their higher education,
these students often have a latent understanding of English, since English was in effect one of their first
languages. Unlike their classmates described previously,
they do not reflect phonological interference in their
spoken English; rather they reflect other nonstandard
speech repertoires, but especially some Chicano English.
Their verbal development in English at the spoken level
is obviously apparent. They are extremely fluent in a
variety of different communicative situations in ways that
the first group of students mentioned are not. For many
of the students in this second group, their lack of
development in written English is also apparent.

We will argue in this paper that the second group
of students described above are in fact a unique type of
bilingual rather than Limited English Proficient students.
In addition, we will illustrate that many of the "errors"
made by this group of bilinguals when writing English may
at first glance appear to reflect syntactic interference
between Spanish and English but in fact are more accurately
attributed to (1) the lack of phonological distinctions
in the particular dialect of the writer (Chicano English);
and (2) an unfamiliarity with the writing conventions of
English.

METHOD

A dozen or so samples of writing were collected from
about 10 students. Ethnographic interviews were conducted
with each student along with the reading aloud of compositions which these same students had previously written.
The purpose of these two types of oral taped-data was to
obtain an adequate sample of natural and reading pronunciation in English. A final source of data included three
years of observation and documentation by the author in
which various aspects of Chicano English were studied
(see Penfield, Joyce and Jacob Ornstein-Galicia. In press.
Chicano English: An Ethnic Contact Dialect. Holland: John

Benjamins Press.) It must be noted that the examples
that will be discussed do not come from code-switching bilinguals but rather from bilinguals whose language acquisition patterns were "sequential" (McLaughlin, 1981) and
whose contact with monolingual-speaking environments involving both English and Spanish was also sequential
with an interruption at various stages in language development.

PROBLEMS IN LITERACY DEVELOPMENT

Orthography
As Herrick (1977) has mentioned in previous publications, many "errors" are the result of inadequate familiarity with the orthographic conventions of English. An
excerpt from one student who falls within the second
category discussed above illustrates the problem of orthography very well (Fig. 2). I have circled those errors
clearly related to spelling and underlined those which
involve the spoken language system on which the written
form was supposedly based.

1.   YOURE LIFE.
2.   LIVING TOGETHER WITH A PERSON WITHOUT
3.   BEEN MRRIADE IS SOMETHING THAT OURE PARENTS DON'T
4.   ACCEPT VERY WELL, BECAUSE THEY WERE RAISE IN
5.   ANOTHER WAY. I THINK IF HADE A GIRL FRIEND AND
6.   SHE WOULD LIKE TO LIVE TOGETHER WITHOUT GETIN
7.   MARRIADE I WOULD ACCEPT AND MOVE WITH HER.
8.   I WOULD DO THESE ONLY IF I LIVE HER IN THE US.
9.   BECAUSE LIKE I SAID BEFORE IN MEXICO MY PARENTS
10.   WOULD NOT APROVE THIS, AND THE SOCIETY WOULD
11.   SEE US LIKE IF WE WERE BREAKING THE ROOLS BY
12.   WICH WE HAVE TO LIVE.

FIGURE 2

In glancing at the underlined errors, the use of
"getin" obviously reflects the informal usage of English
speech on which the writing is based. In other samples
it was common to find "gotta" and "gonna". The use of
"aprove this" raises an interesting question as to
whether the writer is really aware of the entire form of
the expression, i.e. 'approve of' or whether his writing
reflects some type of interference. This example reflects

the deceptiveness of the speech repertoire, since it is
possible to pronounce this expression in rapid, informal
speech by simply lengthening the labio-dental voiced fricative /v/. The vowel in "of" /əv/ would get reduced until it was deleted in Chicano English. Since prepositions
tend to be unstressed and consequently have reduced or
even deleted vowels, Chicano English speakers can simply
slide or lengthen consonants to sound very informal and
still never have any communication problems with more
standard speakers of English; however, the writing system demands the full standard English form. Thus, one
can maintain that for this group of students what interference exists is between the spoken and written systems
of English rather than between Spanish and English. The
examples below somewhat reflect this inference. It can
be argued that they reflect an attempt to map the vernacular base - Chicano English in this case - onto written
English.

(1) "My english was not as good as it supposed to be."(it's)
  2) "Now imaging that the same thing happens to   (imagine)
     a guy."
(3) "The wolf was at bed and he said coming."   (come in)
(4) "The in the night we went to the discotecs   (then)
     and meet a lot of girls every day."
(5) "When we lef to mexico city...."   (left)
(6) "I'm living in Ciudad Juárez right now and
     you are welcome to bisited any time you   (visit it)
     want I will be your host."
(7) "I will trai to maked better."   (make it)
(8) "... because I fall and the water."   (fell in)
(9) "With my parents I private myself of   (prevent)
     doing something because sometimes they
     get angry for just a little."
(10)"I was happy there too because my friend
     had I lot of friend's and for a homecoming   (a)
     they made I lot of party's."   (a)

Example (1) above, I would suggest, illustrates as
most of the others do an attempt to depict spoken Chicano English. In actual pronunciation, there would not
normally be a juncture between the words *it's* and *supposed*.
If written errors as found in (1) were the result of interference between Spanish and English, one would expect
the deletion of the subject pronoun *it* rather than *'s*.
Interference speakers of English in their writing most
typically present the following: "My english was not
so good as *is* supposed to be." Examples (4),(8),(9),and (10)
reflect the writer's attempt to represent in writing those
forms-- given their linguistic context--which are no
doubt homophonous in Chicano speech.

For the group of students, there commonly seemed to
be confusion over the use of *and*, *in*, and *on*. Although at
first glance such errors are treated as grammatical, we

would argue that they merely reflect an error in orthographic choice by a Chicano English speaker who pronounces
all three homophonously. In fact, in rapid speech all three
most typically found in unstressed environments are pronounced in Chicano English as no more than a lengthened
/n/ so that those unfamiliar with the grammar of English
or the orthography often choose the incorrect pattern when
spelling.

Examples (3),(6), and (7) reflect patterns typically
found in the writing of monolingual English speaking children who are not quite familiar with the writing conventions of English. They reflect a confusion with the word
boundaries of the orthographic system but at the same
time they accurately depict the writer's dependence on
his or her pronunciation in terms of rhythm and juncture.

In example (10) it is interesting to note that in one
instance the writer chooses the correct orthographic
form *I* and then equally applies it to those contexts where
unstressed vowels occur and would be pronounced and written
very differently as "a". We would argue that *I* and *a* are
homophonous in Chicano English speech and therefore are
confused orthographically by those yet unfamiliar with
the orthographic conventions of English. Example (11) also
reflects this problem:

(11) "My parents gave me a moral and an education,
     and I know that doing this a would hurt my   (I)
     parents."

Again, some cases of orthographic deletion seem to reflect interference with Spanish as in examples (12)-(15)
below.

(12) "I_ really glad I decided to take this course."   ('m)
(13) "But I think I_ getting it again."   ('m)
(14) "We_ having so much fun."   ('re)
(15) "...and I_ still taking English classes."   ('m)

There is some evidence from typical writing patterns
found in the compositions of new learners of English who
are also native speakers of Spanish to argue that (12)-
(15) do not result from interference with Spanish. Interference speakers (i.e. new learners) tend *not* to produce
such structures as those above, but rather they tend to
delete the progressive ending, forming such structures as
(16).

(16) "I'm still take__ English classes."

Phonological Confusion
The phonological system of Chicano English displays
historical influence of contact with Spanish in ways that
produce confusion for bilinguals becoming literate in
English. However, Chicano English also represented norms

prevalent in Chicano speech communities which can not simply be explained by an interference model. A great deal of literature on Chicano English in the past decade has meticulously pointed this out through detailed field work in Chicano communities (Bills, 1977; Penfield, 1983; Penfield and Ornstein, 1983).

The main point of the discussion which follows is that errors in written compositions are most likely due to a reliance on the phonological system of the writer--in this case Chicano English. Many words which contrast in pronunciation in standard English are homophonous in Chicano English, e.g. *ones* and *once*. As a result, the Chicano English speaker unfamiliar with orthographic/spelling conventions of English will sometimes select the incorrect word. Too often, the teacher interprets this "error" as an incorrect grammatical choice because of interference with Spanish. Given a discourse context of a composition and familiarity with the linguistic system of Chicano English, it is hoped that teachers could become more sensitive to the source of the errors used by this population of students and alter their teaching strategies accordingly. The impact of the phonological and syntactic system of Chicano English on new literates is illustrated below.

/č/ vs. /š/. The /č/ vs. /š/ distinction is rarely phonemic in Chicano English. These two units are apparently in alternation or, as Wald (1976) has suggested, in the process of merging. The result are occasional examples as (17) or (18).

(17) "I never sheat."   (cheat)
(18) "For me it's difficult to shoose."   (choose)

Devoicing. Devoicing occurs in Chicano English both for sibilants and labio-dental fricatives which could possibly explain the orthographic errors in examples (19)-(23).

(19) "They are so sweet and careful with you when
      he's your sweet-heart, but ones you get   (once)
      married with him he turns in a sort of mounster."
(20) "I'll pray for all the people I love and all
      the people I ones hate."   (once)
(21) "Today American doctors are trying to
      proof this theory."   (prove)
(22) "In Mexico we still belief that we have   (believe)
      to get married."
(23) "Once a month he adviced them."   (advised)

It must be noted, however, that devoicing of sibilants has been noted in El Paso even though other parts of the Southwest may have a different trend. Register (1977) noted that in Tucson, Arizona voiceless sibilants were voiced when they preceded voiced consonants, e.g. /ðIz bIg/ for 'this big'. Metcalf (1972) also noted the

voicing of voiceless counterparts in Chicano English in
Riverside, California, e.g. /reIz/ for 'race' and /hauz/
for 'house'.

Defricativization. Some Chicano English speakers follow
a pattern found in Black English by utilizing /d/ and /t/
for the interdental fricative counterpart in standard
English. Orthographic errors based on this pronunciation
are also typical in student compositions, e.g. examples
(24) and (25).

(24) "Tanks to everybody..."   (thanks)
(25) "Even do to many people say that if you   (though)
      have your parents and family love you,
      you don't need friends..."

Consonant cluster deletion. Consonant cluster reduction,
as studies on Black English have shown, affects the
grammatical system a great deal, especially regular verb
endings or past participles. There is much debate in research studies on Chicano English over this aspect, but
from our observations, past tense verb forms are
affected, e.g. examples (26)-(28).

(26) "Workers have loss their jobs."   (lost)
(27) "When I was going to seven grade,   (seventh)
      they close the school..."   (closed)
(28) "She toll me this..."   (told)

Laxing of vowels. Contrary to what new learners of
English do, Chicano English speakers tend to lax vowels
producing a different set of homophonous vowels. Gonzalez (1977) noted this laxing in linguistic environments preceding stops. It can also be noted especially
in those environments preceding /l/, e.g. /sεl/ for 'sale';
/fIl/ for 'feel'; and /pUl/ for 'pool'. Orthographic
errors are numerous which reflect this dialect pattern,
e.g. examples (29)-(34).

(29) "By instinct man stops eating food when
      filling ill."   (feeling)
(30) "This are my reasons why abortion should   (these)
      be legal."
(31) "This is why governments are permitting the
      sell of pornographic magazines."   (sale)
(32) "The role of women in our country has
      being very different..."   (been)
(33) "But know hes being changing in some ways."   (been)
(34) "We are all human beens."   (beings)

Loss of /hw/ vs. /w/ distinction. Many dialects of American English do not make a phonemic distinction between
/w/ and /hw/. Chicano English is one of them. When coupled
with vowel neutralizations significant and frequent words
often get confused, e.g. /wεr/ for 'where' and /wər/ for
'were'. Both are commonly written as *were*. Example (35)
illustrates such a confusion.

(35) "In Mexico women seem to men to incapable
      to accomplish a job were strenght and in-   (where)
      telligents are combine."

Miscellaneous. Other problems are presented for specific
lexical items, e.g. examples (36) and (37).

(36) "I thing I would be one of the more unhappy   (think)
      persons..."
(37) "Most of the youth is learning thinks to   (things)
      early . . ."

One lexical pair which is important grammatically
also seems to be caused by homophony, although in standard
English they would never be pronounced similarly, i.e.
will and *would*. It is very likely that these two items are
homophonous in Chicano English speech of some varieties
and pronounced as /wUl/ resulting in examples like (38).

(38) "What will you like?"   (would)

It is also possible that another pair, *want* and *won't*
may also be homophonous since they are also typically confused orthographically by Chicano English speaking new
literates as illustrated in (39).

(39) "When all the other young man were trying
      to take her out to dance she didn't won't   (want)
      to because she thought that he just
      might take her out to dance."

Nonstandard Syntactic Forms

Many nonstandard syntactic forms which are shared by
other dialects of American English can also be found in
the writing of Chicano English speakers, including: (1)
double negation (examples (40) and (41); (2) topicaliza-
tion (examples (42) and (43); and (3) embedded question
inversion (example (44).

(40) "My four years I spend there I did not
      learn nothing."
(41) "Now that she ain't no more by my side, I still
      remember her with the love she showed me."
(42) "To write about myself, it's a little difficult
      for me."
(43) "I think they taught us pretty good since what I
      know it was from them."
(44) "I ask myself what I would do without a friend."

CONCLUSION

The research study on which the examples and discussion
waged in this paper are based was a small exploratory pilot
study which clearly suggested that for bilingual students
who are speakers of Chicano English and in the process of
learning to write a good deal of their problem lies in

the vernacular base-- Chicano English--on which literacy
development in English rests as well as an unfamiliarity
with the orthographic conventions of English. There are
obvious implications for the teacher of this population.
Although it is quite typical that this population of students would be placed in an academic level class of
English-as-a-second language, they do not have the same
acquisitional background as a new learner of English and
therefore must be taught by teachers with this in mind.
Explanations given and materials used should be specifically adapted to build on their strengths, i.e. a native
knowledge of one variety of English, rather than their
weakness.

REFERENCES

Bills, Garland. 1977. "Vernacular Chicano English: Dialect or In-
     terference?" *Journal of the Linguistic Association of the
     Southwest (LASSO)*, 2(2): pp. 30-36.

Gonzalez, Gustavo. 1977. "Persistent English Language Difficulties
     in the Speech of Chicano College Students." In Paul Wilcott and
     Jacob Ornstein, eds., *College English and the Mexican American*.
     San Antonio, Texas: Trinity University Press, pp. 93-100.

Haugen, Einar. 1956. *Bilingualism in the Americas: A Bibliography
     and Research Guide*. Gainesville, Florida: American Dialect
     Society.

Herrick, Earl. 1977. "Spanish Interference in the English Written
     in South Texas High Schools." In Bates Hoffer and Betty Lou
     Dubois, eds., *Southwest Areal Linguistics Then and Now*. San
     Antonio, Texas: Trinity University Press, pp. 162-9.

McLaughlin, Barry. 1978. *Second-Language Acquisition in Childhood*.
     Hillsdale, New Jersey: Lawrence Erlbaum Associates.

Metcalf, Allan. 1972. "Mexican-American English in Southern Cali-
     fornia." *Western Review*, 9: pp. 13-21.

Ornstein, Jacob. 1971. "Language Varieties Along the U.S./Mexican
     Border." In G.E. Perren and J.L. Trim, eds., *Applications
     of Linguistics: Selected Papers of the Second International
     Congress of Applied Linguistics*. Cambridge: Cambridge Uni-
     versity Press, pp. 349-362.

_____. 1972. "Toward a Classification of Southwest Spanish
     Non-standard Variants," *Linguistics* 93, pp. 70-87.

Penfield, Joyce. 1983. "Chicano English: Implications for Assessment and Literacy Development" *Bilingual Ed. Paper Series* 6(5): pp.1-33.

_____ and Jacob Ornstein-Galicia. In Press. *Chicano English: An Ethnic Contact Dialect*.   Holland: John Benjamins Press.

Register, Norma. 1977. "Some Sound Patterns of Chicano English," *Journal of the Linguistic Association of the Southwest* 2(3/4): pp. 111-122.

Wald, Benji. 1976. "The Process of Unmerger in Bilingual Phonology: The Case of the Voiceless Palatals in the English of Mexican-Americans in Los Angeles," mimeo, National Center for Bilingual Research, Los Alamitos, California.

SECTION II:
THE SOCIOCULTURAL
DIMENSION

8

PARAMETERS OF THE EAST LOS ANGELES SPEECH COMMUNITY*

Maryellen García
National Center for Bilingual Research
Los Alamitos, California

In the course of this conference, we have collectively
been raising the question of what Chicano English is,
considering problems such as the influence of Spanish-
English bilingualism, the relationship of Chicano English
to other nonstandard varieties of English, and the question
of who can properly be called Chicano for inclusion in this
group of speakers. I think that we are too ambitious.
Recent figures show that people of Mexican heritage number
more than 6.5 million in the United States, scattered
throughout the country, although 90 percent are concentrated in the Southwest (Peñalosa, 1980, p.3) in the
states of California, Texas, Arizona, New Mexico, and
Colorado.[1] Approximately 23 percent of that number are
English monolingual (Macías, 1981, p.21). In view of the
social, geographical, and linguistic heterogeneity of such
a group, it seems unlikely that a single definition or
characterization of Chicano English can emerge.

*I would like to thank Benji Wald for our discussions on Chicano
English and for access to recorded data from East Los Angeles,
which provide some of the examples in the text. This paper has also
benefitted from watchful edits by Victor Rodriguez, and helpful
comments from Jacob Ornstein-Galicia.

One approach to the problem is to identify the social and linguistic parameters of a single Chicano English speech community in what will likely prove to be many throughout the United States. A speech community must be socially cohesive, have at least one linguistic variety in common, and share the same norms for the conduct and inter- pretation of speech (and in bilingual communities, this includes language choice), and for the evaluation of linguistic features (c.f., Gumperz 1968, pp. 219-220; Hymes 1972, p. 54; Labov 1972, p. 158; Bailey 1973, p. 65). This discussion considers a 'linguistic variety' to be a set of rules for phonology, morphology, and syntax, and a pool of lexical items, idioms, and expressions in which some rules may hold for the group as a whole, while other rules or lexical usages may be variable across speakers. Further, varieties may be distinguished by a higher fre- quency in the production of a non-standard variant as compared to its frequency in the greater language community. This approach also assumes that Chicanos in a particular locale are socioculturally cohesive, held together by such things as lifestyles, customs, and values, as well as ethnicity.[2] Finally, flexibility is needed in character- izing the geographic parameters of the community, because of the great mobility of modern day societies, and because of the social heterogeneity of people living in the same geographic location. The physical dimension will need to be included as an idealization--a way to identify a parti- cular speech community, East Los Angeles, for example, from another such as El Paso.

THE EAST LOS ANGELES SPEECH COMMUNITY

Indicative of the speech community status of speakers of Chicano English from East Los Angeles is that they are identifiable from Mexican speakers living in the same area, and from Mexican-Americans from the greater Los Angeles suburbs by their speech. There also appear to be norms for English language use versus Spanish language use, and negative evaluation of Mexicans living in the community who speak English with a heavy Spanish accent.

The section of metropolitan Los Angeles known as East Los Angeles is made up of four political divisions, El Sereno, Boyle Heights, Lincoln Heights, and Belvedere. It is a seven-square-mile, unincorporated area bordering the city of Los Angeles on the west and north, Monterey Park to the northeast, Montebello on the east, and the City of Commerce on the south.[3] The area has been Mexican or Mexican-American since the late 1800s, when the land was divided for agricultural use, and later attracted Mexican immigrants in the early 1900s (Macías, 1974). The area is now over 90 percent Spanish surnamed (U.S. Census, 1980). The oppression of Mexicans and Americans of Mexican descent in the area by the mainstream has also been char- acteristic, reflected in the so-called Zoot Suit incidents

of the 1940s. The area has traditionally been working
class, with an overall low income per capita. High school
graduates are expected to go into trades or other manual
labor; there is a high incidence of single-parent families
on the welfare rolls. In some neighborhoods, there is a
youth culture where adolescent boys form gangs with non-
mainstream values such as petty theft, alcoholism, early
sex and fatherhood, and violent crime against members of
rival gangs.[4] For the younger segment of the community,
there is a sense of identity as Chicanos or Mexican-
Americans who are socially and economically distinct from
the new immigrants from Mexico. The latter group tends
to inherit the low rung on the socioeconomic ladder,
taking the low-status jobs and struggling with English as
the parents and grandparents of the second and third
generation Chicanos once did. These factors are presented
as gross indicators of community identity; not all people
who live in these areas would be described by all of these
characteristics.

LINGUISTIC VARIABLES OF EAST LOS ANGELES ENGLISH

Included in the following discussion are phonological
features, morphologically sensitive phonological rules,
syntax, semantics (signaled by unique lexical items), and
nonstandard word formation rules. These various aspects of
East Los Angeles English may prove to characterize its
speakers, although at this preliminary stage the items
are presented as only potentially characteristic and in
need of further investigation.
     As suggested previously here and by other researchers
(c.f., Metcalf, 1979; Wald, 1981), not all features are
used categorically by all speakers. There will be rules
which are used to a large extent by speakers from East
Los Angeles, rules which are shared with speakers of a
more inclusive Southern California English but used with
greater frequency in East Los Angeles, and there are some
aspects of language use which will prove to be shared with
other Chicano English communities. It is the combination of
these features taken together that will contribute to
the characterization of the speaker from East Los Angeles.

     Phonology
     One of the previously noted characteristics of
speakers from the area is the lowering and backing of
/ɛ/ in stressed syllables followed by /l/, so that
helicopter sounds like *halicopter* and *elevator* sounds like
alivator. The openness of the vowel appears to be greater
before *l* in closed syllables, such as in *yell* and *felt*. It
has been described by Wald (1980, 1981) for Los Angeles,
and was noted by Gingras (1978) for speakers in Whittier,
a suburb 15 miles east of Los Angeles. This feature is
perhaps the most distinctive for East Los Angeles speakers,

and has been pointed out as a recognizably Chicano trait
in California (c.f., Metcalf, 1979, p.10).

Also potentially distinctive are tense vowels in
initial, unstressed syllables, where conventional rules
for stress in English predict vocalic reduction. Typical
examples are words containing a one-syllable historical
prefix and stressed root, e.g., *today*, *refuse*, which in ELA
English are [tudéy] and [rifyúz]. This rule also seems
to extend to words which do not contain historical pre-
fixes, e.g., *tomato*, *enough*. It may be that the community
has retained the syllable timing of an earlier generation
of Spanish-English bilinguals. (In Spanish, lack of
stress does not reduce the duration of the syllable, and
vowels retain their underlying quality even though unstressed.) In ELA English, the tensing of initial
unstressed vowels is observed both in words in which the
initial vowel is only variably tensed in Standard
English, e.g., *refuse*, and words in which it is always
lax, e.g., *today*, *tomato*.

Another potential characteristic is the variable
devoicing of intervocalic /z/ (written with s or z).
With words in which the /z/ comes syllable-finally, the
compensatory lengthening of the preceding vowel, and a
universal tendency for devoicing in that position makes
such examples weak evidence, e.g., "It was embarrassing."
However, where the /z/ is syllable-initial the lack of
voicing is especially notable and distinct from other
non-Hispanic varieties of English: "I think I'd try
anything, you know, as a last resort."[5]

Morphologically Sensitive Rules

Other kinds of rules may prove to be sensitive to
the morphemic status of the segment. One affects *the*,
which is conventionally pronounced with a schwa [ə]
before consonants, but a tense /i/ before an initial
vowel, e.g., /ə/ in *the bus*, but /i/ in *the ocean*.
Speakers in ELA variably retain the schwa pronunciation
before vowels, as if written: *thuh ocean*.

Another is the vocalic quality of the present
progressive suffix *-ing*, which in ELA English is often
pronounced with a tense /i/ with no offglide and a dental
/n/. Examples from recorded interviews include: "They'd
see like *gloween* bushes, like," or, "They'd see shadows
goween by." This contrasts with the short i /ɪ/ and velar
nasal /ŋ/ of Standard English, and with the short i and
dental n of other vernaculars, e.g., *fixin' tryin'* (c.f.,
Wolfram and Fasold 1974, p.142; Wolfram and Christian,
1976, pp. 61-63; Feagin, 1979, p.101). While the *-een*
suffix is also heard in the speech of non-Hispanics in
Los Angeles, the frequency of usage, vowel tenseness,
and duration may prove to be distinctive to East Los
Angeles Chicano speakers.[6]

Also observed to be variable in the community is the
glottalization of word-final alveolar stops. This affects

/t/ and /d/ in words that are monomorphemic as well as
those which contain -ed, a marker for past tense or the
past participle. In the following examples from interviews, an apostrophe is used for the glottal stop: "And
I put out the ligh'";"The clothes just parte' like that";
and, "You get loade'." Processes of glottalization and
deletion of syllable-final t and d have been reported in
the English of Puerto Ricans in New Jersey (Ma and
Herasimchuk, 1968) and in New York City (Wolfram, 1974).
Wolfram discovered that the Puerto Rican teenagers he
interviewed deleted /t/ and /d/ more frequently than
Black English speakers from the same area, and suggests
the distribution of these phonemes in Puerto Rican Spanish
as possible influences on their deletion in the English
of the group (1974, pp. 129-131). Wolfram also reports
the deletion of /d/ (not glottalization) in words marked
with -ed, e.g., *raided, cheated*; glottal stop in that
position is observed for ELA. My impression from listening to speakers from the community is that the /d/
glottalization rule applies more frequently to the
syllabic -ed marker than the non-syllabic marker.[7]

Syntax
The syntax of the English of Mexican-Americans has
remained largely unstudied, save for the interference
errors of Spanish-dominant speakers. Syntactic differences from the English speaking mainstream may be far
more subtle than those of phonology. Here I note two
rules which are fairly widely accepted in Standard
English, and appear to be variable for the Chicano
English speech community of East Los Angeles.
One is the obligatory use of the negative word *not*
with *until* in Standard English. Negation with the word
until indicates a period of duration after which something will end or begin. As examples, there are: "He
won't be happy *until* he's tried them all"; "He won't
be home *until* seven o'clock." For some Mexican-Americans
from East Los Angeles, *until* alone can stand as the
negative element in the sentence, so that: "He'll be
home *until* seven o'clock," in the appropriate context,
can mean that, "He won't come home *until* seven o'clock."[8]
Another rule that bears further investigation is the
placement of the indirect object pronoun. While there
are some verbs in English that can take the indirect
object before the direct object, as in, "I gave *her* a
book," "I threw *her* a party," "I saved *her* a seat," it
appears to be a restricted set. In East Los Angeles,
the indirect object pronoun apparently can be pre-posed
with verbs which prohibit it in Standard English such as
put, in "They put *him* a cast," instead of, "They put a
cast on him." The range of verbs which have different
constraints on indirect object placement from those of
Standard English is a suggested area for future
investigation.

Semantics/Lexicon
Empirical investigation has much to contribute to
the study of lexical items that are used in ways peculiar
to particular speech communities. In East Los Angeles,
I can only point out a few that have been observed as
different usages of common vocabulary.

One notable usage is that *all* as an intensifier
before adjectives, as in: "He's *all* proud, passing out
cigars and all." While *all* is commonly used idiomatically
in the speech of other groups of English speakers e.g.,
all done-in, *all* hot and bothered, it appears to be so
used primarily with adjectives or past participles which
indicate a physical or emotional state of the animate
referent. In the East Los Angeles speech community, it
extends to inanimate referents, such as, "The movie was
all weird." Moreover, while colloquial English has words
such as *terribly*, *really*, and *very* as intensifiers, in the
speech of some young people from the community, *all* seems
to be the preferred adjective.

Similarly, colloquialisms used in non-Hispanic
communities may prove to be used to a greater extent in
East Los Angeles. One example is, *for reals*, as in "He
didn't know it was *for reals*." While speakers from non-
Chicano communities might use *really* as a stylistic
variant, a speaker from East Los Angeles may have the
for reals expression in a wider range of syntactic and
semantic environments, as in: "Did you give it to him
for reals?" "*For reals* did you buy it for her?," "Did
you *for reals* sell your car?" This is just one example
of an idiom commonly used in other dialects of colloquial
American English which may serve to distinguish this
speech community by greater frequency of occurrence in a
greater range of environments.

The last item to be suggested for the time being is
the use of *barely* to mean *just* or *only*.[9] While in colloquial American English, *barely* is often used to mean
just did, as in,"He *barely* passed his chemistry exam,"
or "He *barely* made the plane," it seems to be restricted
to verbs that refer to the achievement of a particular
goal. In the Chicano English of East Los Angeles *barely*
appears to be used to emphasize timeliness or scarcity.
Some examples are: "He *barely* came yesterday," meaning,
"He got here *just* yesterday," and "I *barely* have two
pieces," meaning, "I have *only* two pieces." With *barely*
an apparent substitute for *just* and *only*, it would be
interesting to look at the distribution of *barely*, *only*
and *just* in empirical data for the speech community,
comparing the frequency of each with respect to the
semantics of the verb it modifies.

Nonstandard Word-formation or Co-occurrence Rules
Included in this category are those difficult
word-formation rules which may be used very frequently
even by non-Chicano English speakers, but for which

speakers in Mexican-American communities may exhibit
greater variability. One such rule is the voicing of the
labiodental, word-final fricative f in *mischief* when the
adjectival suffix *-ous* is added, as in *mischievous*. The
lack of voicing in the word would make it *mischiefous*, as
in, "She says that there's mischiefous ghosts, too."
Another example of such difficulty is the creation of *-er*
comparative forms in violation of the rule which prohibits
the comparative suffix with words of more than two
syllables, e.g., *politely*. In the following example, the
speaker creates the comparative with the *-er* suffix
rather than with the prescribed comparative word, *more*
(i.e., *more politely*): "I don't talk to them any *politelier*
than I would to anybody else." A last example of unfamiliarity with standard syntactico-semantic co-occurrence rules is the use of a negative polarity phrase *at all*
in a positive context. In the example, "A natural high is
better than *any* high *at all*," the reduced comparative
clause containing *any*. . . *at all* is inappropriate because
there is no negative word in the sentence. Problems
with word-formation and syntactic co-occurrence rules
may be characteristic of speakers in other Chicano
communities as well, as shall be noted subsequently.
Again, not all speakers who have the more easily identifiable phonological features of East Los Angeles English
may have difficulty with rules such as these, but such
difficulty appears to be characteristic of at least a
subset of speakers in the community.

DISCUSSION

In presenting examples of phonology, syntax, lexicon,
and morpho-syntactic rules which are found in East Los
Angeles Chicano English, I emphasize that not all speakers
have all of these characteristics, and the characteristics
presented here are not exhaustive for the community.
Rather, they may be included in a pool of features in
each of the different linguistic categories which
speakers from the community exhibit variably. Moreover,
this discussion of the linguistic parameters of East
Los Angeles English is not enough to support the claim
that the speech community is distinct from that of El
Paso, or Albuquerque, or Denver, for example. Also to
be considered is the sharing of language use norms, such
as community attitudes toward the appropriate use of
Spanish and English in daily life.

Language Use Norms
For many second and third generation Mexican-Americans
in the Los Angeles area, English is very much a home
language. While this domain in some communities means
the use of Spanish or an intrasentential code-switching
style in East Los Angeles, English is also used at home

as an informal speech variety.[10] In East Los Angeles,
parents and grandparents may be addressed in English,
even though they may not speak English themselves. In
other Mexican-American communities, children are repri-
manded for speaking English to elders, and are encouraged
to keep up their Spanish in that domain.[11] In East Los
Angeles, people who look Mexican should be addressed in
English first and then in Spanish if necessary and the
speaker is able to do so. Being addressed in Spanish by a
bilingual who is a fluent English speaker is likely to
offend the native-born, as the implication is that they
are recent immigrants and therefore lower in social and
economic status than the speaker.

Members of other Chicano communities do not necessarily share language use norms with Mexican-Americans
from the Los Angeles area. As evidence, I offer my experience with Spanish-English bilinguals from other
locales. One man I spoke with in Michigan, interviewed in
1973, has lived in a small, semi-rural, factory-centered
community since 1940. Originally from San Antonio, Texas,
there was nothing distinctively Chicano or Texan about
his English. In contrast to second generation speakers
from East Los Angeles, he had the vowel reduction rules
that are common in non-Hispanic vernacular English, and
used the lax i in the present progressive suffix -ing
(-in') also common in the Anglo vernacular. When he spoke
with me, another Mexican-American, he used a Spanish-
English code-switching style rather than English alone,
possibly because I had singled him out to interview because of his Mexican background. To illustrate, I offer
this example, which he offered in response to a question
in English about discrimination:

> No. I don't know. Sometimes *dicen los muchachos*
> *que* they think, you know . . . So I don't know.
> *A los míos no les ha pasado nada,* you know. I can't
> say, you know. Once in a while you hear somethin'.
> Of course, lota people, you know. . . Sometime you
> say somethin' without even knowing what's goin' on.
> *Pero no,* as far as discrimination is concerned,
> *pos aquí 'ondequiera hay . . . Aquí andan juntos*
> *dos 'ondequiera.*

It was clear from remarks addressed to others during the
interview that he also had a non-switching style that he
used with ethnic-group outsiders. I suspect that his
code-switching style had been acquired in San Antonio
with in-group members, and that he had carried over that
speech community language use norm to Michigan.

Another example of speech community language use
norms distinct from those of East Los Angeles is taken
from fieldwork I did in El Paso in 1977. The interviewee
was a woman in her twenties who, when initially contacted
for the interview, had said that she could speak Spanish.
However, she persisted in English throughout our conversation, adding a phrase or two in Spanish in an apparently

sincere attempt to speak Spanish for me. Her preference
for English, due to a far greater facility in that
language, superceded pressure from me to maintain the
conversation in Spanish. I suspect she had said that she
could speak Spanish because Spanish language ability is important in El Paso's Mexican-American speech community.
The following passage contains as much Spanish as she
produced in any one segment of the hour-long interview:

> *No, de ninguna--Bueno, este,* let's say it did have
> some kind of college, you know, school, you know.
> Whatever. *Pero, este,* being a unit secretary and
> giving, you know, computer, it's two completely
> different. . . It has nothing to do with my *edu-
> cación ni nada.*

And, although the next question was also in Spanish, she
responded:

> *No estoy tan segura que,* you know, that my schooling
> did have something to do with getting me my job,
> *este. Pero* I don't do the program, or anything.
> Nothing, nothing that has to do with my classes.

As I persisted in Spanish for a time, the interviewee
continued to begin her turns in Spanish in accordance
with my language choice, and then completed her turns
in English.

There is little that was phonologically distinct
about her English, although she produced the low and
retracted /ε/ before /l/ as is done in East Los Angeles,
and the tense /i/ in the *-ing* suffix, which she pronounced *-een*. She also found the suffixation of adverbs
to be a problem:

> I ran what they call a Modelco, which is similar
> to a computer, but it's very *simplerized*. It's
> very simple to work with.

In these examples, Mexican-Americans from distinct
speech communities show different language behaviors in
similar situations, one using a language switching style
to show ethnic in-group solidarity, the other making an
effort to speak Spanish although Spanish is clearly not
a dominant language. It is the prediction for the East
Los Angeles Chicano English community that such Spanish
language use does not need to be displayed to establish
in-group solidarity. For many, English is the accepted
language for informal settings and situations, with the
possible use of Spanish in tangential functions in the
speech event, such as direct address forms (e.g., *ese,
hombre*) fillers, (e.g., *este*) and tags on questions,
(*¿verdad?*).

CONCLUSION

I think it is premature to delimit what Chicano English is in view of the many social and linguistic factors which shape it in any given community. In order to study any one variety of Chicano English, the speech community must be identified, the social and geographic parameters be loosely designated for purposes of reference, and the pool of linguistic features widely circumscribed. As I have suggested, not everyone in the speech community will use the features identified, nor will every feature be necessary for inclusion of the speaker in the speech community. Attitudes toward the use of English and Spanish in the community will be another factor in the identification of its members. The pool of features identified for East Los Angeles and the language use norms noted are intended as gross parameters for the community and suggest areas in which future empirical investigation has much to contribute.

NOTES

1. Macías (1979, p.74) notes that most of the Mexican population of the United States is concentrated in two states: California, with 40.6 percent, and Texas, with 36.4 percent.
2. The circumscription of a speech community on sociocultural grounds is not new, of course. Barker's study of language use in Tucson (1950) is a prime example of this approach, and other linguists have also used social criteria to indicate linguistic cohesiveness. Sawyer draws sociocultural boundaries around the Mexican community in the San Antonio of the 1950s when she attributes the lack of use of regional vocabulary to their cultural isolation as Mexican-Americans (1971, pp. 380-381). As she sums up at the conclusion of her paper:

> The isolation of the Latin American results in a series of
> social isoglosses separating their speech from that of the
> Anglo community. Although these lines cannot be drawn on the
> map like the geographical isoglosses which separate one dia-
> lect from another, they are quite as real and as enduring.
> (p. 381)

3. Although the Mexican population of Los Angeles has been continuously expanding eastward from East Los Angeles proper, and very dramatically in the last decade, I hesitate to include the adjacent suburbs and those farther to the east in this discussion of the East Los Angeles speech community. Those communities in past years were still ethnically mixed, with relatively low proportions of Mexican residents. The linguistic and sociocultural environment of these communities 20 to 30 years ago when today's adult speakers were children was importantly less Mexican-ethnic than was East Los Angeles of the period, and did not form part of the same speech community. For this reason, East Los Angeles proper is considered to be the locus of the dialect.

4. Problems with male membership in youth gangs in Los Angeles have been attested to as far back as the 1940s (Grebler, Moore, and Guzmán, 1970, p. 458; McWilliams, 1968, pp. 227-258). Although McWilliams may be correct in pointing out that the groups are primarily social in nature and that several of the incidents of the '40s were prompted by the racial prejudice of the authorities of the time, incidents of violent crime in certain neighborhoods continue to be reported in the daily newspapers. While it is not the case that the residents of the community sanction the youth gangs, for many it has been and still is a part of life in some sections of Los Angeles.

5. Other studies report the devoicing of /z/ in Mexican communities, for example, in California (Thrift, 1974), in Arizona (Lynn, 1945), in San Antonio and Austin, Texas (Natalicio and Williams, 1972; Thompson 1975, respectively). Of course, knowledge of Spanish as a first language, with its lack of phonemic contrast between [z] [s] may influence the devoicing for bilinguals but its persistence as a phenomenon for some Chicano monolingual English speakers remains to be explained.

6. It is my impression from listening to local Southern Californian English that non-Chicano speakers under the age of, roughly, forty, have the -een variant (with a tense /i/) as well, but it is not as tense nor used as frequently in non-Hispanic communities. Other conference participants commented during the discussion period that this variant had been heard in Texas and New Mexico by non-Chicanos.

7. This, of course, invites quantitative verification or refutation. A functional explanation is suggested whereby /d/ and /t/ are the only markers of past in words that do not end in alveolar stops, while with /Id/, the added syllabic nucleous serves that purpose. Thus, with glottalization of word-final /t/ and /d/ the loss of information is at greater risk with the single morphophoneme than with the syllabic əd. Likewise, when /Id/ marks a past participle, information as to its function is also conveyed by the fact of being part of a be or get passive construction.

8. This rule may have been influenced by a similar phenomenon in colloquial Spanish, whereby the negative no is deleted with hasta This is nonstandard, but was evidently popular in Mexican Spanish in the 1940s, as one language purist cautioned against the use of hasta without no in a book containing other such "errors" intended for journalists and radio announcers (Alcazar, 1944). In Los Angeles, I have heard until used in this fashion only by bilingual, second generation speakers over the age of 40. It is not clear, however, whether it is restricted to that population.

9. Benji Wald notes this apparently innovative usage of barely in his 1981 research with pre-adolescents, sampled in interviews in two schools in the Los Angeles area (personal communication).

10. See the discussion in Grebler, Moore, and Guzmán (1970, pp. 425-432) for an elaboration of the factors that influence English language use generationally. Apparently, in many Chicano communities--and in Texas in particular--intrasentential code-switching between Spanish and English appears to be an informal conversational style for Chicanos of every age (c.f., discussions on code-switching in Elías-Olivares, 1975; Lance, 1969; Huerta-Macías, 1981, for example). In the Los Angeles area, however, many

second generation bilinguals prefer English language use informally among themselves.
11. Linguistic fieldwork in El Paso allowed me to discover the importance given to Spanish language use in the home by El Paso Mexican-Americans. Several of the people I spoke with had relatives in Los Angeles whom they visited at least yearly. There was a sense of ethnic pride about their own maintenance of Spanish in the home and dismay that it was not spoken well nor required in the homes of relatives in Los Angeles.

REFERENCES

Alcazar, Ricardo. 1944. *Cómo Hablamos en México (Sintaxis sin Tasa, Oral y Escrita. Código al Vuelo)*. Mexico, D.F.: Costa-Mic. (Pen name: Florisel).

Bailey, Charles James. 1973. *Variation and Linguistic Theory*. Arlington, Va.: Center for Applied Linguistics.

Barker, George C. 1972. "Social Functions of Language in a Mexican-American Community." *Anthropological Papers of the University of Arizona*, 22, 1972.

Elías-Olivares, Lucía. 1975. "Ways of Speaking in a Chicano Community: A Sociolinguistic Approach." Ph.D. Dissertation. Austin: University of Texas.

Feagin, Crawford. 1979. *Variation and Change in Alabama English. A Sociolinguistic Study of a White Community*. Washington, D.C.: Georgetown University Press.

Fishman, Joshua, Robert L. Cooper and Roxanna Ma. 1968. *Bilingualism in the Barrio. Final Report*. (U.S. Office of Education Contract No. OEC-1-062817-0297.)

Gingras, Rosario. 1978. "Rule Innovation in Hispanicized English." Paper presented at the annual meeting of the American Dialect Society, Washington, D.C., 1978.

Grebler, Leo, Joan W. Moore and Ralph C. Guzmán. 1970. *The Mexican-American People*. New York: Free Press.

Gumperz, John. 1968. "The Speech Community." In Pier Giglioli, ed., *Language and Social Context*. London: Penguin 1972, 219-231. (Originally in *International Encyclopedia of the Social Sciences*, Macmillan, 381-386.)

Huerta-Macías, Ana. 1981. "Code-Switching: All in the Family." In Richard Durán, ed., *Latino Language and Communicative Behavior*. (Advances in Discourse Processes 6.) Norwood, N.J.: Ablex.

Hymes, Dell. 1972. "Models of the Interaction of Language and Social Life." In John J. Gumperz and Dell Hymes, eds., *Directions in Sociolinguistics*. New York: Holt, Rinehart and Winston.

Jesperson, Otto. 1969. *Essentials of English Grammar*. Fourth Printing. Alabama: University of Alabama Press.

Labov, William. 1972. *Sociolinguistic Patterns*. Philadelphia: University of Pennsylvania Press.

_____, Paul Cohen, Clarence Robins and John Lewis. 1968. *A Study of the Non-Standard English of Negro and Puerto Rican Speakers in the New York City. Vol. 1: Phonological and Grammatical Analysis*. (U.S. Office of Education Cooperative Research Project No. 3288.)

Lance, Donald M. ed. 1969. *A Brief Study of Spanish-English Bilingualism. Final Report*. (Research Project ORR-Liberal Arts-15504.) Bethesda, Md.: U.S. Dept. of HEW/EDRS.

Lynn, Klonda. 1945. "Bilingualism in the Southwest." *Quarterly Journal of Speech*, 31: 175-180.

Ma, Roxanna and Eleanor Herasimchuk. 1968. "The Linguistic Dimensions of a Bilingual Neighborhood." In Joshua A. Fishman, et al., eds., *Bilingualism in the Barrio*, 638-835.

Macías,Reynaldo F. 1974. "East Los Angeles: A Brief History." *La Luz* (October 1974).

_____. 1979. "Mexican/Chicano Sociolinguistic Behavior and Language Policy in the United States." Ph.D. dissertation. Georgetown University, Washington, D.C.

_____. 1981. "Language Diversity Among U.S. Hispanics: Some Background Considerations for Schooling and for Non-Biased Assessment." Paper presented at the Invitational Symposium on Hispanic Diversity, March 14-15, 1981, Michigan State University, East Lansing.

McWilliams, Carey. 1968. *North from Mexico*. New York: Greenwood Press.

Metcalf, Alan A. 1979. *Chicano English. Language in Education: Theory and Practice 21*. Arlington, Va.: Center for Applied Linguistics.

Natalicio, Diana S. and Frederick Williams. 1972. "What Characteristics can 'Experts' Reliably Evaluate in the Speech of Black and Mexican-American Children?" *TESOL QUARTERLY*, 6 (June): 121-7.

Peñalosa, Fernando. 1980. *Chicano Sociolinguistics*. Rowley, Mass.: Newbury House.

Sawyer, Janet. 1971. "Social Aspects of Bilingualism in San Antonio, Texas." In Harold B. Allen and Gary N. Underwood, eds., *Readings in American Dialectology*. New York: Appleton-Century-Crofts, 375-381. (Originally published in *Publication of the American Dialect Society*, 41, 1964, 7-15, University of Arizona Press, Tucson.)

Thompson, Roger M. 1975. "Mexican-American English: Social Correlates of Regional Pronunciation." *American Speech*, 50, (Spring-Summer): 18-24.

Thrift, David. 1974. "Mexican-American Language Studies: A Bibliographical Survey, 1896-1973." *Seminar Paper Series 29*. Department of Linguistics, California State University, Fullerton.

Wald, Benji. 1980. "Dialect Formation in a Bilingual Community: A Preliminary Study of the Evolution of the East Los Angeles Vowel System." Ms., National Center for Bilingual Research, Los Alamitos, Cal. (Paper presented at the Conference on Form and Function in Chicano English, El Paso, Texas, September 1981.)

Wolfram, Walt. 1974. *Sociolinguistic Aspects of Assimilation. Puerto Rican English in New York City*. Arlington, Va.: Center for Applied Linguistics.

_____, and Ralth Fasold. 1974. *The Study of Social Dialects in American English*. Englewood Cliffs, N.J.: Prentice-Hall.

_____, and Donna Christian. 1976. *Appalachian Speech*. Arlington, Va.: Center for Applied Linguistics.

9

THE CHICANO BILINGUAL, CULTURAL DEMOCRACY AND THE MULTICULTURAL PERSONALITY IN A DIVERSE SOCIETY*

Manuel Ramirez III
University of Texas at Austin

In this essay I intend to draw upon my research experience performed with colleagues during the past 15 years or so on the relationship of multiculturalism to flexibility in personality, interethnic skills, and leadership in mixed ethnic groups. My interest in this area is motivated partly by the circumstance that I am Chicano or Mexican-American, and Mexican.

Although I am not a technical linguist, I realize how crucial a role language plays in human relations, whether we are dealing with fairly homogeneous monolinguals or with diverse groups of multilinguals. Language provides the symbols by which humans manifest their feelings, values, and aspirations. As to whether language molds our behavior, as the Whorf-Sapir theory would have us believe, or whether behavior shapes languages is, however, a philosophical question which cannot be resolved here. I have, nevertheless, had ample occasion to work with linguists as a consultant to various bilingual projects both in Texas and California and feel strongly that greater collaboration between the fields of social psychology and linguistics is an urgent need.

---

*This essay is a revision of an Inaugural Lecture delivered by me at Oakes College, University of California, Santa Cruz, October 9, 1979. Some material has also been added.

Those of us who have lived in the border area of South Texas, where my hometown, Roma, is located, sometimes jokingly refer to ourselves as the people that General Santa Ana sold to the United States at the end of the U.S.-Mexico War during the 19th century. At any rate, as Mexican-Americans, we often find ourselves caught in various types of ethnic dilemmas. Our friends and relatives in Mexico call us "pochos," while some Anglos do not accept us. Sometimes we feel like a people without a country. Nevertheless, this is not really so, since we have always referred to South Texas as our "patria chica," or our "little homeland." The folklorist Americo Paredes at the University of Texas at Austin has done extensive research into the history and folklore of the area. In recent years there has been speculation that South Texas was the site of the first nation of the Aztecs, established before they moved south to the Valley of Mexico. Hence, we may be "citizens" of a nation and civilization that dates back several centuries in the history of the Americas.

Be that as it may, this is an interesting locality in which to study the development of multicultural orientations to life. Like many other areas of the country in which many members of minority groups live, it is fertile ground for multicultural development of minority groups. I am, of course, referring to places like Harlem in New York City, the Mission district in San Francisco, East Los Angeles, Chicago, the Santa Fe-Taos area, and southern Colorado. In such places there is constant interaction of different cultures such as Black, Mexican-American, Mexican, South and Central American, Asian-American, Native American, Puerto Rican, Cuban, and Anglo American cultures as well.

In our research we have hypothesized that being socialized amid the diversity reflected in multicultural environments encourages development of multicultural orientations to life. Moreover, we have hypothesized that these culturally diverse environments encourage development of interethnic skills which will be needed by the leaders of the future. Skills such as sensitivity to social cues, cultural facilitation and mediation, and flexibility and adaptability to different conditions of life.

As a psychologist I must freely admit that no matter how rigorous the measures used in testing out hypotheses about people's human behavior, there are so many variables that results can turn out to be ambiguous and subject to different interpretations. There is, unfortunately, much stereotypic thinking in what people readily assume about bilinguals and minority group members - much of it negative and liable to create self-fulfilling prophecies of failure. Nevertheless, empirical research provides our best opportunity of creating a better atmosphere of

belief about non-mainstream members of our society. As a
modest example of this, I would like to point to an experiment conducted by Douglass R. Price-Williams and me
and reported in 1977 in an essay titled "Divergent Thinking, Cultural Differences and Bilingualism" (Price-
Williams and Ramirez, 1977). A total of 183 subjects from
Catholic parochial schools in Houston were tested with
the Unusual Uses Test and the Peabody Picture Vocabulary
Test, both being measures widely used in my field and in
education. An equal number of Mexican-American, Black,
and Anglo fourth-grade children, male and female, were
represented.

Findings from this study were that the Anglos scored
higher than the Blacks and Mexican-Americans on the Peabody test. By contrast, Mexican-American and Black males
scored higher than Anglo males on both fluency and flexibility as measured by the Unusual Uses Test. Black males
tested higher on fluency than any of the other subgroups.
On the other hand, Anglo females scored higher on flexibility than any of the other subgroups. Black females obtained the highest flexibility/fluency ratio. Finally, the
results of the males supported the hypothesis that children of minority groups and children who are "balanced"
bilinguals tend to do better on the Unusual Uses Test -
perhaps attesting to a greater general flexibility and
adaptability. Mysteriously, however, the female results
did not corroborate this hypothesis and could not be explained by data collected in the study.

It is important to emphasize that there are no facile
and ready replies to the whole spectrum of questions revolving about comparative competence and performance of
monolinguals/monoculturals vs. multilinguals/multicul-
turals. Judging from the above experiment, and from
others by now known in the literature, there exists some
reason for believing that multiculturals may have the edge
on monoculturals in significant aspects of behavior, especially as regards coping mechanisms. Is language reflec-
tive of this flexibility in coping mechanisms?

Returning to the topic of cultural models, with which
we are primarily concerned in this essay, we hypothesize
that multicultural persons are the leaders that we need
for the future, because so many of our national and international problems revolve around diversity. Referring
to important international problems which we are facing,
in a newsletter (1979), to voters of the Sixteenth District of California, Congressman Panetta observed:

We live in a world that is rapidly shrinking as the
technologies of communication and transportation
grow more advanced, and as the role of international
economics in our everyday lives becomes increasingly
important. Unless this nation finds ways of improving its knowledge and understanding of foreign

languages and cultures, we will be placing a severe
handicap on our ability to understand, influence and
react to world events.

By way of contrast and at the national level, sociologist
Robert Michels has expressed great concern over the diverse constituencies in the country, stating:

> Democracy and leadership are incompatible. The nation's
> plural interests threaten to turn our country into a
> set of internal Balkan states, into hostile tribes.
> (*Time*,· April 1979)

My colleagues and I disagree with these conclusions. We
are not yet ready to throw in the towel on democracy, but
we do feel that the times call for multicultural leaders.

THE NORTH AMERICAN/WESTERN EUROPEAN WORLD VIEW
AND ASSIMILATION PRESSURES ON MEMBERS OF
MINORITY GROUPS

It seems reasonable to assume that if we have a great
need for multicultural leaders in our country, American
societal institutions would encourage those among our citizens who already have a head start in that direction.

Historically, however, institutions in American society,
specifically educational institutions, have encouraged
assimilation to the mainstream American middle class.
In this respect they have reflected a North American/
Western European world view: the belief that cultures
that are not North American or Western European are inferior. For example, the Latin American and the African
cultures, as well as the cultures of Southern and Eastern
Europe, are believed to be primitive, undeveloped, or
underdeveloped.

According to the North American/Western European
world view, the focus has been upon difficulties, problems, and negative consequences of dual and multiple cultural membership. Bicultural and multicultural persons
have been described as culturally deprived, disadvantaged,
apathetic, pathologically maladjusted, and torn by conflict. The thrust by American societal institutions has
been to assimilate members of minority groups to what is
believed to be the superior sociocultural system of the
mainstream American middle class.

Indeed, the North American/Western European world view
has been rather clearly reflected in the practices of
educational institutions and is well expressed in the
writings of many American educators. An example is E.P.
Cubberly after whom the education building at Stanford
was named. In his book, *Changing Conceptions of Democracy* (1909), Cubberly viewed with alarm and disapproval
the cultural diversity of immigrant parents, and for their
children he recommended in the strongest terms that they

be assimilated and "amalgamated" as part of the American
"race." Moreover, he argued that as part of the American
"race," the offspring of immigrants should be firmly imbued with the Anglo-Saxon conception of righteousness,
law, and order, and with a reverence for our democratic
institutions and for those things in our national life
that we as a people hold to be of abiding worth. Cubberly
is only one example of a deeply assimilationist school of
thought that persisted well into the 20th century, and to
some extent, up to World War II.

In the history of the social sciences in the United
States, the North American/Western European world view
has been expressed as the damaging-culture view - the
theory that the culture and values of members of minority
groups are the ultimate and final cause of the low economic status and low academic achievement of members of
these groups. Specifically, it has been assumed that minority cultures interfere with the intellectual development of children. This belief served as the basis for
compensatory educational progress, such as Head Start,
Title I, and the Parent-Child Development Centers.

Most detrimental to the efforts of encouraging development of multiculturalism among members of minority
groups in the United States was the fact that the North
American/Western European world view was reflected in
models of acculturation developed by social scientists
which my colleagues and I categorized as Conflict/Replace-
ment. The assumptions of these models are as follows:

1. The sociocultural systems and lifestyles of different
   ethnic groups are so opposed to each other that they
   create conflict for the person who participates in
   more than one group.
2. These conflicts result in problems of adjustment such
   as identity crises and split personalities.
3. In order to achieve a happy and successful psychological adjustment the person must reject the minority
   culture and embrace the mainstream American middle
   class.

A picture of the view of acculturation from the perspective of the Conflict/Replacement Models may be seen
in Figure 1. Obviously these are linear models since
growth is believed to occur only in the direction of mainstream American culture. Multicultural development is not
possible under these models; therefore, these are models
of assimilation and not of acculturation.

THE CIVIL RIGHTS MOVEMENT, CULTURAL
DEMOCRACY, AND THE MESTIZO WORLD VIEW

With the advent of the Civil Rights Movement a different philosophy regarding diversity began to emerge in
American society. This is commonly referred to as cultural
pluralism - my colleagues and I prefer the term "cultural
democracy."

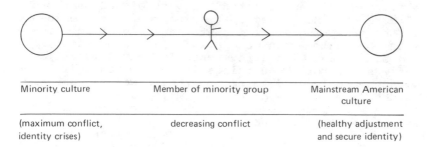

Minority culture	Member of minority group	Mainstream American culture
(maximum conflict, identity crises)	decreasing conflict	(healthy adjustment and secure identity)

FIGURE 1   Conflict/Replacement Models of Acculturation

The concept of cultural democracy introduced by Berkson and Drachsler in the 1920's, has a long history. At that time principal concern in the country was whether members of minority groups would fuse with the majority or decide to remain separate. The choice of whether to assimilate or remain separate, Drachsler felt, should be added to the older American ideas of political and economic democracy and should be referred to as cultural democracy.

Together with Alfredo Castañeda (Ramirez and Castañeda, 1974) I have elaborated on the concept of cultural democracy - we have defined it as the individual's moral and legal right to remain identified with his or her original culture as he or she participates in, and learns to identify with, other cultures in American society. We assume that society and its institutions reflect cultural democracy when policies and practices show respect for cultural diversity and for individual differences.

As the concept of cultural democracy was being introduced by Berkson and Drachsler in the United States, a world view on acculturation different to the North American/Western European was emerging from the unique experience of cultural confluence in Latin America - this is the Mestizo world view. The term "Mestizo" is given to persons and cultures representing the amalgamation of Hispanic and Native American cultures and traditions. The writings of two Mexican scholars have contributed to the basic assumptions of the Mestizo world view - José Vasconcelos (1976), philosopher-educator, and Leopoldo Zea (1974), who is a social historian at the National Autonomous University of Mexico.

The basic tenets of the Mestizo world view, described by Vasconcelos and Zea, are the following:

1. Cultures, sociocultural environments, and people represent a richness in diversity from which everyone can learn.
2. By adding the knowledge and experiences of people

who have grown up in different cultures and environments, the perspective and behavioral repertoires of
a person can be enhanced.
3. These expanded repertoires make the person more
   flexible and adaptable to different life situations
   and sociocultural systems.

RECENT RESEARCH ON MEMBERS OF MINORITY GROUPS IN
DIFFERENT PARTS OF THE WORLD HAVE GIVEN SUPPORT
TO THE MESTIZO WORLD VIEW

For example, McFee (1968), working with American
Indians living in bicultural reservation communities, has
found that, contrary to expectations, there is no substi-
tution or replacement of Indian behaviors and skills with
those of mainstream American culture. Instead, there is
expansion of behavioral repertoires, making for greater
flexibility of behavior and for the ability to participate
competently in both Indian and mainstream American cultures. McFee titled his article "The 150% Man."
Wallace Lambert (1952) and his colleagues studied
French-English bilinguals in the province of Quebec, in
Canada. They found no evidence of replacement of one
language with another as persons became bilingual; instead, they observed expansion of verbal repertoires making for greater mental flexibility. In addition they found
that balanced bilinguals scored significantly higher on
tests of intelligence and were developed in more areas of
cognitive ability than monolinguals.
T.E. Fitzgerald (1971), doing research upon Maoris
in New Zealand, found that his subjects shuttled a great
deal between Maori and European cultures. He also observed a flexibility of identity--he concluded that these
bicultural peoples have a cultural identity which is Maori
and several social identities which are both Maori and
European.
We have done extensive research with bicultural Mexican-Americans in California and Texas and have observed
flexibility of personality in these subjects. Specifically,
we found flexibility of learning styles, including an
ability to do well on tasks requiring both cooperation and
competition. They also performed effectively in learning
situations requiring both discovery and modeling and flexibility of human relational styles (both in close, personal
relationships and in more formal, consultant-type interactions with a teacher). We saw evidence of flexibility
of incentive-motivational styles, including a willingness
to work equally diligently for social and non-social rewards, which we labeled "cognitive flexibility" or bi-
cognition. Abilities to communicate and to mediate between different ethnic groups were also identified.

THE FLEXIBILITY, UNITY, AND EXPANSION
MODEL OF ACCULTURATION

The Mestizo world view and the research findings I
have just reviewed contributed to the development of a
model of acculturation which we have titled the Flexibility, Unity, and Expansion Model. The basic assumptions
of the model are as follows:

1. Acculturation is continued growth and development in
   the person's original culture as well as in the lifestyles and values of other sociocultural systems he
   or she participates in.
2. Growth and development take place in different life
   domains of the different cultures the person interacts
   with (for example, at the same time, a person may be
   developing in the familial domain of one culture, the
   educational domain of another, and the work domain of
   still another.)
3. Growth and development in different cultures and in
   different domains within cultures provides the person
   with personality-building elements which make him or
   her more flexible, adaptable, and understanding of
   others and thereby more able to participate in different sociocultural systems.
4. The personality-building elements which the person ac-
   quires from different cultures have the potential for
   combining to develop multicultural patterns of behavior,
   outlook, and transcendence to life.

Proceeding with our concepts, Figure 2 provides a view
of our Flexibility, Unity, and Expansion Model of Acculturation. The focus of our most recent research is on the
leadership behaviors exhibited by monocultural and multicultural college students in mixed ethnic groups under
conditions of conflict.

Our first task in this leadership research was to develop instruments for identifying people who were multicultural by peers and authority figures who know them well.
From this information we developed items for an inventory,
labeled the Mexican-American Multicultural Experience Inventory. The items on this instrument can be grouped into
three major categories:

1. Ethnographic background and socialization experiences.
2. Extent of participation in different ethnic groups and
   interpersonal experiences with people of different
   ethnic groups.
3. Evidence of sociocultural skills.

One may consult Table 1 for some sample items from
the Mexican-American Multicultural Experience Inventory
(MAMEI). There are five choices which the person can
make in responding to each item; these answers indicate
whether he or she has a predominant Mexican-American,
Anglo, or multicultural orientation.

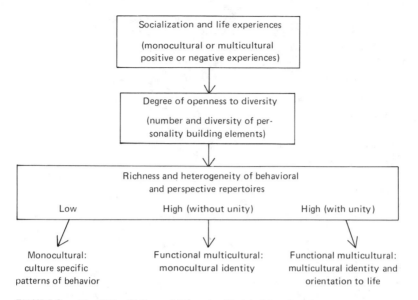

FIGURE 2   Flexibility, Unity, and Expansion Model of Acculturation

In addition to the MAMEI, providing us with a global picture of multiculturalism, we developed the Psychohistory for Assessing Multiculturalism in Mexican-Americans (PAMMA). This provided a detailed, intensive look at multicultural personalities, the development patterns exhibited, and the ways in which multicultural identities were expressed behaviorally.

The psychohistories ranged from one hour and thirty minutes to two hours in length and they focused on five different life periods--preschool, elementary, middle, high school, and college. Questions centered around themes such as language learning and usage, family and community life, school experiences, peer relationships with authority figures, political behavior, religious orientation, life crisis experiences, identity crises, sociocultural identity, perceived advantages and disadvantages of Anglo, Mexican-American, and other cultures, degree of comfort experienced when participating in Anglo, Mexican-American, and other cultures, preference for ethnic background of marriage partner, philosophy of life, and career goals.

The interviews were recorded, transcribed, and scored on several variables. From these scores we identified five different historical development patterns or paths of development of multiculturalism. These are shown in Table 2.

We also were able to identify different contemporary multicultural identities. Our multicultural subjects varied considerably from one another in their contemporary identities. These ranged from almost exclusively Chicano or Anglo to thoroughly multicultural, strongly identified

Table 1. Sample Items from the
Multicultural Experience Inventory

In high school, my close friends were:

_____1. All Chicanos   _____4. Mostly Anglos

_____2. Mostly Chicanos   _____5. All Anglos

_____3. Chicanos and Anglos, about equal

The people with whom I have established close and meaningful relationships have been:

_____1. All Chicanos   _____4. Mostly Anglos

_____2. Mostly Chicanos   _____5. All Anglos

_____3. Chicanos and Anglos, about equal

When I am with my friends, I usually attend functions
where people are:

_____1. All Chicanos   _____4. Mostly Anglos

_____2. Mostly Chicanos   _____5. All Anglos

_____3. Chicanos and Anglos, about equal

When I discuss personal problems or issues, I prefer to
discuss them with:

_____1. All Chicanos   _____4. Mostly Anglos

_____2. Mostly Chicanos   _____5. All Anglos

_____3. Chicanos and Anglos, about equal

When I write poetry or other personal material, I write
in:

_____1. Spanish only   _____4. Mostly English

_____2. Mostly Spanish   _____5. English only

_____3. Spanish and English, about equal

---

with Mexican-American and Anglo cultures, and often with
other cultures as expressing a transcendent philosophy of
life.

The different contemporary multicultural identities
are shown in Table 3.

LEADERSHIP BEHAVIOR IN MIXED ETHNIC GROUPS

Once we had developed instruments for identifying multiculturals and for assessing degree of multiculturalism,
we were ready for the next step - to study leadership
effectiveness in mixed ethnic groups.

Table 2. Historical Development Pattern

Parallel	Extensive and continuous exposure to Mexican-American and Anglo cultures beginning in preschool period or before, and continuing for at least two more life periods.
Early Chicano/Abrupt Anglo	Extensive, almost total exposure to Mexican-American culture in the first two or three periods of life, followed by sudden immersion in Anglo culture.
Early Chicano/Gradual Anglo	Extensive, almost total exposure to Mexican-American culture throughout all life periods with gradually increasing exposure to Anglo culture as subject becomes older.
Early Anglo/Abrupt Chicano	Reverse of Early Chicano/Abrupt Anglo.
Early Anglo/Gradual Chicano	Reverse of Early Chicano/Gradual Anglo

Table 3. Contemporary Multicultural Identity

Contemporary Multicultural Identity	Defining Characteristics
Synthesized Multicultural	Positive attitudes toward both Chicano and Anglo cultures; competent functioning in both cultures, feels accepted by members of both cultures; transcendent philosophy of life and world view.
Functional Multicultural/ Anglo Orientation	Functions competently in both Chicano and Anglo cultures; more comfortable in Anglo culture.
Functional Multicultural/ Chicano Orientation	Functions competently in both Chicano and Anglo cultures; more comfortable in Chicano culture.

Our hypothesis for this study was that persons who are more multicultural would use more effective behaviors to get a group composed of members of different ethnic groups to reach consensus of opinion under conditions of conflict.

Effective leadership behaviors have been described as including the following:

1. Permitting all group members to express their opinions.
2. Giving equal status to opinions expressed by others.
3. Clarifying opinions expressed by individual group members as necessary.
4. Being assertive without being authoritarian.
5. Attempting to mediate between members.
6. Personalizing relationships with the members.
7. Seeking compromises or intermediate solutions.

The procedure for the group session was as follows: Three students, a Black, an Anglo, and a Mexican-American were selected and trained to assume each of three roles involving a pro, a con, and a fence-sitting position on a controversial problem dealing with the preservation of the cultural integrity of a hypothetical nonindustrialized society. The problem as it was presented to the subjects was as follows: contact has been made with a traditional society in which mortality rates and malnutrition are high, but the people have a very supportive and cohesive family life and religion. Should we intervene, offering advantages of technology in food production and health care, or leave them alone? The subjects were Mexican-American male college students from either Texas or California who had been identified as being either high or low on multicultural experience. Degree of multicultural experience was determined by the MAMEI and the PAMMA. The subjects were assigned to be coordinators for the four-person groups, although it appeared that they were selected by chance.

The procedure was as follows: The coordinator was instructor to do everything possible to get his or her group to achieve consensus on the controversial problem.

Each member of the group read a summary of the problem. The group then had 20 minutes into the discussion; exchanges between the confederates holding the con and pro positions were very heated. Fifteen minutes into the discussion the student playing the fence-sitter role switched to either the pro or con position, leaving one member of the group who was in disagreement. This member maintained his or her opinion, so the group never achieved consensus. Then, after the group session had been completed, the coordinator was interviewed by an experimenter. The group sessions were tape-recorded as well as observed in order to rate the coordinator on the leadership behaviors. Data showing differences in leadership behaviors between high

and low multicultural experience subjects are summarized
in Table 4.

As can be seen, the findings show that leaders with
high multicultural experience were more effective in most
of the criterion behaviors. Leaders with high multicultural experience:

1. were more active and assertive;
2. asked members for their opinions, evaluations, and
   feelings more often;
3. clarified statements made by members more often;
4. acknowledged contributions made by members more frequently;
5. more often made attempts to clarify the issues under
   discussion;
6. assessed group progress more frequently;
7. tended to mediate more among the members;

Table 4. Leadership Behaviors of Subjects of
High and Low Multicultural Experience

Leadership Behaviors in Mixed Ethnic Groups	High M.E. Mean (N=15)	Low M.E. Mean (N=21)	F
More active and assertive	5.53	3.29	3.12 (p.09)
Asks members for opinions, evaluations, feelings	13.40	11.14	1.65
Clarifies statements of members	3.20	1.65	2.47 (p.13)
Acknowledges contributions of members	1.80	.67	2.96 (p.09)
Clarifies issue under discussion	2.93	2.05	2.76 (p.11)
Assesses group progress	1.33	1.00	1.21
Mediates between members	2.13	1.14	2.75 (p.11)
Seeks compromise of intermediate solution	1.87	1.52	
Addresses members by their names	2.67	.57	5.92 (p.02)
Shows tension, jokes, and laughs inappropriately	.53*	.81	
General leadership style:	41% autocratic 24% democratic 18% laissez-faire	58% autocratic 10% democratic 21% laissez-faire	

*A low score on this variable indicated a more favorable
leadership behavior.

8. sought more compromises or intermediate solutions;
9. were more likely to address members by their names;
10. showed less evidence of tension and less tendency to joke and laugh inappropriately.

On our ratings of general leadership style, leaders with high multicultural experience were less autocratic and laissez-faire and more democratic than their low-multicultural-experience counterparts.

Results of the post-group interviews showed that leaders of high multicultural experience were more accurate in reporting what had actually transpired in their groups. In the actual group process 59 percent of the high multiculturals were accurate, while only 37 percent of the low multiculturals were accurate.

When asked to speculate as to why their group had failed to achieve consensus in the allotted time, the highly multicultural subjects stated they would most certainly succeed if given a second chance. Fifty-three percent of these subjects gave self-responsibility attributions; that is, "I should have worked harder on the person who couldn't make up his mind," or "I should have asked the two members who were arguing to try to assume each other's points of view." In contrast to this, 69 percent of the low multicultural leaders gave other-directed responsibility attributions; that is, they said things like, "The members are too stubborn to ever agree with each other" or "They just can't get along with each other."

CONCLUSIONS

Our ultimate objective is to train people to use effective interethnic leadership skills which lead to less alienation and greater understanding in conflict situations in mixed ethnic groups. However, training in multiculturalism is extremely difficult. Thus, the need is for all societal institutions who are involved in the socialization of our citizens to reflect the ideas of the Mestizo world view and of cultural democracy in their policies and practices.

Our life history research has established that early socialization and life experiences are of great importance in encouraging development of multiculturalism. Also important are parental and teacher attitudes toward diversity in people and in sociocultural environments. It is important to give children the message that *they can learn from everybody*.

Our findings show that education experiences are crucial - meeting and interacting with people of different ethnic groups and socioeconomic backgrounds while at the same time maintaining close ties with people of the original group leads to a multicultural orientation. Also important is placing the person in a position in which he or she can teach others about culture and language and have the opportunity to interact with adults and peers of

different backgrounds and ethnic groups early in life
under conditions of mutual cooperation and equal status.
    In recent years much has been learned about multi-
cultural development processes in children and adults.
However, little progress has been made in our knowledge
as to the development of multilingual skills. For example,
the following questions are still largely unanswered:
What relationship do the variations of Chicano English
have on multicultural development and functioning? Can
fluency in the different sub-dialects of Chicano English
be used as a predictor of flexible leadership behavior in
mixed ethnic group situations? How is Chicano English related to academic achievement? Clearly, there is need for
more investigation.
    It is perhaps not too absurd to suggest that we might
be better able to cope with the complex events of an ex-
ploding international scene, be it the Iranian hostage
situation, revolution in Central America, or the Detroit
"inner city" back home, if we would learn to make maximum
use of the insights of our own multicultural and multilingual Americans. These Americans have had the *advantage*
of growing up and becoming socialized in settings where
not one language but several are spoken, and where the
cultural symbols are not homogeneous but pluralistic.

REFERENCES

Baldwin, James. 1979. *Los Angeles Times*, September, 1979.

Berkson, I.B. 1978. *Theories of Assimilation: A Critical Study with Special Reference to the Jewish Group*. New York: Penguin.

Cubberly, E.P. 1909. *Changing Conceptions of Education*. Boston, Mass.: Houghton.

Fitzergerald, T.K. 1971. *Education and Identity - A Reconsideration of Some Models of Acculturation and Identity*. New Zealand Council of Educational Studies, pp. 45-57.

Michels, Robert. 1979. *Time*, October, 1979.

Panetta, Leon. 1978. *Newsletter to Voters of the 16th District*. July, 1979.

Price-Williams, Douglass R., and Manuel Ramirez, III. 1977. "Divergent Thinking in Children of Three Ethnic Groups." *The Journal of Social Psychology*, 103: 3-11.

Ramirez, Manuel, III, and Alfredo Castañeda. 1974. *Cultural Democracy, Bicognitive Development and Education*. New York: Academic Press.

Vasconcelos, José. 1976. *La Raza Cósmica* (4th ed.). México, D.F.: Espasa-Calpe Mexicana, S.A.

Zea, L. 1974. *Dependéncia y Liberación en La Cultural Latinoamericana.* México, D.F.: Editorial Joaquin Mortiz, S.A.

NOTES

In addition to writings by Ramirez cited above, attention is called to the following publications, all dealing with significant aspects of the psychology of bilinguals, particularly Mexican-Americans:

Ramirez, Manuel, III, and Clark Taylor, Jr. 1971. "Mexican-American Cultural Membership and Adjustment to School." *Developmental Psychology*, 4(2): 141-148.

Ramirez, Manuel, III and Douglass Price-Williams. 1974. "Cognitive Styles in Children: Two Mexican Communities." *Interamerican Journal of Psychology*, 8(1-2): 93-101.

Ramirez, Manuel, III and Alfredo Castañeda, and P. Leslie Herold. 1974. "The Relationship of Acculturation to Cognitive Style among Mexican-Americans." *Journal of Cross-Cultural Psychology*, 5(4): 424-433.

Ramirez, Manuel, III and Douglass R. Price-Williams. 1974. "Cognitive Styles of Children of Three Ethnic Groups in the United States." *Journal of Cross-Cultural Psychology*, 5(2): 212-219.

Ramirez, Manuel, III. "Recognizing and Understanding Diversity: Multiculturalism and the Chicano Movement in Psychology." *Chicano Psychology*, New York: Academic Press, pp. 343-353.

SECTION III:
INVESTIGATING
CHICANO ENGLISH

10

LESSONS LEARNED IN A HALF CENTURY: EXPERIENCES OF A PRACTICING DIALECTOLOGIST[*]

Raven I. McDavid, Jr.
University of Chicago and
Linguistic Atlas of the United States and Canada

* * *

In line with the general broadness of scope of this volume, we also include the following Guest Essay by a scholar who may perhaps be considered America's outstanding dialectologist, certainly one of the most prolific to our times. The rationale for his appearance here is his decades of rich experience with the *Linguistic Atlas of the U.S. and Canada,* and his general feel for the topic of dialects. While he has not worked personally on Chicano English as such, his sharing of his exhaustive experience here should be useful to any and all who work in the areas of both Chicano English and Spanish. In this essay, it is to be noted that he deplores the lack in the United States of in-depth research and writing on ethnic dialects, which are so much a part of the American Mosaic.

* * *

[*]The author expresses his appreciation to Hans Kurath, for guidance and inspiration for nearly half a century, to his colleagues on the Atlas staff - notably A. L. Davis, Gail Hankins, William Kretzschmar, Theodore Lerud, Virginia McDavid and Martha Ratliff, and to Dr. Kenneth Toombs, Librarian and Director of Libraries at the University of South Carolina, where the principal archives are housed, and to the American Council of Learned Societies and the University of Chicago for continuing support.

So many have set themselves up as experts on linguistic, educational, and social problems that for my professional integrity I must dissociate myself from the lot.
In my native South Carolina we often define an expert as
a damned fool a thousand miles from home, and it is much
more than a thousand miles from El Paso to either Chicago
or Greenville. I will not offer solutions for the problems
of a regional culture or a community about which I know
little. I was in El Paso only once before, for a couple
of hours in 1964, while the late "Golden State," then in
its penultimate agonies, waited in the station to resume
its journey to Chicago. Spanish is not one of the languages that I have studied; I have left that to my sister
and my late brother-in-law. What I will say is derived
from my interest in history, both of the profession and
of the complex which we call the civilization of the United States. This interest has given me a profound respect
for the integrity of regional and local cultures, including my own, basically derived from the Ulster Scots settlement of Up-Country South Carolina, but diluted with
admixtures of other ethnic stocks. But to show that I am
not utterly a stranger, I recall that more than half a
century ago a cousin who had studied the history and culture of the Southwest pointed out the full name of this
city, *El Paso del Rio Grande del Norte,* "the pass of the
great North River," and observed that many people in this
region call it simply *Del Norte.* Some day I may learn
where one can find the great river of the South.

This curiosity about history helped me to commit my
life to the study of regional varieties of American speech,
once I learned that this study was a serious academic discipline. The epiphany came to me during the Linguistic
Institute of 1937, two years after I had received my Ph.D.
in English. Though I had had somewhat more of formal language study than is now fashionable for the Ph.D. in English literature, even in the most prestigious institutions--
a year each of Old and Middle English and a semester of
Gothic--I had had no chance to study the structure and
history of English. Moreover, those of us who were taking
our degrees in English literature generally resented the
language courses we had to take; and once we were past the
six-hour preliminary examination in the medieval field -
an examination which heavily emphasized traditional philology -- we tried to put our unhappy memories behind us.

But I had other advantages. I had the good fortune to
grow up in a small community where one was necessarily
exposed to all sorts of Southern American English.[1] And my
first teaching assignment--which I got because I had had
slightly more work in language than the competition --took
me to Charleston, at the other end of the state and with
an assortment of dialects strikingly different from anything I had known as a child. Naturally, I wondered about
how such differences could have arisen. When a friend per-

suaded me to be interviewed, at the Institute, as a demon-
stration Southerner for Bloch's seminar in linguistic geography (R. McDavid, 1980) I realized that this kind of
study offered answers to questions I had been asking. And
I set out to become competent in the field. I studied
first how to gather the kinds of data the Atlas project
was concerned with; then I went back to school, as it were,
to learn how to interpret what I had gathered. Fortunately,
I served this second apprenticeship as the junior colleague
of Hans Kurath on the *Pronunciation* volume (Kurath and R.
McDavid, 1961).

My studies have continued ever since. They take me in
many directions: English settlement in the Caribbean;
shipbuilding in Maine and the cutting of timber for those
ships in Tidewater Virginia; railroad building in the 19th
century; migrations of Germans to Texas. The implications
multiply as one continues study.

My work did not stop with South Carolina. I was asked
to work in other regions, and to my delight I found it
easy to interview Michiganders and Upstate Yorkers. As evidence piled up, I began trying to interpret it, and I
lured students into doing similar work. Regrettably, this
immediate region--West Texas and New Mexico--is least
adequately investigated (for practical purposes, Atwood,
1962, stands alone), and the evidence gathered so far is
hardly accessible. But we may extrapolate from what we
have learned elsewhere.

I am far from a pioneer in the study of American dialects: the Atlas project, launched in 1929, became a working reality when fieldwork started half a century ago.
Before that lay a long history, largely with anecdotal and
informal concern for language variety. Sometimes the varieties were regional, like the differences between the
spirant systems of Gilead and Ephraim in ancient Hebrew
(the *shibboleth* episode of Judges 12:6); sometimes they
were social, as in Catullus's satirical picture of the
Roman cockney *Arrius,* who pronounced his name *Harrius,* and
was troubled by *hambushes* on the *Hionian Hocean.* These
informal concerns, and more serious ones (see the history
of dialectology in Pop, 1950) were brought to a focus at
the end of the 18th century, when comparative and historical linguistics arose. This new discipline was abetted in
part by the Romantic Movement (see Wordsworth's notion
that the folk speech of England was clearer and more emphatic than that of the privileged classes), in part by
the study of folklore,[2] in part by the rise of ethnic
nationalism. In the 19th century, many scholars urged the
recording of the salient features of all the dialects of
each linguistic community; toward the end of the century
two major projects were set in motion--the German *Sprachatlas* and the *Atlas linguistique de la France.* Their methods agreed in many respects--a network of communities, a

selection of items to be investigated, and the publication
of the recorded data in cartographic form. They differed
strikingly in others: an attempt to cover every German-
speaking village, as opposed to a selection of some 650
in France; a questionnaire of 40 sentences of standard
German, to be put into the local dialects, as opposed to
the selection of some 2,000 words and phrases of standard
French, for which the dialectal equivalents were sought.
Most of all they differed in the way the evidence was
elicited: German village schoolmasters were asked to set
down local speech (the speakers were not identified in any
way) on forms sent out from *Sprachatlas* headquarters at
Marburg; in France, a single trained investigator, Edmond
Edmont, interviewed selected speakers with identifiable
backgrounds and recorded their responses on the spot in
phonetic transcription. Both German and French investigations were confined to village speech; dialect was not
at that time considered to exist in urban society. To some
extent the feeling that dialect can be studied only in villages and in the countryside is still with us; of more
than 300 interviews for the *Survey of English Dialects*
(Orton et al., 1962-71) only five were conducted in urban
areas--two in Greater London and one each in Leeds, Shef-
field, and York.

Urban areas were first included in the survey of
Italy and southern Switzerland (1925-40), organized by two
Swiss scholars, Karl Jaberg and Jakob Jud, with interview-
ing conducted by three of their students - -Paul Scheuermeier, Gerhard Rohlfs, and Max Leopold Wagner. Both Jaberg
and Jud had studied with Jules Gilliéron, director of the
French Atlas; in turn, Jud and Scheuermeier were to help
train the first cadre of American investigators. Unlike
Edmont, a good phonetician but not a professional linguist -
Gilliéron felt that training in linguistics might prejudice a field-worker--the investigators in Italy went on
to distinguished scholarly careers; surviving correspond-
ence suggests that the naturalness of their interviews did
not suffer from their learning. More important, Jaberg and
Jud included cities as well as villages; and in the cities
they departed from the older notion of a single speaker in
a community. Nevertheless, they kept up the tradition that
dialect was the province of the least sophisticated. This
is not surprising; in Europe it has been traditional to
think of a polar opposition between a diversity of local
dialects and a more or less uniform standard language. It
was not till after World War II that scholars in Europe
began to investigate the intermediate types, which American scholars have come to call the common speech, and the
Germans *Umgangsprache*.

When the Linguistic Atlas of the United States and
Canada was launched in 1929, the designers agreed that it
could not follow European practice and rely on single folk
informants in each community.[3] In Europe the dialects had

been in place for a long time (though naturally there had
been mutual infiltration from region to region and from
class to class); in the United States there had been native speakers of English only since the 17th century.
Furthermore, there had been many social forces to compli-
cate the distribution of speech patterns:

1. Mixture of British dialects in every Atlantic Seaboard
    settlement, a process repeated with every stage of the
    westward movement (local patterns are very hard to
    find in the Rockies and the Pacific States).
2. Practically no representation of the aristocracy or
    the peasantry --the two extremes of English society--
    but heavy representation of the middle and upper
    working classes, with a large proportion of the rest-
    less, the uprooted, the misfits according to the ortho-
    doxy of their times.
3. Leavening of every colony with speakers of other lan-
    guages, especially in such colonial centers as New
    York, Philadelphia, and Charleston.
4. Geographical and social mobility, as witnessed by the
    careers of Daniel Boone and Sam Houston on the one
    hand, and on the other by the backgrounds of nearly
    all the presidents since Buchanan.[4]
5. Industrialization, realized in a variety of labor-
    saving devices, from the American ax-handle to the
    computerized blast furnace.[5]
6. Urbanization, with a larger proportion of Americans
    than of Britons living in cities in 1776.
7. A tradition of the most generous commitment to popu-
    lar education the world has ever known - however
    flawed it may be in practice.

Each colonial center developed its own elite and its own
standards of good usage--a reality frustrating to would-
be pundits of propriety from Noah Webster to John Simon.
Consequently, one interested in varieties of American
English cannot do as the Europeans were wont to do: concentrate on folk usage and take standard usage for granted.[6]
And because the usage of intermediate groups differs from
community to community in its relationship to cultivated
and folk usage, it was found necessary to sample such
groups as well, to suggest the direction of change at the
time of the survey.
     As the design of the American regional atlases was
sketched by Hans Kurath and his associates, they were
aware that it was incomplete, as any survey must be. Joseph Wright long hindered the systematic investigation of
British folk speech because in his *English Dialect Dictionary* (1898-1905) he asserted that he had recorded all the
dialect words of English. The American regional atlases
were not designed to provide the complete statement of regional and social usage that no investigation of a living
tongue can provide. They could only offer a framework, to

be filled in by later investigations, and a record valid
at a given time, which in many ways is bound to be super-
seded by the inexorable processes of linguistic and social
change, but which, by being set down, provides a way of
interpreting the significance of such changes.[7] That the
American atlases chose to investigate three varieties of
usage - -folk, common, and cultivated -- marks an important
innovation in dialect investigation. The folk speech represents, if we will, the Wordsworthian notion that somehow the folk reflect more clearly than the more affluent
the traditional patterns of the language, uncluttered by
formal education and travel; the cultivated speech represents the usage of the local elite at the time of the
investigation; the common speech reflects the dynamics
of cultural interchange. But this is only a frame, not a
definitive statement of class differences in America; even
in tribal villages with little contamination from the West,
anthropologists have found many-layered social hierarchies.
In the United States the comfortable triad of upper, middle, and lower classes, with which students were content
in the 1920s, has given way to a bewildering array of differences, with no community exactly replicating the orders
and degrees of its neighbors. In a slum neighborhood near
the University of Chicago, sociologists working in the
later 1960s not only distinguished between the traditional
lower class and its contemporary euphemism *working class,*
but have come up with a dozen subdivisions below the lower
middle class that seem to represent the reality of the
community.

    Thus the decision to limit the investigation of
American dialects to three main social levels does not
imply that there are only three levels in American society. It is a practical limit, imposed not only by the
need to have an adequate geographical distribution of communities in each region and an adequate questionnaire for
covering pronunciation and grammar and vocabulary, but
also by the impossibility of sketching the real class
differences in every community (some 200 in New England
alone) before beginning the fieldwork. Alert observers
will always find new things that need to be studied - not
merely refinements on social distinctions but the distribution of features of vocabulary (whether a road is *slick*
or *slippery* after a rain), or pronunciation (whether the
first syllable of *apricot* rhymes with *cap* or with *cape*) [8]
or grammar (such multiple auxiliaries as *used to could*).
It is the purpose of a linguistic atlas not to provide all
the answers but to suggest further questions that need
answering. An atlas properly designed and executed lays
out the data and leaves most of the interpretation to
those who use it.

    The first purpose of the regional atlases- -to go
over the ground and record usage as of the time of inves-
tigation- -has been pretty well accomplished for the con-

tinental United States (this region, as we pointed out, is
an exception). New England has been investigated and the
evidence published -- within 12 years of the beginning of
fieldwork, a remarkable achievement in dialectology. In
the Upper Midwest there has been a good summation of the
data, with publication of a fair amount of it. In California and Nevada, the North-Central States, and the Gulf
States the field records are available in microcopies;
microcopying is underway for the materials, from the Middle and South Atlantic States, even as traditional editing
and publication continues; the records for Oklahoma are
being transcribed from tapes, with microcopying the next
stage of editing. A good many records have been made, on
tape and otherwise, in Arizona, New Mexico, Colorado,
Washington, Missouri, Montana, and Utah, and in various
parts of Canada. Editorial work proceeds slowly, for the
most part, since the first duty of linguistic geographers
is to set forth their evidence in a form useful to future
scholars. The form may be cartographic, as in the *Linguistic Atlas of New England*, tabular, as in the first fasci-
cles from the Middle and South Atlantic States, or micro-
photographic like the data from other regions. In every
region the materials need a considerable amount of inter-
pretive apparatus; how much depends on the interests of
the editors and the kinds of materials they have to work
with.

Serious dialect work in America was inspired by Joseph Wright's dictionary, of which we have already spoken.
In fact, the American Dialect Society was founded in 1889
to produce an analog to Wright's work. That never came to
pass: there was no body of eager volunteers like those
who had provided Wright's collections, nor at that time
was there anyone with Wright's drive who could contract
to publish on a rigorous schedule and meet the deadlines.
But almost a century later this dream is being fulfilled
by Frederic Cassidy, who worked on the North Central Atlas
before World War II and--settling down at Wisconsin--
drafted plans for a Dictionary of American Regional English. Drawing on the experience of the regional atlases,
he relies primarily on field interviews -- 1,002 in all 50
states and the District of Columbia-- with a three-tiered
social classification, equal representation of men and
women, and attention to blacks and American Indians as
significant cultural groups. To supplement the field records, he includes almost any clearly documented kind of
evidence, so long as it is identified as regional or local.

The regional atlases and Cassidy's DARE have paid
more attention to the humble and everyday side of the vocabulary, and more to rural than to urban life, simply
because their aim is historical, looking back. But from
the beginnings of dialect study in America there has been
attention to urban culture, the amount varying according
to the area and the investigator's interests. Perhaps the

most careful probing of urban areas has been provided by
Lee Pederson, whose *Linguistic Atlas of the Gulf States*
(1981), the latest for which field work has been done,
includes an urban supplement of more than 200 questions
in addition to the basic questionnaire used in the field.
This urban supplement seeks to probe for details of urban
life that may yield different terms in Memphis, Atlanta,
New Orleans, and Houston. In fact, Pederson has recorded
so much evidence on vocabulary variation that his concor-
dance will in effect be another dialect dictionary, less
extensive in scope than Cassidy's but more intensive in
its investigation of the region.

All of these regional investigations are concerned
primarily with American English. They do not shrink from
the bilingual or multilingual; they only insist that
everyone interviewed, regardless of how many other languages each one speaks and how well, should be a native
speaker of American English. Yet all those concerned with
the Atlas projects have felt from the beginning that the
study of regional and social language variety in North
America should not ignore other tongues. They are aware
that, taken all together, the territorial claims of France
and Spain once embraced over 80 percent of what is now the
continental United States, and that within the Atlantic
Seaboard area dominated by the English there were viable
Dutch and Swedish settlements before the English came on
the scene. Many of us know Fr. Jogues's remark that in the
1650s in New Amsterdam--Manhattan Island--with hardly
2,000 people, some 15 languages and dialects could be
heard; fewer realize that there was the same language diversity in Philadelphia and Charleston, or that the white
creoles of Louisiana included not merely Frenchmen and
Spaniards but Germans and Irish. Despite the necessary
emphasis on English, the original planning of the Atlas
surveys advised that other colonial and immigrant languages deserved attention; it was Kurath, as Director of
the Atlas, who interested his students in the investigation of these other languages, and who sponsored the first
serious investigation of Gullah (Turner, 1949). My first
encounter with Kurath came at the Linguistic Institute of
1940 (I was then studying field methods with Bloch),
during the conference on non-English dialects in the United States. At this conference--sponsored by the American
Council of Learned Societies and published in its 1942
Bulletin--many significant projects were described; but
thanks to the pressure of world events, few of them came
to fruition; of those that did, one thinks chiefly of the
various projects in Pennsylvania German, Gaston Dulong's
Atlas of Canadian French, and Haugen's study of American
Norwegian. Despite the number of speakers, there has been
no coordinated survey of North American Spanish, or of any
of the Slavic languages transplanted across the Atlantic;
just as Trager was beginning work on the latter project

in 1941 he was summoned to make an introductory text in
Russian, and he never went back to the field. Likewise,
Vogelin's plan to enlist Hockett for fieldwork toward a
survey of dialect variation in Ojibwa (Hockett was another
student in Bloch's 1940 seminar at the Institute) was forgotten when Hockett was drafted by the Army and assigned
to study Chinese. The winds of World War II swept away
many of the languages spoken by smaller groups in the United States, but brought reinforcements - -especially to
urban areas - -of languages from the Russian client states.
The admission of Hawaii as a state called attention to the
kaleidoscopic assortment of tongues spoken on our Pacific
frontier; more recently our overseas involvements have
brought fresh accretions of Koreans, Vietnamese, and Cam-
bodians. Yet till now the broad-gauge studies of these
immigrant languages have been few. Almost every such study
has been an individual effort, confined to a single city
or at most a state. Still, there have been significant
revelations: both Haugen's classical study of American
Norwegian (1953) and Larmouth's more recent investigation
of American Finnish (1972) have shown how structural ir-
regularities of the immigrant tongue have been simplified,
and often rearranged, under the influence of the new
model of linguistic prestige offered by American English.
Haugen's own work, from his 1953 study of American Norwegian to his 1973 overview, provides models for others to
emulate. Regrettably, there is nothing comparable for
Spanish-English bilingualism in North America; we must
still begin with Janet Sawyer's 1957 study in San Antonio.
     We have mentioned that, in recognition of the social
complexity of American life and language behavior, the
regional linguistic atlases have tried to provide a three-
tiered model. It was assumed by Kurath and his associates
that if this framework was provided, later generations of
scholars would start from the Atlas statements and fill
in the interstices. A few such intensive studies were
possible on the basis of the Atlas records alone: with 25
full-length records from the five boroughs of New York
City and a dozen or so more from suburban counties, Yakira
Frank (1949) was able to make statements about the linguistic structure of the city as of 1940.[9] Allan Hubbell
(1950), supplementing a selection of Atlas interviews with
fresh work of his own (largely electronic recordings),
adds some details and generally confirms Frank's conclusions. Labov (1966), highly praised, also starts from the
Atlas records in New York. Other investigations, filling
in details in the picture broadly sketched by the regional
atlases, have been conducted in Boston (Carlson, Parslow),
Chicago (Pederson), Akron (Udell), Louisville (Howren),
Terre Haute (Carmony), Charleston (O'Cain), Savannah (Hopkins), Augusta, Georgia (Michael Miller), and San Francisco (DeCamp). Since the Atlas recordings are generally
good, since their coverage of any community is bound to

be sketchy with so much territory to be covered, and since
time has elapsed since the fieldwork for the regional surveys, there are hundreds of significant studies waiting to
be done, each with a good framework from which a competent
investigator may start.

Nor does the completion of one study in a given community take the opportunity away from later scholars; we
have seen this in the investigations of New York City, and
O'Cain's study of Charleston (1972) was a third generation
effort. Axiomatically, there is room for successively more
intensive work almost everywhere. The Chicago field records
for the North-Central survey, from 1949 to 1961, provided
the groundwork for Pederson's more intensive study of
1962-64; these in turn led to two strikingly different
studies, Uskup (1974), treating the local elites (so far,
the only sociolinguistic study in America to single out
the prestigious class), and Herndobler (1977), treating
intensively the speech of one Chicago neighborhood, East
Side -- a four-generation white working-class enclave, pro-
tected from invasions by blacks and Spanish-Americans by
industrial developments and the Calumet River. Uskup confined her work to pronunciation; Herndobler sought to explore the social implications of differences between men's
and women's usage in a rather compact neighborhood. There
is again almost no limit to the kinds of investigations
one may undertake, starting from what has been set forth
in the regional surveys. The materials from the Gulf
States, particularly, provide many such openings, since
Pederson has been especially careful to obtain generous
assortments of interviews from every urban center in the
Gulf States.

But there are other investigations -- and regrettably
not so dispassionately concerned with objective evidence
as those which begin with the regional atlases. These
might be characterized as activist sociolinguistics, particularly attentive to the cultural and educational problems of those who so far have not yet entered the main
economic and social currents of American society, but are
floundering in disturbing cultural eddies and backwaters.
Most of the popular sociolinguistic work of the past two
decades is of this type. Its quality varies, even in the
work of a single investigator, according to how seriously
the scholar is able to differentiate between the various
hats appropriate on different occasions, a choice not easy
when research is set up with practical pedagogical results
in mind. As Norman McQuown and George Faust stated about
1960, the building of a successful teaching program --
whatever the source and the target language or dialect--
involves several labors: a theoretical framework; a serious
gathering of data and organizing it into an objective description; a reordering of the description into a pedagogi-
cally viable presentation, with ample exercises; the
training of teachers in the use of the materials; and the

development of institutional and community support for the
classroom. Sometimes a scholar involved in this kind of
work has to operate on every one of these levels to get
the work done; if so, it is essential to recognize in each
part of the work which level the scholar is dealing with.[10]
Each level offers its own hazards: the theoretical sketch
may become so abstruse that it alienates many of those who
ought to be interested; and the appeal to the community,
or to some sections of the community, may reek of dema-
goguery. It takes courage, cool nerves, and an overwhelm-
ing commitment to objectivity to resist the temptation to
confuse the roles of scholar and advocate; and few there
are in sociolinguistics who can resist this.

Part of the problem is that sociolinguistics, as it
has developed in America, has not grown out of cumulative
experience as has much of more traditional linguistics,
including linguistic geography. It has been too much the
creature of sudden demand for instant miracles, of failed
school systems and crisis-ridden neighborhoods. In American sociolinguistics there has been none of the cumulative
scholarship that should ideally have developed --working
from small homogeneous communities in the center of well-
defined dialect areas, adding one complication at a time
till the investigators reached the urban monstrosities of
Washington and Chicago and Detroit and New York (Kurath,
1968). Nor as a rule was there a cadre of experienced
workers with awareness of previous relevant scholarship.
Haste marked their operations, from design through publication. Field-workers were sent out without adequate prep-
aration to work in situations where natural rapport with
informants would be difficult to achieve, and where some
of the most important categories of informants were excluded by the design:[11] relevant investigations, whether
in the same region (the same community or adjacent ones)
or in the regions from which the problem groups have come,
were ignored. Once a sweeping conclusion was proclaimed,
it became a part of *pseudodoxia epidemica,* accepted by
those with a vested interest in the new statements; when
the scholars from older disciplines raised mild questions,
they were shouted down.[12] Perhaps worst of all, there is
a reluctance of the newer breed to set out primary data in
detail, so that others can test their procedures and replicate their conclusions.[13] It is this, above all, that
leads one to skepticism, but of course I am spoilt by
being trained by someone who ruthlessly insisted that the
skills and deficiencies of his field-workers, and their
idiosyncracies in phonetic transcription, be set out in
detail, so that one who read might understand. As a result
of this training, I would much sooner hear cassettes of
the interviews than look at charts and graphs of the conclusions.

Here one may offer examples of the kinds of cautions
built into the work I have been doing. Kurath, 1949, Map

163, omitted the considerable evidence on *carry you home*
from northeastern New England; Kurath himself insisted
that the full evidence be published, to set the record
aright (R. McDavid, 1972). In the same spirit, it was necessary to review considerable evidence bearing on the
state of the low-back vowels in the Providence area: on
the basis of the field records Kurath and R. McDavid (1961)
asserted neutralization of the syllabics of *cot* and *caught*,
but William Moulton, an aboriginal as well as a trained
phonetician, had demonstrated that the contrast exists in
his speech. Not surprisingly, it was found that the contrast did not exist in the speech of the field-worker who
had had made the Providence records in the 1930s, but
phonographic records made independently from her informants by Miles Hanley and others showed such a contrast;
and a carefully detailed examination of the records of the
original field-worker suggests that she did recognize the
existence of the difference and was trying to record it,
though she had not had the same kind of training which
Bloch and Lowman had brought to their investigations (R.
McDavid, 1981a).

It would seem that, though we should not rest content
with the amount of evidence already recorded from various
regions, communities, and social groups--there will never
be enough --we should first concentrate on getting our
evidence accessible to those who should use it. A first
order of business would seem to be the making of microcopies of all the records from all the surveys launched so
far; if the evidence is still found only on tapes or cassettes, these should be duplicated for safety and then
transcribed as fully as possible, so that microcopying can
take place. In undertaking these archival operations we
will probably have to go back to basics in our training
of linguists, to give a new generation both the kind of
training in field transcription that was once commonplace,
and the ability to read and interpret the field transcriptions of others. This will require a kind of patience now
too rarely possessed: after transcribing or retranscribing
about 200 taped interviews, I conclude that if the interview approaches natural speech conditions, the scribe must
spend at least five hours for each hour of tape. As we
handle these materials, we must be particularly wary of
letting our own phonemic systems blind us to the significance of potential differences in the speech of others.
For years I have been troubled at the insistence of Midwestern colleagues that underprivileged Southerners do not
distinguish *rat* and *right*; the explanation I would offer
is that because the difference in Southern speech is signaled differently, by lower tongue position for *right*
than for *rat,* rather than by diphthongization of the vowel
in the in the former, the Midwesterner does not hear the
way the Southerner distinguishes the pair. And sure enough,
a story surfaced in the South of the social contretemps

that arose when a male Up-Country South Carolinian, having
a drink in a Michigan coed's apartment, asked the hostess
for a piece of *ice*.[14]

With Moulton, I agree that one must not merely have
good phonetic transcriptions but seek to set forth the
structural differences in the various dialects. In two
recent reviews (R. McDavid, 1981b; 1981c), I recalled the
embarrassment of the Michigan young woman, and suggested
in both publications that more attention might have been
paid to the organization of the dialectal phonemic systems,
and their contrasts, since the evidence, if not published
so far, can be provided by an examination of the *Basic
Material*. In fact, for every exotic linguistic feature one
may chance upon in Harlan, Kentucky, or Harlem, New York,
there is a trail of evidence leading back over the centuries. Though the social problems may not be less acute
when the knowledge is made accessible, at least the perspective on the nature and origin of differences will help
dispel superstitions. It should certainly help dispel
pious frauds-- deliberately teaching historical inaccura-
cies in the hope of developing greater self-respect among
one's students: what respect for their teachers will they
have when they learn they have been bamboozled?[15] Not only
is the study of language variety interesting and often
amusing, but one thing can be said by all who have studied
it seriously: greater awareness and more intensive study
make these problems of variation more complicated than
they were before. For the way each of us uses our language
and thinks about it is the result of all our intellectual
and social experience; and the way a community uses its
language is the result of all the experience of those in
the community.

As I promised, I have said little about Spanish: I
prefer a confession of honest ignorance to a glib parrot-
ing of somebody else's slogans. I grew up too close to
Buncombe County. As a part-time historian, I know that all
the complexities of American English are parralleled in
those of American Spanish, with a somewhat longer history
and spread over a larger territory. Practically speaking,
having participated in the language programs of World War
II and afterwards, I see nothing to be gained by attempted
suppression of another tongue, or by patronizing endorsement of "bilingual" education which in fact is but a per-
petuation of parallel monolingualism in both language
communities.[16] For genuine bilingualism, on the other hand,
the example of the Haugens and those like them has given
me only the greatest respect. Any approach to the kind of
bicultural understanding their competence has given them
needs to be encouraged.

All of those who use a language are entitled to describe their dreams. Mine are simple. I would like to see
the time when everyone in childhood begins to study a

language other than his own, and keeps it up long enough
to acquire a modicum of fluency, facility, and versatility:
my four children were fortunate enough to begin German in
the third grade and continue it through high school. What
language the child studies may be a matter of personal
choice, even of accident:[17] however small may be the speech
community this language represents, an introduction to
another culture through a mastery of its language will
make one a better citizen of a shrinking world. In this
world, it is ludicrous, if not tragic, that any classroom
teachers, confronted with the language variety that now
characterizes almost every classroom, should be certified
without a knowledge of how languages work, and a decent
command of at least one language of which they are not
native speakers. If this is Utopian, I had rather be bri-
gaded with St. Thomas More than with the time-servers who
have too often made our educational system an expensive
mockery.

NOTES

1. The sociolinguistic situation in Greenville, S.C., has been described many times, notably in R. McDavid, 1966. The perspective of
these investigations is set forth at greater length in "Langue et
société aux États-Unis; nouvelles perspectives," as co-author with
Guy Jan Forgue of *La langue des Américains*. This collaboration, along
with the active interest of M. Forgue and his colleagues in France,
led to the award, January 7, 1983, of the degree Docteur de l'Univer-
sité de la Sorbonne Nouvelle, one of the most coveted distinctions
in the scholarly world.

2. Many linguists overlook the interest of the Grimms in fairy tales
as well as in philology.

3. Although Orton (1962-71) emphasized the single interview in a
community, hardly 10 percent of the interviews were conducted with
single speakers: the average is at least three, and there may be as
many as seven speakers for a single record; the difference in age
between oldest and youngest may be as much as four decades.

4. Only Taft and the two Roosevelts came from families of long-time
wealth and social position.

5. The coexistence of considerable poverty and unfilled jobs during
the Reagan administration is nothing new, but has occurred repeatedly
during the history of English-speaking settlers in the New World. The
high wages for skilled labor, caused by its scarcity, were noted by
observers of the colonial scene.

6. John Fisher suggests (conversation at Knoxville, 1979) that in
America it is probably best to limit the term "standard" to written
usage, since it implies something undeviating. As I indicated in the
discussion, my mode of discourse differs a great deal from that of
my fellow Southerner, President-Reject Jimmy Carter, let alone that
of President-Eject Nixon.

7. Kurath points out that an aerial survey at a given time is like
a census, whose data for 1900 are extremely useful to the demographers
of 1980.

8. *Slick* is my normal usage; in Michigan and Upstate New York, when I used the term with my informants, it was identified as Indiana and Pennsylvania usage, as opposed to their normal *slippery*. The item has been incorporated in later surveys, such as Allen, 1973-76.

For *apricot* I knew only the vowel of *cape*; but my Minnesota-raised wife has the vowel of *cap*. Her pronunciation is apparently restricted to the area settled from New England.

For my father and his professional associates, all college educated and of established social position in the Up Country of South Carolina, *used to could* was normal in informal usage. So was it for my childhood associates.

9. Some details of the speech of the metropolitan area are treated more exhaustively in Wetmore, 1956, and Van Riper, 1958.

10. Kenneth Pike is one of the few linguists who have worked successfully on all levels.

11. Shuy, Wolfram, and Riley (1968)--one of the frankest expositions of a sociolinguistic survey--indicates that the design of the Detroit investigation, by excluding students in non-Roman Catholic private schools and restricting the coverage to the area within the city limits (including the enclaves of Highland Park and Hamtramck), effectively excluded the upper class, who generally live in the suburbs or send their children to non-Roman private schools, or both. Similar demographic patterns exist in most of the large metropolitan areas. A design that excludes the upper class removes the local models of excellence.

12. A number of the new breed have made their reputations by bad-mouthing the kind of work with which I have been associated.

13. Two successive issues of *Science* (October 3, 10, 1981) describe situations in the biological sciences where conclusions were considered invalid because the investigators did not make available the primary data from which their conclusions were drawn, so that others would have an opportunity to replicate the work.

14. Kurath et al. (1939) is ruthless in its presentation of the strengths and weaknesses of the various investigators in New England.

Southerners have a number of amusing indications of what happens when one speaker has as homonyms, or perceives as homonyms, what other speakers distinguish. When the Wepman Auditory Discrimination Test was used as a measure of reading readiness in Chicago, students with Southern-derived speech forms were penalized. But when a group of Chicago-born teachers were tested on discriminations made by Southerners, they did just as badly.

15. The origins of the varieties of English spoken by urban blacks in the Northern United States are extremely complex, as are the origins of all forms of New World speech. Yet I have heard an activist sociolinguist advocate teaching the Africanist-Creolist position, as a matter of principle, regardless of evidence.

16. In Chicago, some of the proponents of what they call "bilingual education" simply mean that when children come from Spanish-speaking homes all classroom activities should be conducted in Spanish, not that both English and Spanish-speaking groups should become proficient in a second language.

17. Such an accident determined the choice of German as the foreign language our children studied. The oldest had had a summer of French after his kindergarten year, and did well. But in the second grade

he became very seriously interested in dinosaurs, and on learning
that most of the important books in paleontology were in German, he
decided for that - and the others naturally followed.

REFERENCES

Allen, Harold B. 1973-76. *Linguistic Atlas of the Upper Midwest.*
3 vols. Minneapolis: University of Minnesota Press.

Atwood, E. Bagby. 1962. *The Regional Vocabulary of Texas.* Austin:
University of Texas Press.

Carlson, David B. 1973. "The Common Speech of Boston." Ph.D. dissertation, University of Massachusetts.

Carmony, Marvin. 1965. "The Speech of Terre Haute: A Hoosier Dialect
Study." Ph.D. dissertation, Indiana University.

Cassidy, Frederic G. 1983. *Dictionary of American Regional English.*
Cambridge, Massachusetts: The Belknap Press of Harvard University.

DeCamp, David. 1954. "The Speech of San Francisco." Ph.D. dissertation, University of California, Berkeley.

_____. 1958-59. "The Pronunciation of English in San Francisco."
Orbis, 7: 372-391; 8: 54-77.

Frank, Yakira. 1949. "The Speech of New York City." Ph.D. dissertation, University of Michigan, Ann Arbor.

Gilliéron, Jules, and Edmond Edmont. 1902-10. *Atlas linguistique de
la France.* Paris: Champion.

Haugen, Einar. 1953. *The Norwegian Language in America.* 2 vols. Philadelphia: University of Pennsylvania Press.

_____. 1956. "Bilingualism in the Americas: A Bibliography and Re-
search Guide." *Papers of the American Dialect Society,* 26.

_____. 1973. "Bilingualism, Language Contact, and Immigrant Languages
in the United States: A Research Report 1956-70." *Current Trends
in Linguistics,* Vol. 10. In Thomas A. Sebeok et al. The Hague:
Mouton, pp. 1.2.505-591.

Herndobler, Robin. 1977. "White Working-Class Speech of Savannah,
Georgia: A Phonological Analysis." Ph.D. dissertation, University of Chicago.

Howren, Robert R. 1956. "The Speech of Louisville, Kentucky." Ph.D.
dissertation, Indiana University.

Hubbell, Allan F. 1950. *The Pronunciation of English in New York
City: Consonants and Vowels.* New York: King's Crown.

Jaberg, Karl, and Jakob Jud. 1928-40. *Sprach- und Sachatlas Italiens under der Sudschweiz*. 8 vols. Zofingen, Switzerland: Ringier.

Kurath, Hans. 1949. *A Word Geography of the Eastern United States*. Ann Arbor: University of Michigan Press.

_____. 1968. "The Investigation of Urban Speech." *Papers of the American Dialect Society,* 49: 1-7.

_____, and Raven I. McDavid, Jr. 1961. *The Pronunciation of English in the Atlantic States*. Ann Arbor: University of Michigan Press.

_____, et al. 1939. *Handbook of the Linguistic Geography of New England*. Providence: Brown University Press. For the American Council of Learned Societies (2nd ed., rev. by Audrey Duckert. New York: AMS, 1973).

_____, et al. 1939-43. *Linguistic Atlas of New England*. 3 vols., bound as 6. Providence: Brown University Press. For the American Council of Learned Societies (repr. 3 vols. New York: AMS, 1972).

Labov, William. 1966. *The Social Stratification of English in New York City*. Washington D.C.: Center for Applied Linguistics.

Larmouth, Donald W. 1972. "Grammatical Interference in American Finnish." Ph.D. dissertation, University of Chicago.

McDavid, Raven I., Jr. 1966. "Dialect Differences and Social Differences in an Urban Society." In William Bright, ed., *Sociolinguistics*. The Hague: Mouton, 72-83.

_____. 1972. "Carry You Home Once More." *Neophilologische Mitteilungen,* 73 (1-2) (studies presented to Tauho F. Mustanoja on his sixtieth birthday): 192-196.

_____. 1980. "Linguistics Through the Kitchen Door." *First Person Singular:* Papers from the conference on an oral archive for the history of American linguistics, ed. by Boyd David and Raymond K. O'Cain. Amsterdam Studies in the Theory and History of Linguistics. *LLL: Studies in the History of Linguistics,* Vol. 21. Amsterdam: John Benjamins, pp. 1-16.

_____. 1981a. "Low-Back Vowels in Providence: A Note in Structural Dialectology." *Journal of English Linguistics,* 15: 21-29.

_____. 1981b. (Review) "Eduard Kolb, et al., Atlas of English Sounds." *Journal of English Linguistics,* 15: 45-52.

_____. 1981c. (Review) "Harold Orton, et al., Linguistic Atlas of England." *American Speech,* 57: 219-254.

Miller, Michael I. 1978. "Inflectional Morphology in the Speech of Augusta, Georgia: A Sociolinguistic Description." Ph.D. dissertation, University of Chicago.

O'Cain, Raymond K. 1972. "A Social Dialect Study of Charleston, South Carolina." Ph.D. dissertation, University of Chicago.

Orton, Harold. 1962-71. *Survey of English Dialects: Basic Material.* Introduction, 4 vols. (each in 3 parts). Leeds, England: E. J. Arnold.

Parslow, Robert L. 1967. "The Pronunciation of English in Boston, Massachusetts: Vowels and Consonants." Ph.D. dissertation, University of Michigan, Ann Arbor.

Pederson, Lee. 1965. "The Pronunciation of English in Metropolitan Chicago: Consonants and Vowels." *Papers of the American Dialect Society,* 44.

_____. 1981. *Linguistic Atlas of the Gulf States.*

Pop, Sever. 1950. *La dialectologies.* 2 vols. Louvain, Belgium: University of Louvain.

Sawyer, Janet. 1957. "A Dialect Study of San Antonio, Texas: A Bilingual Community." Ph.D. dissertation, University of Texas at Austin.

Shuy, Roger W., Walter A. Wolfram, and William K. Riley. 1968. *Field Techniques in an Urban Language Study.* Washington: Center for Applied Linguistics.

Turner, Lorenzo B. 1949. *Africanisms in the Gullah Dialect.* Chicago: University of Chicago Press.

Udell, Gerald R. 1966. "The Speech of Akron, Ohio: A Study in Urbanization." Ph.D. dissertation, University of Chicago.

Uskup, Frances. 1974. "Social Markers of Urban Speech: A Study of Elites in Chicago." Ph.D. dissertation, Illinois Institute of Technology, Chicago, Illinois.

Van Riper, W. R. 1958. "The Loss of Postvocalic *r* in the Eastern United States." Ph.D. dissertation, University of Michigan, Ann Arbor.

Wetmore, Thomas H. 1959. "The Low-Central and Low-Back Vowels in the English of the Eastern United States." *Papers of the American Dialect Society,* 32.

Wrede, Ferdinand. 1927-56. *Deutscher Sprachatlas.* Marburg/Lahn, Germany: Elwert.

Wright, Joseph. 1898-1905. *English Dialect Dictionary.* 6 vols. London: Frowde.

11

THE PAN AMERICAN PROJECT

Jon Amastae
Department of Linguistics
University of Texas at El Paso

The Pan American Project, which ran from 1975 to 1979, was begun to investigate the aspects of bilingualism of Pan American University (=PAU) students, as well as the effect of these aspects on their general academic performance. An especially important objective was to determine the kinds of problems PAU students had in writing and the degree, if any, to which Spanish interference accounted for these.

Pan American University is located in Edinburg, Texas, in the lower Rio Grande Valley of south Texas only about 15 miles from the U.S./Mexican border. The majority of its students come from the four-county (Starr, Hidalgo, Cameron, Willacy) area immediately surrounding the university. The student body typically reflects the composition of the surrounding community, being 76.7 percent Spanish surname (SS) and primarily lower socioeconomic status (=SES) (Amastae, 1978a).

At the initial stage of the project, several different types of data were collected under the auspices of the Language and Linguistics Research Center, which was funded in great part by an AIDP grant. A *Sociolinguistic Background Questionnaire* (=SBQ), adapted from one used in a similar study at the University of Texas at El Paso, was administered to a stratified, systematic sample comprising 7.6 percent (n=679) of the PAU student body. Writing samples were collected along with an interview in

Spanish and English as well. In addition, Nicholas Sobin
developed a syntax elicitation device (=SQE) to help us
assess certain aspects of the ways in which the students
commanded English (Sobin, 1977b). This part of the project will be described in more detail later in this work.

SBQ

The SBQ (Brooks et al, 1972) covered several areas,
including general background and SES (socioeconomic status), family structure, and history; academic background
including academic experience, major, career aspirations,
and university attitudes; and language-related matters
such as language-use scales, language fluency rating
scales, and linguistic attitudes. All in all, the SBQ
provided us with an extremely interesting portrait of the
bilingual situation in the area, since we assumed that
PAU students accurately reflected the surrounding community. For example, we learned that, of the Spanish
surname students, 74 percent spoke first in Spanish
while 14 percent learned both Spanish and English simultaneously. Almost all reported high identification with
Spanish and loyalty to it in both practical and aesthetic
terms. Nevertheless, many expressed a certain negative
attitude toward the local variety of Spanish, which was
seen as inferior to the local variety of English. Few
had literacy training in Spanish, with the result that
many students could be said to be dominant in English
even though Spanish was the first and still the home language. In summary, the SBQ provided us with necessary
background for a more direct examination of language and
writing. (See Amastae 1978a; 1978b; 1980; 1981, for
further discussion of the sociolinguistic data.)

ANALYSIS OF WRITING SAMPLES

A large portion of time and effort was directed toward the analysis of the writing samples. This analysis
took two forms. First, we examined actual errors. In
doing this we did not preselect errors to analyze, but
defined categories of errors as we proceeded. In this
way, 73 error types were isolated, ranging from errors of
literacy convention (including punctuation) through
errors of standard usage to basic language errors. We
discovered in the sample as a whole, including both
Spanish-speaking (SS) and non-Spanish-speaking (NSS)
groups, that there were remarkably few language errors,
as opposed to punctuation and other errors of orthographic convention. Thus it seemed that these Spanish-
speaking students were making the same errors everyone
else makes, for the most part.

Secondly, we analyzed the students' writing from the
point of view of elaboration, using techniques developed

by Hunt (1965) and Loban (1976). These techniques analyze the degree to which a sentence structure is elaborated beyond a simple sentence using such devices as
modifying works, phrases, clauses, and complements.
Using an index of elaboration, called a communication-
unit (c-unit), which was similar to Hunt's "t-unit",
allowed us to quantify the degree of syntactic elaboration. The c-unit is composed of an independent clause
with all attendant modifiers, including modifying
clauses. Within this unit, we counted the number of
words and this index quantitatively measured syntactic
maturity. Comparing quantitative data from PAU students
to Loban's high school seniors, we found that PAU freshmen very closely matched the Loban low group in their use
of syntactic elaboration (McQuade, 1978).

    Since we were interested in searching for relation-
ships between error types and elaboration types, we
subjected both to a factor analysis procedure using SPSS
(Nie et al., 1975).* It is interesting to note that in
the factoring of the 23 elaboration types, the first five
factors were strongly related, and these factors included
those elements found by Loban to appear first in the
developmental sequence. In other words, the informants
were early in their development of syntactic elaboration
in English (McQuade, 1980). The stronger factors were
exclusively literacy and standard usage errors of the
type all students have trouble with—not just bilingual
students.

SQE

    The general lack of association between most lan-
guage errors and elaboration which the factor analysis
revealed raised questions about the students' command
of Standard English syntax. Since many possible forms
simply did not occur in a given corpus, we could not conclude that the writers did not know them, but merely that
they had just not used them in the sample collected. We
realized that the absence of certain forms could imply
any of three interpretations: (1) the writer did not in
fact know the construction; (2) the writer did not command it completely; or (3) the writer simply avoided it.
    In order to address the questions raised by the fac-
tor analysis in regard to the students' command of
syntax, Sobin (1977a; 1977b) developed a device (SQE) to
force students to manipulate patterns which simply might
not have occurred in their writing samples and to allow

---

*We have taken the liberty of including in our References still
other works expecially useful in our study.

us to learn more about possible interference from
Spanish to English. The SQE queried students' ability to
perform operations corresponding to different sorts of
syntactic rules, e.g., insertion, deletion, movement,
etc. Other parts of the SQE asked respondents to mark
acceptable vs. nonacceptable sentences and others to
choose an item, e.g., a preposition. Many types of operations were selected expressly for their difference or
similarity in English and Spanish. A few sample items
are given below:

(1)   Check (√) any acceptable sentence. Put an X before
      any sentence that sounds unnatural.

      a.   Jack has kissed Jill.
      b.   Jill has been kissed by Jack.

      a.   To leave home scares Sally.
      b.   Sally is scare by to leave home.

(2)   Combine the separate sentences in each group into
      one natural sentence.

      a.   I want this. You write to your mother.
      b.   Sheila pointed this out. She left early last
           night.

(3)   Write the form of the word in ( )'s which will com-
      plete the sentence:

      a.   (push)_____your friend wasn't
           nice.
      b.   (resign) They asked for her _____.
      c.   (write) Good_____is important.

      It is important to note that most of our informants
were able to perform these syntactic operations using an
elicitation device similar to the sample items given
previously. One interesting finding resulting from an
analysis of the SQE data is that, while some aspects of
linguistic structure (e.g., preposition usage and lexi-
cal/semantic selection) may transfer, there is little
or no evidence that transformational rules transfer.
Specifically, in English question formation, the variant
forms look nothing like Spanish, but are just those that
English monolingual and all other learners of English
produce (Sobin, 1977c). The case for nontransference of
transformational rules is dealt with in detail by Sobin
(1980).

EDUCATIONAL IMPLICATIONS OF THE PROJECT

      The three main data sources used in the PAU Project,
the SBQ, writing samples, and the SQE, strongly revealed
that, although more than a majority of the students were
bilingual, many of their problems in writing English

could not be attributed to interference.   Therefore,
educationally a contrastive approach was not the solution.   And since the data showed very few basic language
errors, an approach emphasizing basic competence would
not be called for.   Yet freshmen obviously needed some
solution other than what they were getting.   PAU is an
open admissions institution.   The ACT scores of entering
freshmen were in the bottom 1-2 percentiles nationally.
Average reading levels have been at the ninth-tenth
grade level and the failure rate in freshman composition
courses was approximately 50 percent.

The solution we proposed was to emphasize development in writing over remediation, and we chose to do this
by using sentence-combining as a method of instruction
to increase morpho-syntactic flexibility, to iron out
basic orthographic problems, and to put the writing process in the context of meaningful communication.
Sentence-combining was considered a logical strategy for
teaching PAU students how to write, since our data had
revealed that most students showed little interference
from Spanish or other characteristics of basic deficiency
in English, but they did not use all the syntactic resources in writing English.

Instruction over a semester with the sentence-
combining method revealed that almost all the students
had some knowledge of the structures at some level, but
they often failed to see the myriad possibilities of
combinations. Sentence-combining seemed to spark a late
stage of language acquisition in which structures known
passively (and perhaps often avoided) became structures
known actively and productively.   In short, what we found
was completely in accord with what several recent investigations of later phases of first language acquisition
have found (Ingram, 1975; Limber, 1973).

SUMMARY

The PAU Project, a complex research study, found few
special language problems with English among the predominantly bilingual student population; however, it did
discover a lack of literacy in at least three senses:
(1) lack of orthographical practice and awareness; (2)
lack of standard usage; and most important, (3) lack of
variety and embedding in syntax (which like the other
two, is hardly unique to Hispanic students).   Our experience was that sentence-combining was a useful technique
for fostering development in all three areas.

REFERENCES

Amastae, Jon. 1977. "The Use of Phonology in the Study of
Bilingualism." In Bates Hoffer and Betty Lou Dubois, eds.,
Southwest Areal Linguistics Then and Now (SWALLOW V). San
Antonio, Tex.: Trinity University Press, pp. 229-247.

_____. 1978. "Sociolinguistic Background of Pan American
University Students." In Anthony Lozano, ed., *Bilingual and
Biliterate Perspectives* (SWALLOW VII). Boulder: University of
Colorado, pp. 132-141.

_____. 1978b. "Attitudes Towards Varieties of Spanish."
(with Lucía Elías-Olivares). In Michel Paradis, ed., *Fourth
LACUS Forum 1977*. Columbia, S.C.: Hornbeam Press, pp. 286-304.

_____. 1978c. "The Acquisition of English Vowels." *Papers
in Linguistics*, 11(3-4): 423-457.

_____. 1979. "Family Background and Bilingualism." *The
Journal of the Linguistic Association of the Southwest*, 3(2):
132-150.

_____. 1980a. "First Language." In Florence Barkin and
Elizabeth Brandt, eds., *Speaking, Singing, and Teaching: A
Multidisciplinary Approach to Language Variation* (SWALLOW VIII).
Tempe: Arizona State University. Anthropological Research
Papers #20.

_____. 1980b. "Sociolinguistic Variation and Markedness."
In Edward Blansitt, Jr., and Richard V. Teschner, eds., *A
Festschrift for Jacob Ornstein*. Rowley, Mass.: Newbury House,
pp. 10-17.

_____. 1980c. "Phonological Theory and Bilingualism." Pre-
sented at the IV International Symposium on Spanish and
Portuguese Bilingualism, Juárez, Chih., Mexico.

_____. 1981. "Learner Continuums and Speech Communities."
Papers in Linguistics, 14(1-2): 155-196.

_____. 1982. "Language Maintenance and Shift in the Lower
Rio Grande Valley of South Texas." In Florence Barkin, Elizabeth
Brandt, and Jacob Ornstein, eds., *Bilingualism in the Border-
lands*. New York: Teachers College Press.

Brooks, Bonnie, Gary Brooks, Paul Goodman, and Jacob Ornstein.
1972. *Sociolinguistic Background Questionnaire*. El Paso:
Cross-Cultural Southwest Ethnic Study Center, University of
Texas at El Paso.

Combs, Warren. 1977. "Sentence-combining Practice Aids Reading
Comprehension." *Journal of Reading*, October: 18-24.

Hunt, Kellogg. 1965. *Grammatical Structures Written at Three Grade Levels*. Urbana, Ill.: National Council of Teachers of English.

Ingram, David. 1975. "If and When Transformations Are Acquired by Children." In D.P. Dato, ed., *Developmental Psycholinguistics: Theory and Application*. Washington, D.C.: Georgetown University Press, pp. 99-127.

Keenan, Edward, and Bernard Comrie. 1977. "Noun Phrase Accessibility and Universal Grammar." *Linguistic Inquiry*, 8:63-99.

Lawlor, Joseph. 1980. "Improving Student Writing through Sentence Combining: A Literature Review," *ERIC* (ED 1972 356).

Limber, John. 1973. "The Genesis of Complex Sentences." In Timothy Moore, ed., *Cognitive Development and the Acquisition of Language*. New York: Academic Press, pp. 169-185.

Loban, Walter. 1976. *Language Development*. Urbana: National Council of Teachers of English.

McQuade, Judy. 1978. "On Errors and Elaboration in Freshman Themes." In Anthony Lozano, ed., *Bilingual and Biliterate Perspectives* (SWALLOW VII). Boulder: University of Colorado, pp. 122-131.

_____. 1979. "Factors Affecting Performance in Pan American University Compositions." In Florence Barkin and Elizabeth Brandt, eds., *Speaking, Singing, and Teaching: A Multidisciplinary Approach to Language Variation* (SWALLOW VIII). Anthropological Research Papers #20. Tempe: Arizona State University.

_____. 1981. "Writing Development: Monolinguals vs. Bilinguals." In Charles Elerick, ed., *Southwest Areal Linguistics* (SWALLOW IX). El Paso: Texas Western Press.

Mejías, Hugo. 1978. "Errors and Variants in Spanish Compositions." In Anthony Lozano, ed., *Bilingual and Biliterate Perspectives* (SWALLOW VII). Boulder: University of Colorado, pp. 88-111.

_____, and Gloria Garza-Swan. *Nuestro español: curso para Estudiantes Bilingües*. New York: Macmillan.

Nie, Norman, et al. 1975. *Statistical Package for the Social Sciences*. New York: McGraw-Hill.

Ornstein, Jacob, and Paul Goodman. 1974. "Bilingualism/Biculturism Viewed in the Light of Socio-educational Correlates." Paper presented at the World Congress of Sociology, Toronto.

Sobin, Nicholas. 1976. "Texas Spanish and Lexical Borrowing." *Papers in Linguistics*, 9(1-2): 15-47.

_____. 1977a. "On the Study of Syntax and Bilingualism."
In Bates Hoffer and Betty Lou Dubois, eds., *Southwest Areal Lin-
guistics Then and Now* (SWALLOW V). San Antonio, Tex.: Trinity
University Press, pp. 247-263.

_____. 1977b. *English Syntax Questionnaire*. Edinburg,
Tex.: Pan American University.

_____. 1977c. "Notes on the Acquisition of Interrogative
Questions." Paper presented at SWALLOW VI. *ERIC* (ED 144 377).

_____. 1977d. "On Echo questions in English." In Donald
Lance and Dan Gulstad, ed., *The Proceedings of the 1977 Mid-
America Linguistics Conference*. Columbia: University of
Missouri, pp. 247-259.

_____. 1978. "On Complex Sentence Construction." In
Anthony Lozano, ed., *Bilingual and Biliterate Perspectives*
(SWALLOW VII). Boulder: University of Colorado, pp. 112-121.

_____. 1980a. "On Transference and Inversion." In Edward
Blansitt, Jr., and Richard V. Teschner, eds., *A Festschrift for
Jacob Ornstein*. Rowley, Mass.: Newbury House, pp. 265-273.

_____. 1980b. "On Deletion Rules and Transference." In
Florence Barkin and Elizabeth Brandt, eds., *Speaking, Singing,
and Teaching: A Multidisciplinary Approach to Language Variation* (SWALLOW VIII). Tempe: Arizona State University,
Anthropological Research Papers #20, pp. 409-419.

_____. 1980c. "Gapping as Evidence of Distinct L2 Acqui-
sition." Paper presented at the Conference on Spanish in the
U.S. Setting: Beyond the Southwest, University of Illinois,
Chicago Circle.

_____. 1980d. "Theoretical Implications of Bilingualism:
The Lexicon." Paper presented at the International Symposium on
Spanish and Portuguese Bilingualism, Juárez, Chih., Mexico.

12

THE EL PASO SOCIOLINGUISTIC MICROSURVEY OF BILINGUALISM

Jacob Ornstein-Galicia
University of Texas at El Paso

Betty Lou Dubois
New Mexico State University, Las Cruces

Bates Hoffer
Trinity University, San Antonio

This paper describes one type of sociolinguistic study --localized microsurvey--carried out by a team initially consisting of an educational psychologist, an educational administration specialist, a sociologist specializing in the "culture of poverty," and a linguist. This inter-disciplinary team, formed in 1969, set out to carry out a comparative survey of the two major ethnic groups attending the University of Texas at El Paso: Chicanos, or Mexican-Americans, and Anglos. The need for data cor-relating language and societal dimensions was urgent, primarily because of the uniqueness of this university, which is the most bilingual/bicultural of any larger in-stitution of higher education in the U.S., with an en-rollment of 15,000. Over one-third of the students at UT-El Paso (UTEP) are Mexican-Americans and, quite commonly, individual classes may reflect over 90 per-cent Spanish-surname constituency. Matching this pattern, Spanish is heard in the halls of UTEP buildings as fre-quently as English, perhaps more so. We concluded there was a need for better understanding of the differences between monolingual Anglo (English-speaking) and bi-lingual Mexican-American (Spanish and English) students at this university. Thus, the Sociolinguistic Studies on Southwest Bilingualism (SSSB) was born.

COLLECTION OF MICROSURVEY DATA

The broad goal of the microsurvey was to carry out a comparative survey of the leading traits of Mexican-Americans and Anglos enrolled at this university in 1970-71. Initially concerned with probing the socio-educational correlates of local bilingualism, we attempted to devise an instrument for this purpose. After a certain amount of trial and error, the team succeeded in elaborating the *Sociolinguistic Background Questionnaire: An Instrument for the Measurement of Bilingualism* (Brooks et al., rev. 1972). Adaptations of this instrument have been used in other microsurveys and research studies, as well as Ph.D. dissertations.

The *Sociolinguistic Background Questionnaire* (SBQ) consisted of two parts. Part A consisted of 106 items in multiple-choice format covering the following dimensions:

A. Demography
B. Educational history
C. Vocational and lifestyle goals
D. Cultural value systems (Mexican-American vs. Anglo)
E. Language patterns and attitudes (Spanish, English, and bilingual dialects)
   1. Self-assessment of fluency
   2. Self-assessment of dominance
   3. Comparative use (in some 20 domains)
   4. Perceptions and value judgments of regional varieties (stigmatizing effects of Mexican-American accent)

Although we attempted an approximate balance between linguistic and social items, heavy emphasis was placed on attitudinal questions in both dimensions as a basis for comparing perceptions of the two groups. Of special relevance is the attention paid to attitudes and opinions regarding Southwest Spanish, a particular non-standard dialect typical in the Southwest. A six-point scale for socioeconomic status combining features from Duncan and Hollingshead's system was developed by Goodman.

Part B of the SBQ, which was optional, consisted of language elicitation among bilinguals in order to assess linguistic performance in both Spanish and English or in a code-switching variety. This consisted of an open-ended oral interview and a written sample. The open-ended interview was conducted by a bilingual peer who broached a variety of topics intended to bring the former to the highest level of their competence as reflected, of course, in their actual performance. The topics ranged from elementary discussion of daily living ("A Day in My Life") to topics of intermediate difficulty and complexity ("Comparison of Life in Mexico and the United States") to the more advanced levels of

abstraction and conceptualization, such as existentialist
and other philosophies, religion as a force in life, and
Chicano and other ethnic movements. Following the oral interview came the written portion. Again respondents could
choose from three levels of topics, but they were asked
to write on the same themes in both Spanish and English.
The object of the written component was to provide a dimension too often neglected in American sociolinguistics,
i.e., writing skill as an important aspect of one's communication equipment.

All subjects also completed the CUES test (*College
and University Environment Scales*), a commercial instrument prepared by Pace et al. for the Educational Testing
Service, Princeton, New Jersey (1969). The CUES test
consisted of 160 true-false items attempting to measure
students' perception of their home institution in terms
of: (1) practicality; (2) propriety; (3) community; (4)
awareness; and (5) scholarship. From these responses,
a profile of the perceived climate on these five dimensions was constructed and comparisons made with other
institutions.

In order to cope with the socioeducational side of
bilingualism, our team undertook a stratified random
sample of the entire, full-time, undergraduate, un-
married student body of UT-El Paso, subdivided into 16
homogeneous groups according to age, sex, year of school,
school in which enrolled, and ethnic affiliation. Two
general populations were targeted: Spanish-surnamed individuals, or Mexican-Americans, and the others known
in the Southwest by the portmanteau term, of Anglos.
Approximately 5 percent of the undergraduate students
present at this university in the academic year 1970-71
--301 in all--completed Part A of the SBQ and the CUES
Test. Of these 301, 154 were Spanish-surnamed and 147,
Anglos. A 10 percent sub-sample of the original total
sample--all bilinguals completed the entire battery of
SBQ Parts, A and B and the CUES Test. Thus, 30 subjects
in all completed the entire elicitation battery. Part B
of the SBQ, which consisted of the taped bilingual corpus and the compositions, is known as the V Series.
(Analysis of the V Series will be discussed in detail
later.)

ANALYSIS OF DATA

As Goodman and Brooks (1973) point out, following
the data collection, the SBQ-Part A questionnaires were
coded and the information entered on key-punched cards
to facilitate compuational computer processing. Comparisons between Anglos and Mexican-Americans were
analyzed statistically, using nonparametric statistical
techniques proposed by Siegel (1956). Reported differences between the two groups were considered significant at the .05 level of confidence.

Socioeconomic status was measured in the SBQ according to a scale combining and modifying the Hollingshead and Redlich system (Hollingshead and Redlich, 1958). The scale numbers were reversed, and somewhat different categories of educational training were employed. An eighth point was added to their seven for "possession of a professional degree." Duncan's system assigns number from 1 to 100 for each occupation. Accordingly, for each subject, scores from the two socioeconomic measures were added together and assigned to one of eight categories (for detailed discussion of this method, see Goodman, 1970).

Five socioeconomic categories were then employed: lower-upper; upper-middle; lower-middle; upper-lower; and lower-lower. The upper-upper category was deleted since it depended upon old-family affiliation and wealth --scarcely present in such a combination in a city mostly settled since the 1870s.

Not unsurprisingly, it turned out that in our sample only 18 percent of Anglos were qualified for upper-lower, as contrasted with 37 percent of Mexican-Americans for that category. There were, moreover, more Anglo respondents who were lower-middle, upper-middle, and lower-upper than Chicanos--32 and 28 percent, 37 and 9 percent, and 12 and 2 percent respectively. Goodman and Brooks (1973) note that, while each social class was represented in each ethnic group, more than 60 percent of the Mexican-American subjects turned out to be in the lower-lower and upper-lower SES (socio-economic status), as contrasted with a mere 19 percent of Anglos.

SOME RESULTS

Wayne Murray analyzed the CUES data, and these results are discussed in detail in his doctoral dissertation (Murray, 1972a) and elsewhere (Murray, 1972b). In regard to the various dimensions of attitudes treated in the instrument, Murray found a significant difference of outlook between Chicanos and Anglos only in that towards scholarship. To our surprise, the Mexican-American respondents did not regard the university more reverently than Anglos, in contrast to stereotypic beliefs that they do. In fact, Mexican-American respondents evaluated the university, its faculty, and teaching efforts lower than did their Anglo peers. Murray also found that, among our subjects, sex rather than ethnicity was the only variable making for any significant difference throughout the questionnaire.

A section of the *Sociolinguistic Background Questionnaire* dealt with the question of language loyalty and usage. We asked students to indicate how much English and/or Spanish they used in various settings: the home, at school, during recreation, at work, and in the environment, i.e., shopping, writing letters, etc. We hypothesized that for Mexican-American students the higher the social class, the more use of English there would be in any of these settings. Our data results clearly indicated that in three life settings out of five (at school, during recreation, and at work) there was little social class difference in the use of language by our Mexican-American respondents. In other words, Mexican-American students tended to use equal amounts of Spanish or English in certain life settings regardless of social class. In general, we concluded that if upper class status represents assimilation, it does not represent non-use of Spanish language in our community. Spanish in El Paso is not disappearing with assimilation.

Additionally, we had hypothesized that with upper social classes there would be less loyalty to Spanish language and Chicano customs and few assimilation problems. As a matter of fact, this hypothesis did not hold up. Loyalty to Chicano customs showed no social class differences, nor did loyalty to Spanish language. Quite to our surprise, we found a positive significant correlation indicating that the higher the social class the higher the degree of assimilation problems. Thus, the lack of social class correlation with loyalty to Spanish language and customs seemed to strengthen our proposition that language usage is not connected strongly to social class and/or assimilation in this geographical area.

A panel of three bilingual judges evaluated the taped interviews and written portions of the SBQ data using the following scale, which was a modified version of that used in the Department of State, Foreign Service Institute:

1. Slight
2. Elementary
3. Intermediate
4. Advanced
5. Educated Native

The results are given in Table 1 below.

Table 1
(N=30)
Distribution of oral and written scores

Scale	Spanish Oral	Spanish Written	English Oral	English Written	Combined Spanish	Combined English
1. 0 - 1.9		1				
2. 0 - 2.9	10	13		1	13	1
3. 0 - 3.9	15	15	17	20	16	21
4. 0 - 4.9	-	-	-	-	-	-
5. 0	5	1	13	9	1	8
	30	30	30	30	30	30

It should not surprise linguists to note that English performance was in general appreciably higher than was the case in Spanish. Nevertheless, scores in both languages were clustered at well above the intermediate level and indeed between 3.0 and 3.9 on a 5-point scale. We inferred that the overall performance in Spanish of this sub-sample was poorer because the majority of the students had had most of their schooling with English as the language of instruction.

We were obviously interested in discovering how language performance ratings correlated with other kinds of scholastic performance. The only correlations significant at the .05 level of confidence, however, were English performance with Spanish performance and English performance with grade point average.

In addition to ascertaining students' evaluation of types of Spanish used in this geographically bilingual area, we also attempted to determine the students' self-evaluation of the varieties of Spanish and English controlled by them. Table 2 reports these results.

Table 2.

Student self-evaluation of English and Spanish capability

| | English* | | Spanish** | |
	Anglo	Mexican-American	Anglo	Mexican-American
Formal, educated	121 (82%)	112 (73%)	21 (14%)	48 (31%)
Informal, everyday	24 (16%)	41 (27%)	32 (22%)	87 (57%)
Southwest dialect	1*(1%)	0 (0%)	6 (4%)	14 (9%)
Border slang	0 (0%)	0 (0%)	18 (13%)	3 (2%)
Cannot handle	1*(1%)	0 (0%)	69 (47%)	1 (1%)
Totals	147 (100%)	152 (100%)	146 (100%)	153 (100%)

*p < .05 > .02
**pp<.001 (Kolmogorov-Smirnov one-tailed test)

In general, Chicanos rated themselves lower than their performance, at least in the language sample as basis of comparison. It is obvious that they feel less confident in their English language skills than their monolingual peers. In addition, more Chicanos than Anglos felt their proficiency in English was of the informal, everyday style. This despite the fact already noted, that tested proficiency of the sub-sample in English was quite high. We infer that these results suggest an insecurity either with Standard English or written English or both. This insecurity is corroborated by Goodman and Brooks (1973) in their analysis

of the overall sample. They found that 52 percent of
Mexican-American students--a majority--indicated having
made special efforts to improve English as compared with
only 39 percent of the Anglos (see Table 3).

Table 3.

Students' reported efforts to improve English

Efforts to Improve English	Anglo No.	%	Mexican-American No.	%	Total No.	%
Have made an effort	58	(39%)	79	(52%)	137	(46%)
Have not made an effort	90	(61%)	73	(48%)	163	(54%)
Totals	148	(100%)	152	(100%)	300	(100%)

p<.05 > .02 Kolmogorov-Smirnov one-tailed test)

Other aspects of language and culture in the Southwest as they are reflected in our Sociolinguistic Studies
on Southwest Bilingualism are discussed in greater length
by team members of the project (Goodman, 1970; Goodman
and Brooks, 1973; Goodman and Renner, 1979; and Ornstein,
1971; 1972, 1973a, 1973b, 1973c).

THE V SERIES

The most extensive analyses of the English compositions obtained from bilinguals in the project have been
performed by Betty Lou Dubois. Dubois (1975a) analyzed
the 90 English essays written by the survey's sub-sample
of 30 bilinguals. On the basis of grammatical and
spelling phenomena, as well as the mechanics of punctuation, Dubois was able to distinguish four categories of
competence: (1) educated native; (2) poorly educated
native; (3) dialectal or non-native; and (4) English
learner, poorly educated. Those familiar with Chicano
students could almost predict the sorts of features that
occurred, such as the use of *this* for *these*, deletion
of past marker, spelling digraphs as single-letter
grapheme, and the like. Nevertheless, although unnative
rhetorical turns of phrase were found, some of it possibly reflecting Spanish, Dubois (1975b) concludes:

As for my preliminary assessment of the written,
communicative competence of Chicanos writing in
English: what I have read nearly always conveys a
message to me. None of the features I am studying
interferes with the message but many of them trans-
mit the signal "bad English" or "non-English."
What message interference I encounter is in word
choice.

In another writing, Dubois (1975b), with the help of a colleague in the Department of Experimental Statistics, relates the formal English writing competence of the stratified group to some important socioeducational correlates. In effect, she found very little statistical evidence of relationship between language and leading indicators of educational progress, except in the case of the following three variables: (1) mother's birthplace (U.S. vs. Mexico); (2) college in which enrolled; and (3) total hours attempted. As for the last named, it turned out that the fewer the grammatical errors displayed by a student, the more courses he or she was liable to be carrying.

On the language side, Dubois notes the elusiveness of assessing differences between Chicanos and Anglo peers, but feels that these are to be found in stylistic phenomena, such as a tendency to repeat the noun phrase rather than to substitute a pronoun when the same referent is alluded to. Among these phenomena are echos of the subjunctive, inversion of subject and verb, and reflexive verbs. Finally, Dubois suggests that there is need to compare the compositions of bilinguals with those of Anglo peers. She mentions the possibility of determining relative frequency of various phenomena by a count of the Brown University Standard Corpus of Present-Day American English Prose. However, Dubois (1978) also conducted an experiment on verb usage using a multiple-choice CLOZE procedure which she developed. The students were presented with a series of passages and asked to choose from one of several verb possibilities where a blank occurred. This was administered to a group of Anglo and Chicano undergraduates at New Mexico State University in order to study stylistic and qualitative judgment of a highly subjective matter. She found no significant differences between Anglos and Chicanos, although trends were evident.

Hoffer (1975) is another linguist who has examined most of the Sociolinguistic Studies on Southwest Bilingualism corpora. Hoffer dealt with six types of nonstandard features found in the V Series. The first three he associated with a generally weak command of English: (1) prepositional misuses, such as substituting *of* for *from*; (2) grammatical order, as exemplified by substituting the indicative for the subjunctive; and (3) syntactic agreement, such as "the people is." The next three may stem from contrastive problems: (1) confusion of syntactic rules involving *be* and *have* so that one writer of a composition realizes the existential *there is/are*, as "In El Paso are many stores"; (2) problems with "dummy verb" rules, exemplified by confusion of the two *do* verbs; and (3) problems with embedded clauses, particularly with the relativizers *that*, *who*, and *which*. Beyond this Hoffer notes that the rhetoric of a large proportion of the compositions reflected a pattern of basic sentences without embedding

and that those students who did attack embedding demonstrated a high level of performance in all other areas
of syntax.

A working hypothesis of Hoffer's research was that
there is a continuum of varieties of Mexican-American
English, such that they range from maximal interference
as defined by a number of features through various
stages to minimal interference defined by an occasional
intonation feature. His model defines an implicational
scaling in which a syntactic feature Z always occurs
with features X and Y, feature Y with X, but X may
occur alone. Hoffer thus suggests an implicational scaling of some syntactic features based on the UT-El Paso
corpus. For example, he notes that sentences with well-
formed complicated relative clause constructions such
as "the room in which I found. . ." occur only where
the active/passive and other relatively easy constructions were well formed. In conclusion, Hoffer offers a
unique solution to the analysis of the bilingual corpus:

> ...if we can show that the second language acqui-
> sition schema follows a general sequence between
> maximal contrast to minimal contrast AND that
> ethnic dialects in general correspond to one struc-
> tural state between maximal and minimal contrast,
> then we have an extremely powerful diagnostic
> tool. Once we have this acquisition schema better
> delineated, we can spend our linguistic observa-
> tion time looking for the maximal interference
> errors--or "difference" if you prefer--and pre-
> dict the rest of the dialect system from those.
> (Hoffer, 1975, p. 66).

We might also mention here that a variety of other
bilingual corpora were collected as a result of the
Sociolinguistic Studies on Southwest Bilingualism.
These are listed in the Appendix at the conclusion of
the essay. They are currently on file with the Cross-
Cultural Southwest Ethnic Study Center, which was the
original impetus for the Studies on Southwest Bilingual-
ism and still exists at the University of Texas at El
Paso co-directed by Z. Anthony Kruczewski and Jacob
Ornstein-Galicia.

PUBLICATION RESULTING FROM THE SSSB

Much of the data analyzed from the Sociolinguistic
Studies on Southwest Bilingualism has been published in
various Proceedings of the Southwest Areal Language and
Linguistics Workshops, or SWALLOW (Appendix B). These
workshops are a direct result of the SSSB, but they
contain as well articles devoted to the full range of
possibile approaches to the study of the extraordinary
number of languages and their varieties spoken in the

Southwest. In addition to the "national" languages--English and Spanish--most of the European languages are represented, and there are large numbers of speakers of Asian languages. There are, of course, a large number of publications on Amerindian languages. The SWALLOW workshops are the occasions for the coming together of the "Southwest Circle"--a non-organization without officers, dues, or funds, but with an active group of non-members, devoted to the full range of possible approaches to the languages and varieties spoken in the U.S. Southwest. The first two workshops, the former held at the University of Texas at El Paso in 1972 and the latter at the University of New Mexico, Albuquerque, in 1973, were organized by the two prime movers of the Southwest Circle, Jacob Ornstein (UT-EP) and Garland Bills (University of New Mexico). To date, there have been a total of ten SWALLOW workshops held at different host universities in the Southwest and resulting in nine publications so far, many of which contain various articles dealing with Chicano English and bilingualism in particular.

In addition to the SWALLOW proceedings, Trinity University (Dept. of English), under the guidance and direction of Bates Hoffer, has supported the publication of nine volumes, primarily on varieties of English in the Southwest but also on applications of the research to real-world situations. In particular, Chicano English has been dealt with in this series--entitled *Papers in Southwest English* or PISE (Appendix C)--perhaps more extensively than any other series of publications in the U.S. Consequently, this series remains one of the major sources for work on Chicano English (to obtain any one of these, contact Bates Hoffer at Trinity University, Department of English, San Antonio, Texas). The PISE series has been intricately connected with the team effort of the El Paso survey and also that of Pan American University in some respects. For example, PISE V resulted from a Conference on College English and the Mexican-American which was co-sponsored by the Language and Linguistics Research Center at Pan American University and the Cross-Cultural Southwest Ethnic Study Center of the University of Texas at El Paso. In summary, we must note that the PISE series has contributed much through its publication of work on varieties of English found in the Southwest in general.

CONCLUSION

The El Paso sociolinguistic microsurvey of bilingualism was a major effort involving not only a team of researchers in El Paso but others throughout the Southwest area. Extending over several years time and actually even into the present through its child, SWALLOW, the microsurvey data results have appeared in numerous publications which were stimulated primarily by the joint

efforts of those involved with the microsurvey. But even
given all of this productivity over a span of some 10 or
more years, there is much work and data collection to be
done on Chicano English and Spanish in the Southwest
which future scholars must undertake, hopefully with
the enthusiasm and rigor of those of the past.

REFERENCES

Brooks, Bonnie S., Gary Brooks, Paul W. Goodman, and Jacob Ornstein.
1972. *Sociolinguistic Backgroung Questionnaire. An Instrument
for the Measurement of Bilingualism.* Rev. ed. El Paso: Southwest Ethnic Study Center, Univ. of Texas at El Paso.

_____, and Dick Calkins. 1980. "Mexican-Americans at a
Southwest University--How Do They Fare Academically?" In
Jacob Ornstein-Galicia and Robert St. Clair, eds., *Bilingualism
and Bilingual Education: New Readings and Insights,* (PISE VIII).
San Antonio, Tex.: Trinity University Press.

Dubois, Betty Lou. 1974. "Written English Communicative Competence
of UTEP Chicanos: A Preliminary Report," *System* 2(2): 49-56.

_____. 1975a. "A Plan to Study the Written English of
Chicanos." In Gina Cantoni-Harvey and M. F. Heiser, eds.,
Southwest Languages and Linguistics in Educational Perspective,
(SWALLOW III). San Diego, Calif.: Institute of Cultural Plura-
lism, San Diego State University.

_____. 1975b. "Further Studies in Southwest English."
In Betty Lou Dubois and Bates Hoffer, eds., *Research Techniques
and Prospects,* (PISE I). San Antonio, Tex.: Trinity University
Press.

_____. 1978. "A Cloze Study of Verb Usage in Context.
Anglos and Chicanos." In Michel Paradis, ed., *The Fourth LACUS
Forum 1977.* Columbia, S.C.: Hornbeam Press, pp. 604-614.

_____. 1979. "Societal and Linguistic Correlates in an
Investigation of the English Writing of a Selected Group of
University Level Chicanos." In William F. Mackey and Jacob
Ornstein, eds., *Sociolinguistic Studies in Language Contact.*
The Hague: Mouton, pp. 347-361.

_____, and Bates Hoffer, eds. 1975. *Research Techniques
and Prospects,* (PISE I). San Antonio, Tex.: Trinity University
Press.

Goodman, Paul. 1970. "A Comparison of Spanish-Surnamed and Anglo
College Students." Paper presented at the Rocky Mountain Social
Science Association, Annual Meeting, Boulder, Colorado.

_____, and Bonnie S. Brooks. 1973. "A Comparison of Anglo and Mexican-American Students Attending the Same University." *Kansas Journal of Sociology*, 10: 181-203.

_____, and Kathryn Renner. 1979. "Social Factors and Language in the Southwest." In Glenn Gilbert and Jacob Ornstein, eds., *Problems in Applied Educational Sociolinguistics: Readings in Language and Cultural Problems of U.S. Ethnic Groups*, (SWALLOW I). Hague: Mouton, pp. 55-62.

Hoffer, Bates. 1975. "Towards Implicational Scales for Use in Chicano English Composition." In Betty Lou Dubois and Bates Hoffer, eds., *Research Techniques and Prospects*, (PISE I). San Antonio, Tex.: Trinity University Press.

_____, and Betty Lou Dubois, eds. 1977. *Southwest Areal Linguistics Then and Now*, (SWALLOW V). San Antonio, Tex.: Trinity University Press.

_____, and Jacob Ornstein, eds. 1974. *Sociolinguistics in the Southwest*. San Antonio, Tex.: Trinity University Press.

Hollingshead, August B., and Frederick C. Redlich. 1958. *Social Class and Mental Illness: A Community Study*. New York: Wiley.

Jacobson, Rodolfo. 1975. "Research in Southwestern English and the Sociolinguistic Perspective." In Betty Lou Dubois and Bates Hoffer, eds., *Research Techniques and Prospects*, (PISE I). San Antonio, Tex.: Trinity University Press.

Murray, Wayne. 1972a. Ethnic and Sex Differences as Related to Perceptions of a University Environment. Ph.D. dissertation, New Mexico State University, Las Cruces.

_____. 1972b. "Research in Progress." *Bulletin of the Cross-Cultural Southwest Ethnic Study Center*, 1(March): 3.

Ornstein, Jacob. 1971. "Sociolinguistic Investigation of Language Diversity in the U.S. Southwest and its Educational Implications," *Modern Language Journal*, 55 (April): 224-229.

_____. 1972. "Applying Sociolinguistic Research to the Educational Needs of Mexican-American Bilinguals/Biculturals in the U.S. Southwest." Paper presented at Third International Congress of Applied Linguistics, Copenhagen, Denmark, August 22-27.

_____. 1973a. "Toward an Inventory of Interdisciplinary Tasks in Research on U.S. Southwest Bilingualism/Biculturalism." In Paul Turner, ed., *Bilingualism in the Southwest*. Tucson, Ariz.: University of Arizona Press.

_____. 1973b. "Mexican-American Sociolinguistics: A Well-Kept Scholarly and Public Secret." In Bates Hoffer and Jacob Ornstein, eds., *Sociolinguistics in the Southwest--A Symposium*. San Antonio, Tex.: Trinity University Press.

_____. 1974. "The Sociolinguistic Studies on Southwest Bilingualism: A Status Report." In Garland Bills, ed., *Southwest Areal Linguistics*, (SWALLOW II). San Diego, Calif.: Institute for Cultural Pluralism, pp. 11-34.

_____. 1975. "Sociolinguistics and the Study of Spanish and English Language Varieties and Their Use in the U.S. Southwest (with a proposed plan of research)." In Jacob Ornstein, ed., *Three Essays on Linguistic Diversity in the Spanish-Speaking World*. The Hague: Mouton, pp. 9-46.

_____. 1976. "A Sociolinguistic Study of Mexican-American and Anglo Students in a Border University." Will Kennedy, ed., Occasional Paper No. 3. San Diego, Calf.: Institute of Public and Urban Affairs, San Diego State University.

_____. 1976b. "A Cross-Cultural Sociolinguistic Investigation of Mexican-American Bilinguals/Biculturals at a U.S. Border University." *La Linguistique*, (Paris) 12: 131-145.

_____. 1978. "Relational Bilingualism--A New Approach to Linguistic-Cultural Diversity and a Mexican-American Case Study," *Ethnicity* 5: 148-166.

_____, and Bethany Dumas. 1975. "A Broad-Gauge Pattern for Investigating Mexican-American Spanish-English Bilinguals: A Sociolinguistic Approach." In Betty Lou Dubois and Bates Hoffer, eds., *Research Techniques and Prospects*. San Antonio, Tex.: Trinity University Press, pp. 43-45.

_____, and Betty Lou Dubois. 1977. "Mexican-American English: Prolegomena to a Neglected Regional Variety." In R. J. DiPietro and Edward Blansitt, Jr., eds., *Third LACUS Forum 1976*. Columbia, S.C.: Hornbeam Press, pp. 95-107.

_____, and Paul Goodman. 1979. "Socio-educational Correlates of Mexican-American Bilingualism." In William F. Mackey and Jacob Ornstein, eds., *Sociolinguistic Studies in Language Contact*. The Hague: Mouton, pp. 393-421.

Ornstein-Galicia, Jacob, and Robert St. Clair, eds. 1980. *Bilingualism and Bilingual Education*, New Trends and Insight (PISE VIII). San Antonio, Tex.: Trinity University Press.

Pace, C. Robert, et al. 1969. *College and University Environment Scales (CUES, form X-2)*. Princeton, N.J.: Educational Testing Service.

Siegel, Sidney. 1956. *Nonparametric Statistics for the Behavioral Sciences*. New York: McGraw-Hill.

Teel, Tommy Lou. 1971. "A Sociolinguistic Study of Spanish Linguistic Interference and Nonstandard Grammatical Phenomena in the Written English of Selected Mexican-American Bilinguals." Master's thesis, University of Texas at El Paso.

Willcott, Paul, and Jacob Ornstein, eds. 1977. *College English and the Mexican-American,* (PISE V). San Antonio, Tex.: Trinity University Press.

APPENDIX A

Inventory of Bilingual Corpora of Sociolinguistic Studies on Southwest Bilingualism, University of Texas at El Paso, 79968.

V Series--Taped oral interviews and written compositions. A total of 30 respectively, representing 10% out of the almost 5% of the overall undergraduate sampling (1970-71) of 301 students.

A Series--This represents the results of a "trial run" in 1969-1970 when we wished to ascertain how our elicitation materials functioned. Subjects represented students in four Spanish classes, two of them elementary, one intermediate, and one advanced. Two-thirds of the students had Spanish-surnames. A total of 35 of the Mexican-Americans completed Spanish-language essay writing, and in all 27 produced compositions in both Spanish and English. Oral elicitation of 18 students was carried out.

Z Series--Represents elicitation of Mexican-American students at the University who appeared to be fairly well balanced bilinguals. The corpus represents 13 taped interviews as well as 4 Spanish, and 30 Spanish and English compositions.

X Series--Represents a "windfall" of essays written by Mexican-American students as part of an examination for advanced standing in Spanish (along with the standardized Stanford objective type Spanish test). These compositions, unclassified as to year of college or any demographic data, represent "tests" taken during the years 1969-1970). (Compositions from previous years are also available.) The essays, totaling in all 290 were written upon topics made available in a list by the Department of Modern Languages, and are mostly of elementary or intermediate levels.

Y Series--This consists almost entirely of the results of projects
    carried out by graduate students, mostly teachers themselves,
    in local public schools, either junior or senior levels. Al-
    together 108 taped interviews of individuals have been re-
    corded, in both Spanish and English, with extensive code-
    switching if that was the way the subject communicated in
    either language. A total of 105 subjects produced compositions
    in both English and Spanish respectively, each containing
    identical topics. These have been accumulated as well as the
    corresponding term papers describing code-switching, lexical
    borrowing, and other aspects of local language use.

The Sociolinguistic Background Questionnaires have been modified for pre-college use by various of the public school teachers-
graduate students, and are available upon request.

APPENDIX B

SWALLOW WORKSHOPS

SWALLOW I   Gilbert, Glenn, and Jacob Ornstein, eds. 1979.
 in 1972   *Problems in Applied Educational Sociolinguis-*
at UT-El Paso   *tics: Readings in Language and Cultural*
                      Problems of U.S. Ethnic Groups. The Hague:
                      Mouton.

SWALLOW II   Bills, Garland, ed. 1974. *Southwest Areal Lin-*
 in 1973   *guistics*. San Diego, Calif.: San Diego State
at U. New Mexico   University, Institute for Cultural Pluralism.
Albuquerque

SWALLOW III   Cantoni-Harvey, Gina, and M. F. Heiser, eds. 1975.
 in 1974   *Southwest Languages and Linguistics in Educa-*
at Flagstaff,   *tional Perspective*. San Diego, Calif.: San
 Arizona   Diego State University, Institute for Cultural
                     Pluralism.

SWALLOW IV   Mazon, Reyes, ed. 1976. *Proceedings of the*
 in 1975   *Fourth Southwest Areal Language and Linguis-*
at San Diego   *tics Conference*. San Diego, Calif.: San Diego
                     State University, Institute for Cultural
                     Pluralism.

SWALLOW V   Hoffer, Bates, and Betty Lou Dubois, eds. 1977
 in 1976   *Southwest Areal Linguistics Then and Now*.
at San Antonio   San Antonio, Texas: Trinity University Press.

SWALLOW VI   Key, Harold, Gloria McCullough, and Janet Sawyer,
 in 1977   eds. 1978. *The Bilingual in a Pluralistic*
at Long Beach   *Society*. Long Beach: California State Univer-
                     sity.

SWALLOW VII   Lozano, Anthony, ed. 1978. *Bilingual and Bili-*
  in 1978   *terate Perspectives.* Boulder: University of
at UC-Boulder   Colorado.

SWALLOW VIII   Barkin, Florence, and Elizabeth Brandt, eds. 1980.
  in 1979   *Speaking, Singing, and Teaching: A Multidisci-*
at Arizona State *plinary Approach to Language Variation.* Tempe:
Univ.-Tempe   Arizona State Univ., Anthropological Series.

SWALLOW IX   Elerick, Charles, ed. 1981. *Southwest Areal Lin-*
  in 1980   *guistics.* El Paso: Texas Western Press.
at UT-El Paso

SWALLOW X   Cantoni-Harvey, Gina, and M. F. Heiser, eds. 1982.
  in 1981   *Proceedings of the Tenth Southwest Areal Lin-*
at Los Angeles   *guistics Workshop.* Los Angeles: UCLA.

APPENDIX C

Papers in Southwest English (=PISE)

PISE I   Dubois, Betty Lou, and Bates Hoffer, eds. 1975.
            Research Techniques and Prospects. San Antonio,
            Tex.: Trinity University.

PISE II   Valdes-Fallis, Guadalupe, and Rodolfo Garcia-Moya, eds.
            1976. *Teaching Spanish to the Spanish-speaking.*
            San Antonio, Tex.: Trinity University.

PISE III   Leap, William, ed. 1977. *Studies in Southwestern
            Indian English.* San Antonio: Trinity University.

PISE IV   Dubois, Betty Lou, and Isabel Crouch, eds. 1979. *The
            Sociology of the Languages of American Women.* San
            Antonio, Tex.: Trinity University.

PISE V   Willcott, Paul, and Jacob Ornstein, eds. 1977. *College
            English and the Mexican-American.* San Antonio:
            Trinity University.

PISE VI   Raffler-Engel, Walburga von, and Bates Hoffer, eds.
            1977. *Aspects of Non-verbal Communication.* San
            Antonio: Trinity University.

PISE VII   Hoffer, Bates, and Betty Lou Dubois, eds. 1977. *South-
            west Areal Linguistics Then and Now.* San Antonio,
            Tex.: Trinity University.

PISE VIII   Ornstein, Jacob, and Robert St. Clair, eds. 1979.
                 Bilingualism and Bilingual Education. San Antonio,
                 Tex.: Trinity University.

PISE IX   Bartel, Guillermo, Susan Jasper, and Bates Hoffer, eds.
                 1982. *Essays on Indian English.* San Antonio, Tex.:
                 Trinity University.

PISE X   Cantoni-Harvey, Gina, and M. F. Heiser, eds. 1982.
                 Proceedings of SWALLOW X. Los Angeles, Calif.:
                 UCLA.

13

NETWORKING:
A NEEDED RESEARCH DIRECTION

Jacob Ornstein-Galicia
University of Texas at El Paso

Just as research problems in Chicano Spanish are shared
in large measure by other varieties of U.S. Spanish, so
are research problems in Chicano English shared by other
varieties of Hispanic and non-Hispanic English variation.
A prime difficulty in conducting research is that there
is hardly any collaboration among investigators, each of
whom functions independently, perhaps with the assistance of students. While this is not to suggest that personal initiative should in any way be curbed, this unexplored and underexplored area calls for some sort of coordinated effort. Thus, we suggest that regional networks
be set up in the Southwest and other parts of the country
to study various aspects of Chicano English. Such networks
could also explore aspects of Spanish varieties as well,
since the two are intricately related. Such a regional
effort would allow comparative regional data on Chicano
English, something the field has never approached to date.

These networks could be made up of groups of cooperating sociolinguistic research teams, consisting minimally
of a linguist and a social scientist. (For further discussion, see Ornstein, 1975.) Teams would then be based
at different colleges and universities which would investigate the Chicano English and Spanish in their area. Each
network would operate with some guidance from a coordinating committee which would provide some unity to
the efforts of the teams and also feed selected data

into a computerized central data bank. Use of common instruments and questionnaires would be encouraged and information exchanged. On the basis of funds and manpower
available, the Coordinating Committee would also develop
a research design appropriate to the Southwest as a sociolinguistic area. It would then determine priority targets
and a general methodology, and a format for reporting to
all would be incorporated into a Research Kit. Orientation and training sessions would be organized at different points in the Southwest. Sociolinguistic research thus
far indicates that work of teams could be carried out with
relatively small samples of the targeted ethnic groups of
the area, if they indeed reflect much larger statistical
cross-sections.

The types of data the teams would collect and relay to
the Coordinating Committee could be broad enough to cover
related areas of interest, e.g., bilingualism, varieties
of Spanish, and sociopsychological interests. We suggest
the following types of data: (1) language variation; (2)
bilingual/bidialectal communication patterns; and (3)
socio-attitudinal information. To every extent possible,
attempts would be made to relate linguistic and societal
factors, but in our view, efforts would not be exclusively
restricted to the correlation of variables in a statistical sense. Collection activities ought to be broad in
scope with adequate attention paid to the acquisition of
"fugitive" materials, both of oral and written type. For
example, many linguistic descriptions of Chicano English
especially related to child language acquisition are
available for the most part in the form of Master's theses
and Ph.D. dissertations. (See the Annotated Bibliography
at the end of this book.)

Although "Mainstream" dialectology is constantly
attacked as old-fashioned, it, at least, mounted and maintained some sort of regional networks of cooperating
scholars. The same cannot be said of sociolinguistic projects, which often reflect extreme fragmentation. For
example, even the results obtained by the El Paso microsurvey tend to have little meaning until they can be compared with replications of similar studies carried out
elsewhere - let us say, on groups of similar and different demographic characteristics in both the Upper and Lower
Rio Grande Valley, or Los Angeles and Tucson, or in re-
mote mountain communities of northern New Mexico. Our own
sampling, needless to say, showed an elitist bias in consisting exclusively of college students. Eventually, it
would be hoped that profiles could be drawn of representative samplings of the leading ethnic groups within a
given region, thus constituting a much-needed data bank.
In this day of ethnic competition and strife, along with
the Bilingual Education Movement, consumers of such sociolinguistic information are numerous in the fields of education, politics, and social work.

The potential of team efforts and networking has been well-articulated by Bethany Dumas:

> In view of the action taken at the national meeting of the Conference on College Composition and Communication in adopting the resolution entitled: "The Students' Right to Their Own Language" held in April 1974, it would seem particularly important for local research teams to initiate or continue research designed to let us know among other things just what the sociolinguistic facts about students' language and language use are. (Ornstein and Dumas, 1975)

It is not suggested that the range of targets should be limited to language variation in the school contexts or that linguistic geographers have been unaware all these years of social factors. The contrary is true as one may realize abundantly by consulting essays by McDavid, Davis, Pederson, and others in a book of representative readings such as that of Allen and Underwood (1971), or the survey by the writer and Paul Murphy (1976). Our advocacy of sociolinguistic regional networking brings us back in spirit and form to the *Sprachatlas* team concept, although with a much greater societal orientation. Accordingly, it would seem that a symbiosis is possible between dialect geography, with its fullness of description, and sociolinguistics, with its focus on small sets of implicational features and their multiple interrelations.

Moreover, in view of the growing ethnic frictions witnessed in the United States, a nation supposedly dedicated to cultural pluralism, pressure might be put on funding agencies, public and private, to provide more substantial support for "social dialectology." Unfortunately, in the U.S. at this point there would appear to be a clear imbalance in the share of funds allocated to pure linguistics research and those to dialectological work, of whatsoever orientation.

REPLICATIONS

It would be gratifying to boast here of a stampede to replicate the El Paso microsurvey research design, but such is not the case. Although a bit of a dent has been made by our team in this vast region of the Southwest and Rocky Mountain states, we must settle for this. In all about 30 to 40 copies of the *Sociolinguistic Background Questionnaire* (=SBQ) have been requested or ordered by individuals or departments of schools in North America, Latin America, Africa, Asia, and Europe. To what extent these have been put to use is not well-known by us. At the University of Texas at El Paso, at least two graduate students have utilized it as the basis for their master's theses (de Porras, 1971; Teel, 1971). At least 25 term papers in various graduate seminars on dialectology and/or sociolinguistics have also carried out field projects

using and modifying the SBQ. Two in particular were
carried out by a Spanish teacher and a principal in Ysle-
ta, outside of El Paso. These small papers are especially
informative and worthwhile, as are portions of the others.

The most considerable replication made of the El Paso
broad-gauge design was that carried out by the Language
and Linguistics Center at Pan American University, some
900 miles distant from El Paso (see Amastae in this section for a description). This replication does afford
some contrasts since the student population is different,
with the Pan American Project drawing on a predominantly
rural-agricultural population and the El Paso survey on
an urban/semi-urban milieu. Although both are almost immediately on the U.S./Mexico border, the University of
Texas at El Paso reflects a somewhat more advanced stage
of development, with more upper-division and graduate offerings.

A partial replication of the El Paso survey is represented by the work of Earl Herrick who applied the SBQ in
somewhat modified form to several high schools around
Kingsville, Texas (Herrick, 1977). Supported by a Texas
A. & I. University Research Grant and assisted by several
graduate students, Herrick also elicited knowledge of
English structures on the part of bilinguals. Considerable
computerized unexploited data was gathered, which now are
housed in the writer's office.

It is important to mention, along with the notion of
replicational studies, that attempts to secure critiques
and feedback of our *Sociolinguistic Background Questionnaire* have only produced a limited number of reactions.
While this cannot be taken to mean that it is well-nigh
perfect, it appears to be a viable and productive instrument for its purposes and one which can be administered
in a fairly brief period of time, although linguistic
elicitation, if used, is obviously more time-consuming.
The SBQ, in short, can be utilized independently or as
part of a larger battery. It thus provides potential for
cross-regional comparisons if networking set-ups existed
throughout the Southwest.

WHITHER NOW?

There is no doubt that the 1,200 square miles of the
Southwest are the least exploited dialectologically and
sociolinguistically in the United States. Chicano English
remains at the bottom of the research list of language
issues treated in the Southwest. Even now, the Southwest
remains a region yet to be fully explored in language
variation.

For those who wish to inform themselves regarding the
investigations already performed on language variation in
the Southwest - related to variation in both English and

Spanish - a good beginning is Atwood's *Methods in American Dialectology* (1971, pp. 28-31). One may also find studies bearing on the area in *Orbis, American Speech,* and *PADS (Paper of the American Dialect Society),* with a growing number of sociolinguistically-oriented writings in the more recent *Journal of the Linguistic Association of the Southwest (LASSO).* The annual proceedings of the Southwest Areal Language and Linguistics Workshop (SWALLOW) which have been held each year at a different regional university since 1972 contain many articles addressing research on Chicano English and Spanish. In addition, pertinent essays are to be found in such regional journals as the *Western Review,* and *The Rocky Mountain MLA Review.* In addition, regional meetings of the American Dialect Society are often held in conjunction with those of the South Central Modern Language Association. (For a more exhaustive source reference, see Teschner et al., 1975.)

An endemic problem to networking has been for each region to follow a sort of Western "rugged individualism" --eschewing joint efforts because of scant funding, great distances, and the like. Along with this trend is the lack of cooperation between U.S. and Mexican scholars. Unlike American and Canadian dialectologists, there are far fewer linguistically oriented colleagues south of the border with whom to collaborate. However, the foremost linguist and dialectologist of Mexico, Juan Lope Blanch, has urged joint efforts and the establishment of a documentation center on the Spanish varieties of the United States which would presumably involve scholars from Latin America (Lope Blanch, 1978). Blanch, who coordinated the Norma Culta project at both the Universidad Autónoma de México and the Colegio de México, has access to a wealth of computerized data on 19 dialect zones of Mexico. His colleagues, José Moreno de Alba and Oscar Uribe Villegas, are also becoming well-known in the field. Thus, at least for language variation studies of Spanish, there is great potential for collaborative endeavors across the border as another type of networking which remains as yet unexplored.

In summary, we might note that microsurveys are only one of the possible approaches to studying language diversity, specifically Chicano English, in the vast, far-flung, and largely sparsely inhabited areas of the Southwest and Rocky Mountain states. As such, mircosurveys are perhaps the easiest means to use in bringing the concept of networking to fruition, simply because standardized questionnaires already exist which could be used, at least as a beginning. Networking is a concept that requires cooperation and common interests and that could far advance our limited resources and resulting knowledge through comparative studies. Thus, we close noting that networking is a viable concept, but it is people with time and effort collaborating together who must bring it to life and make it work.

REFERENCES

Allen, Harold, and Gary Underwood. 1971. *Readings in American Dialectology*. New York: Appleton-Century-Crofts

Brooks, Bonnie S., Gary Brooks, Paul Goodman, and Jacob Ornstein. 1972. *Sociolinguistic Background Questionnaire: A Measurement Instrument for Studying Bilingualism*. El Paso: Cross-Cultural Southwest Ethnic Study Center, University of Texas at El Paso.

Herrick, Earl. 1977. "Spanish Interference in the English Written in South Texas High Schools." In Bates Hoffer and Betty Lou Dubois, eds., *Southwest Areal Linguistics Then and Now (SWALLOW V)*. San Antonio, Tex.: Trinity University, pp. 162–169.

Lope Blanch, Juan. 1978. "La investigación del español en México y en el suroeste de los Estados Unidos: Posibilidades de aproximación." Border Linguistics Symposium, University of Texas at El Paso.

Murphy, R. Paul, and Jacob Ornstein. 1976. "A Survey of Research on Language Diversity: A Partial Who's Who in Linguistics." In Peter A. Reich, ed., *Second LACUS Forum 1975*. Columbia, S.C.: Hornbeam Press, pp. 423–461.

Ornstein, Jacob. 1975. "Sociolinguistics and the Study of Spanish and English Language Varieties and Their Use in the U.S. Southwest (with a proposed plan of research)." In Jacob Ornstein, ed., *Three Essays on Linguistic Diversity in the Spanish-Speaking World*. The Hague: Mouton, pp. 9–46.

_____ and Bethany Dumas. 1975. "A Broad-Gauge Pattern for Investigating Mexican-American Spanish-English Bilinguals: A Sociolinguistic Approach." In Betty Lou Dubois and Bates Hoffer, eds., *Research Techniques and Prospects (PISE I)*. San Antonio, Tex.: Trinity University, pp. 43–45.

de Porras, Normina Wolff. 1971. "Anomalías Lingüísticas en el español de un grupo de estudiantes bilingües" (Linguistic Divergences in a Group of Bilingual Students). Master's thesis, University of Texas at El Paso.

Teel, Tommy Lou. 1971. "A Sociolinguistic Study of Spanish Linguistic Interference and Nonstandard Grammatical Phenomena in the Written English of Selected Mexican-American Bilinguals." Master's thesis, University of Texas at El Paso.

Teschner, Richard V., Garland Bills, and Jerry Craddock. 1975. *Spanish and English of U.S. Hispanos: A Critical, Annotated, Linguistic Bibliography*. Arlington, Va.: Center for Applied Linguistics.

SECTION IV:
CHICANO ENGLISH
IN THE MAINSTREAM

14

THE RIGHT TO HAVE AN ETHNIC ACCENT: SOME VIEWS OF SPEECH TEACHERS AND A SPEECH THERAPIST

Joseph Perozzi, Moderator
University of Texas at El Paso

Hector Serrano
Director of Southwest Repertory Company

Gilda Peña
Socorro Independent Schools

Joe Martinez
El Paso Community College

PEROZZI: Each of the three panel members will give their viewpoint on the ramifications of an ethnic accent as related to their professional area: theatre, speech/language pathology, and speech communication. I would first like to introduce Hector Serrano who is Director of the Southwest Repertory Company (our Bilingual Theatre), Director of Viva El Paso -- a magnificent historical-based theatre pageantry held outdoors in the summer in El Paso and who is also instructor at El Paso Community College.

SERRANO: I want to first talk about the arts in general and to let you know my feelings on the arts as far as accents are concerned. It seems that many of us who are non-native speakers of English are in the arts because we can express ourselves naturally, without any hang-ups. Many of us have some difficulties in expressing ourselves in at least two of the art forms - -drama and literature -- because of our "accent." In the other arts, e.g. painting, sculpture, dance, and architecture, our ethnic accent is not very apparent, and when it is, it is in fact widely accepted not only by our peers but by people of nations all over the world. I'm sure that all of you understand and appreciate Ballet Folklórico and you understand and appreciate painters like Manuel La Costa. But once we get to poetry or fiction or even the language of theatre, many individuals do not accept the accent of the Chicano. That is one of the main difficulties that I have had in the

world of theatre, specifically Chicano theatre. I'd like
to compare this "accent" used in this genre to spice used
on a meal. Only the people who are raised with a particular spice, who are given a taste of it when they are
young, appreciate the taste and accept it and digest it
accurately. To those who come upon it accidentally or
later on in life, spice is sometimes a little hard to take
and it is pushed aside.

I have observed three different types of Hispanic
"accents" related to theatre. First is what I call accent
A. That is the accent the Mexican-American has, or any
Hispanic has, if he studies English in his native country.
It's a very pleasant type of Latin accent. It's charming;
it's romantic; and everyone accepts it. Ricardo Montalban
made a fortune using it previously. That is accent A and
I'm sure that all of you, if you think about it, know
several others who use it.

Accent B is what I call the accent that I have. It's
a bilingual accent that is derived by all of us who come
to learn English from ESL (English as a Second Language)
classes. We have tapes that we listen to; we have sounds
that we imitate; we have sentences that we practice; we
have dialogues and we learn how to speak English properly
in an accepted way. That is what I call the ESL bilingual
accent.

The third accent, accent C, is the Chicano accent.
This is the accent that individuals develop as a result of
going through bilingual education or just being raised bi-
lingually. It is the least accepted of the three --perhaps
because it is the spiciest of all. Although all three
types of "accents" are used and heard not only in theatre
but in neighborhoods throughout the Southwest, I'd like to
comment on only accent C --the Chicano accent --in theatre,
film, and television.

In theatre, there has been only one Chicano play,
"Zoot Suit," that ever reached national prominence and
played on Broadway. "Zoot Suit" is based in the 1940s and
is set in the Southwest. It has music and dancing and it
is a very worthwhile production. Unfortunately, its theme
is something with which not everyone can identify. It
played for four months to packed houses in Los Angeles,
but when it was taken to Broadway in New York City- -the
hub of American theatre --it closed in less than two weeks
after very unfavorable reviews. The play was a failure on
Broadway because the ideas it represented were too strong
for people to accept. They have now made a movie of "Zoot
Suit" which will no doubt suffer the same kind of doom
that the play experienced. There was also a previous film
called "The Children of Sanchez" which was enthusiastically
produced by Anthony Quinn, who, by the way, is a Chihuahua
native and comes from the bilingual school that I come from.

Although the film was given a tremendous amount of publicity, it lasted about six days in El Paso and I haven't heard about the film since.

With respect to television, two different groups from Los Angeles have consulted me. The first was Warner Brothers who wanted to produce a situation comedy based on the typical life of a Chicano family. Unfortunately, the typical life of a Chicano family does not lend itself to a situation comedy, but that is what they wanted to produce. I understand that a pilot was made and was played in several cities. I don't think we got it here in El Paso but it did not sell and as far as I know Warner Brothers has abandoned all plans of doing any television programs based on the typical Chicano life. The other group was ABC, who went so far as to send a writer to El Paso. He spent a week with us, meeting families and writing situations. I have not heard from the writer or about his project for the last six months so I'm pretty sure that they've also abandoned their project.

PEROZZI: There are some current Chicano playwrights such as Carlos Morton and Jorgé Huerta who are writing plays about the Chicano experience. Do you think the efforts of these new playwrights will in some way make the Chicano accent more acceptable in the future? In other words, will there be a place for this type of accent in live theatre because of the impetus that these new playwrights are giving to the Chicano experience?

SERRANO: I think that if there is a place for this type of theatre, it will rather be in the educational institutions where the audience will be primarily made up of people who are aware of the situation and who want to better the situation. I don't think that a Chicano play will ever have national acceptance in the United States, and certainly not worldwide. The only exception is if there is no emphasis on spoken language, say through pantomime, dance, or other arts.

AUDIENCE SPEAKER: I want to comment on what Hector said about a play called "Zoot Suit" and the film "The Children of Sanchez." I think we have to distinguish between production and artistic qualities and between the ethnic material that we are looking at. I saw "Zoot Suit" in Los Angeles. It was fabulous and great fun because it was very much a local, community happening. Even though it flopped on Broadway, for the Chicano community in Los Angeles it was a very important thing. We must note the importance of those types of artistic endeavors to the locale from which they come. I also saw "The Children of Sanchez." It was an uneven movie and I was disappointed in it. I really wanted to like it. I admired Quinn for taking it on but I don't think it was artistically successful.

Another very important movie which you didn't mention

was "Boulevard Nights." The producer was Anglo, but I
think he did a tremendous job of reflecting what life in
East LA can be like. The movie was criticized by people in
the community because they felt it was too much a mirror
on their society and they realized the way that they would
be evaluated if people thought this was what life was like
in their community. Eric de La Posta, an important character in that movie, has addressed this problem to a similar conference in UCLA, noting that there has been a
lot of reaction to the movie that is hard to ignore. He,
as a matter of fact, grew up in the suburbs of Los Angeles and does not have a Chicano accent, but he adopted
one for the movie.

SERRANO: I think a primary function or an underlying purpose in Chicano theatre and Chicano films is more than to
entertain. They want to teach. They want to present a
message, but I think that most of the audience is not
willing to hear the message, or to accept the lesson.
That's why "Zoot Suit" was tremendously popular in LA, because so many people could identify with it. Then it went
to Broadway expecting the same kind of success and folded.

PEROZZI: Our second panelist is Gilda Peña who has been
a public speech pathologist with El Paso Independent
Schools for over seven years and is currently working with
the oral language development program in the Socorro Independent School district as a lead teacher and speech
pathologist.

PEÑA: For the seven years I worked with El Paso Schools
as a language pathologist, I faced the same dilemma that
speech and language pathologists across the country are
faced with - What do we do with a dialect? Who handles it?
How is it to be handled? As recently as the 1978 American
Speech, Hearing and Language Convention in San Francisco
people were still asking the question: "Whose problem is
it?" Many of us who were hoping to get some help in how
to deal with Spanish-speakers attended a particular session entitled: "Dialect and How to Deal with It." Unfortunately, the session turned out to be on how to deal with
Black speech so we left with our question unanswered.
    Actually, the truth is that in the public school dis-
tricts, speech and language pathologists are not allowed
to deal with Hispanic dialects because a speech and language disorder is considered a disorder only when the
child cannot communicate in his native tongue. If a child
cannot make his needs known in his native tongue, then he
is looked at as being language delayed and he is taken
care of in that respect. If that same child, however, can
speak very well in his native tongue but cannot communicate in English then he goes to another program, i.e., ESL.
There are programs galore for ESL in the district. If that
same child becomes bilingual and has a problem with

switching over between the *ch* and *sh* in English, this is
not viewed as a problem for the speech and language pathologist. This is viewed as a dialect issue which should be
dealt with by a diction specialist. Once a child can communicate his or her needs but has a dialect, then the dialect is to be handled "outside the school district." This
is the rule or law.

AUDIENCE SPEAKER: Are there any set special circumstances
under which a public school speech language pathologist
can work with the youngsters to help them achieve Standard American dialect?

PEÑA: There are various ways that we do get around this
particular rule. We can go to the teacher and offer various
ideas related to improving speech that they can use when
teaching that child in the classroom. Also, if a child cannot pronounce a sound in both his native language and English, say [š], then that child is qualified for speech therapy and he can be helped to articulate the sound. Most
of the time, children who are in speech therapy understand the gist of what is going on and then they begin to
generalize what they learn to other areas. For example,
auditory training which includes discrimination of speech
sounds is part of articulation therapy and can be very useful in other areas of language acquisition.

   I also might mention that the oral language development program that I am now affiliated with in Socorro is
hoping to develop, through the teachers, the very essential skills of listening and discrimination in children
at a very young age. This program is begun in kindergarten
and goes all the way through the high schools. Eventually
we hope that at least in Socorro, some of the problems
brought on by the Chicano accent can be redressed.

AUDIENCE SPEAKER: Are sound substitutions the only aspect of a dialect recognized by speech and language pathologists in the schools?

PEÑA: No. I mentioned sound substitutions because these
are what most people associate with "accent." It goes beyond sounds. Accents vary from the Standard in terms of
syntax, morphology, rate of speech, and inflection. Speech
and language pathologists in the schools are prepared to
work with all aspects of communicative delay or deviancy,
all of which are defined by the fact that the child cannot communicate his or her needs.

PEROZZI: Our third panelist is Joe Martinez who is instructor of speech communication at El Paso Community
College.

MARTINEZ: One of the things I am concerned with is the impact that adult speakers with an accent have upon the listener. Many studies have been conducted regarding speaker
influences on audiences. My interest is not so much

whether minority groups, Chicanos in this case, have a
right to a certain accent, but rather how they are perceived by listeners who may not understand or appreciate
the accent. Robert McCloskey's study looked diligently into the impact of foreign accent.[1] He found that audiences
perceive speakers with accents to be less-qualified, less-
knowledgeable and less-effective than speakers without
accents. McCloskey also found that, for speakers with an
accent, communication experiences have been unrewarding
and even punishing. He noted that as a consequence those
individuals who spoke with a foreign accent avoided situations where they had to communicate. This would explain
why many Chicano lawyers and successful Chicano business-
men refuse to participate in politics. They also refuse
to become parts of large organizations where their speech
will affect their power and authority as perceived by
their listeners. George Barker's work in Tucson, Arizona,
also indicated that individuals who speak with a Chicano
accent are perceived by audiences to be of lesser status
than speakers without an accent.[2] In a limited study that
I, myself, conducted, I spoke with some would-be Chicano
politicians and asked them how they felt audiences perceived them. One of the most common answers to that question was "I don't think they are listening to me. I'm
not getting across. I'm well-prepared and well-educated
but people do not listen to me."

Perhaps the reason that an audience does not listen to
a speaker with an accent is that people in the audience
may not identify with what the speaker has to say or the
way in which the message is delivered. As Kenneth Burke
stated, effective communication occurs at a point where
we share, where we identify with the speaker's background,
past experience or interests.[3] Oftentimes, a student or
politician that I work with comes to me and says: "How do
I get away from this? How long will it take? Can I take
one of your courses and at the end of the term I'll get
rid of my accent and I'll no longer have this problem?"
But there are no quick answers that I can formulate. However, it appears that there is a considerable amount of
concern on the part of individuals who speak with an accent.
They want to participate in the political and business
worlds but are very aware of the negative impact their
speech has on many listeners.

PATRICIA CANO: I am very troubled by what all three
panelists have said. The impression I get is that we
don't have a right to an ethnic accent! Why do we have to
spend so much time trying to get rid of it? If anybody
can't identify with us, I think it's *their* problem. What
we have to show is that it doesn't bother us. They should
be the ones to make the effort to understand us. We communicate because the content is there.

AUDIENCE SPEAKER: About three years ago, Bernard Spolsky
published an article entitled "The Limits of Language."[4]
In the article he noted a word of caution to speakers who

wish to change accents since social facts indicate that it is often skin pigmentation which determines perception of an accent rather than the ethnic accent itself. Even the slightest ethnic accent, apparently, will cause the speaker to be rejected by a prejudiced person on the basis of pigmentation.

ORNSTEIN-GALICIA: I personally sympathize with what you are saying. I'm an ethnic myself because I grew up in an English-Yiddish-speaking home. I had a very bad accent in Yiddish so they made fun of me. But I personally feel that ethnicity needs to push through. Let's quote some people with accents who have made it big, like Henry Kissinger or even Hitler, not one of my heroes. But Hitler had an accent that was considered low-class in Berlin, a Bavarian-Austrian accent. Stalin had an accent too. . . well, we'ere getting into dictators now. Suffice it to say, there are many individuals who have been very successful despite their ethnic accents.

MARTINEZ: Just one final comment. The fact is that I have been asked many times by students who have Chicano accents: "How do you operate? How do you set yourself up? How do you feel when you are with different types of individuals from different kinds of backgrounds?" My response is that I adapt myself to any given situation. After I know that I have done this successfully, I can go home with confidence. And that makes me feel good. This is the only answer I can offer.

15

CHICANO ENGLISH IN LITERARY AND ORAL MEDIA

Fritz G. Hensey
University of Texas at Austin

"What is Chicano English?" asks the El Paso *Times* of September 11, 1981, in reference to a three-day conference on Form and Function in Mexican-American (Chicano) English. Chicano English is the subject of an article in the Dallas *Morning News* four days later. An American social dialect has been recognized by a sector of the mass media.

M.A.K. Halliday states that dialects are defined by reference to their speakers, and that social dialects stand as symbols for objectively definable social groups; "the dialect you speak is a function of who you are."[1] This approach agrees with Fernando Peñalosa's observation that, while the term "Chicano English" is ambiguous, it is generally reserved for varieties of English exclusive to Chicanos.[2]

There has been increasing scholarly interest in Chicano English since the mid-seventies. The study of Chicano *Spanish* has certainly been extensive, but by now it is possible to gather a reasonably lengthy bibliography of publications concentrating on some variety of Chicano *English* usage. Some of the work deals with phonological or morphosyntactic variables;[3] some with sociolinguistic themes, and particularly with attitude studies;[4] and some with comparisons of Chicano English with Standard English for pedagogical purposes.[5]

With the growing interest in ethnic studies, there has
arisen a body of social science literature relating to
the Chicano: history, psychology, politics, anthropology,
and other areas of study are increasingly present.[6] The
linguistic dimension is generally under-represented in
such treatments. When there is a linguistic component, it
is likely to focus on Chicano *Spanish* or the linguistic
side of education or of such civil rights issues as access
to goods and services, employment, and the like.[7] Chicano
English as such seems to be virtually ignored by scholars
outside the field of (socio)linguistics. Such appears to
be the case as well in the more general area of U.S. ethnicity studies.[8] This is hardly surprising when a specifically *Chicano* English social dialect has not yet been
recognized to any great extent.

Another product of the sixties and particularly the
seventies has been Chicano literature and related criticism, some of it sociolinguistic in nature.[9] A great deal
of that literature is in English; some, especially poetry,
in Spanish or in both languages (literary code-switching).
Some of the English used shows traits which analysis may
reveal as exclusive to Chicano usage. If Chicano literature can be recognized as such on linguistic as well as
thematic grounds, we will be presented with a major instance of Chicano English in the mass media. A similar
observation applies to media other than print, such as
movies or television, in which there is a Chicano English
presence.

While there is a good variety of studies discussing
the relationships between mass media and their societies,
there has been less attention to the mutual effects of
ethnic pluralism and the power of print and electronic
media. Aside from the question of Spanish-language publication or broadcasting, most studies of Chicanos and
the media have dealt with issues other than Chicano English. An area in which social dialectology becomes quite
relevant is that of negative stereotyping, which in turn
bears on denial of civil rights or other forms of discrimination which ultimately relate to racism. Interven-
tion by or on behalf of Chicanos in the mass media has
addressed such issues as Chicano access to media, im-
proved coverage of community needs, and elimination of
degrading imagery. Educational and other public services
form a separate dimension which will not concern us
here, since most of the corresponding publication or
programming is in Spanish or addresses itself to issues
of bilingualism other than that of social dialects.[10]

An important recent work which joins the historical
realities of socioeconomic oppression with the reinforc-
ing stereotypes is Pettit's *Images of the Mexican
American in Fiction and Film* (1980). Pettit presents a
well-documented history of literary and cinematic degradation of Mexicans in the prose fiction of the 19th and

20th centuries. Beginning with writing (mostly novels), he
passes on to the movies and, by implication, to television.
The audio-visual media continue in the same molds developed
by the writers of over a century ago. Part of the image
involves the form of English which writers place in the
mouths of their fictional characters. Decades of literary
production, some of it by leading Anglo-American writers,
have no doubt helped to form the public image of Mexican/
Chicano English *qua* social dialect associated with and
helping to define this major U.S. ethnic community.[11]

Linguistic descriptions of Chicano English are apt to
deal with (1) accentedness, in terms of phonological
variables; (2) nonstandard morphosyntactic processes; (3)
code-switching, an overgeneralized term which requires
qualification and possibly replacement by a more complex
and sensitive terminology, as did the former use of the
term "bilingualism". A characteristic of Chicano varieties
of English which remains to be well defined is stylistic
incongruity, i.e., uses which are grammatically standard
but which may be inappropriate in context, usually in
terms of formality.[12]

These traits relate in part to bilingualism, in that
accentedness and nonstandard morphosyntax *may* be attributed to interference from Spanish. Code-switching and
stylistic incongruity (e.g., bookish usage in informal
contexts) can be related to diglossic factors.

As an initial contribution to the study of Chicano
English as a *product* of certain mass media, we will consider sample texts from two sources: Anglo-American
writers and Chicanos identified with Chicano literature.
Only dialogue will be considered. Thus, even though the
material is in writing, it purports to represent speech
by Mexicans or Mexican-Americans. This media version of a
form of English attributed to either or both ethnic
groups may be termed MeChicano English, i.e., a *media*
variety associated with *Mexicans* and/or *Chicanos*. It
remains to be seen whether or not other forms of Hispanic
English can be identified as precisely as this one. Texts
and accompanying analyses appear as an appendix to this
essay.

For texts produced by Anglo-American writers we will
use the term A-Texts and for those done by Chicano writers,
C-Texts. Each will be further subdivided into Stages 1 and
2 for reasons to be discussed below. There are four texts:
A1, A2, C1, and C2. Each consists of three randomly selected samples by different writers. Each text type, with its
subtexts, will be described in terms of accentedness,
morphosyntactic deviance from standard, code-switching,
and stylistic incongruity. We relate the A-Texts, those
produced by Anglo-American writers, to the images of the
Mexican/Chicano which Pettit attributes to popular fiction.

Some Chicanos may share Richard Rodríguez's mis-
givings about the possibility or the desirability of

"going public" with what is traditionally a vernacular, a language of the ingroup.[13] There is so far no good evidence that a given usage by Chicano writers will be considered representative of Chicano English. The point is rather that as long as crude caricatures of Chicano speech . . . MeChicano. . .dominate the popular consciousness, popular writing is likely to go on contributing to this form of linguistic degradation.

The samples comprising Text Al date from the first third of the twentieth century. The speakers are a bandit ...rather, a *bandido*..., a housewife, and a gambler. Observations of their MeChicano usage are limited to direct quotes from dialogue. The stories all deal with criminality: a rape scene, an interview about Billy the Kid, and the befriending by a Mexican family of a good-hearted Anglo bankrobber. Text Al presents the MeChicano as Bandido or accomplice of Bandidos. The Al texts (see Appendix A) show numerous conventional spellings indicating accentedness and eye dialect. Clearly the one on which the writers most rely is the raising of standard /i/ to /iy/, as in *heem*, *leetle*, *weeked*, etc. Most morphosyntactic deviations involve the verb phrase, particularly the -*s* deletion in third person singular and nonstandard uses of auxiliaries.

Code-switching is of the sort that requires little knowledge of Spanish on the part of the reader; most of the words used would most likely be known to monolingual Anglo-Americans with some experience of western writing (*caballero*, *hidalgo*, *señorita*, etc.). Stylistic incongruities are more likely to be syntactic than lexical, assuming *inter alia* that questions involving the copula and modal auxiliaries are assigned to the domain of syntax.

Text A2 (Appendix A) samples show much greater fluency and syntactic sophistication than those of Al. The analyses show important differences between Al and A2. In the latter, the speakers are two old men, a ranch woman, and a cowboy or ranchhand. The two old men are traveling through New Mexico; the woman addresses her son, who has just killed a man; and the cowboy(*peon*?) is engaging the writer in philosophic conversation about the innocence of nature. Here, according to Pettit, the MeChicano takes on some variant of the Noble Savage image: Jolly Loafer, Doomed Rebel, or Accepter-of-his-Lot.

There are several major differences between the Al and A2 texts, in terms of the four descriptors used in the respective analyses. First, A2 writers appear to drop accentedness as an overt marker of MeChicano English. Few of the A2 morphosyntactic deviations are of the type that predominate in Al: the latter are mostly low-level morphophonemics, while those of A2 (particularly the Lummis sample) are calques of Spanish, easily backtranslated:

it is truth: *es verdad*
without to drink: *sin tomar*

but that thou not rememberest our compromise: *pero que tu no recuerdas nuestro compromiso* of the gente uninstructed: *de la gente inculta* (or, *sin instruccion*)

Writers of A2 texts show a greater familiarity with Spanish than do those of A1; consequently, their readers are more apt to need both linguistic and cultural back- grounds of far greater scope. The Lummis passage in some places would verge on gibberish if the reader cannot ap- preciate the calques (including drinklet/*traguito*). Stein- beck inserts complete, untranslated Spanish utterances. Dobis assumes that his readers have some notion of the im- portance of the *dicho* in Mexican popular culture.

Stylistic incongruities include the curious convention that Spanish *tu* be rendered as *thou/thee*. The characters in A2 texts speak in a dignified, even elegant fashion, such as befits Noble Savages in their subroles of Jolly Drunkard, Stoic Earth Mother, or Vaquero-cum-Homespun- Philosopher.

Texts A1 and A2 differ particularly in their reliance on accentedness, in what they demand of their readers in terms of knowledge of MeChicano language and culture, and in the sort of stereotypes they present. The A1 materials rely heavily on eye-dialect to indicate certain stigmatized pronunciations of English; they do not require knowledge of Spanish beyond that of a few lexical items; and they pre- sent a blatantly racist portrayal of MeChicanos as Bandits, Bitches, and/or Buffoons. The A2 texts shift accentedness from phonology to morphosyntax; they assume a certain amount of cultural awareness; and they project a more sym- pathetic, if perhaps condescending, image of the MeChicano as Noble and non-threatening.

In considering the samples of Chicano writing listed as Texts C1 and C2, it must be pointed out that the criti- cism of Chicano literature lies far beyond the scope of the present treatment. Here, we will apply the four de- scriptors to material whose proper analysis requires a radical change in critical philosophy, particularly as regards interlingualism. Bruce-Novoa's survey of Chicano writers provides not only a valuable overview of Chicano literature from the mid-sixties on, but more germane to the language issue, a wide range of answers to the ques- tion of whether Chicano literature has a particular lin- guistic identity.[14]

It is valuable to summarize the comments of leading Chicano novelists, playwrights, and poets, fourteen in all, since they give substance to the more general state- ments by students of Chicano literature that linguistic matters are fundamental to such criticism. Since much of this literature is in English, in the sense of being cast in an English-language matrix despite the presence of Spanish, Chicano writing has come to form an important subset of American letters.

To Bruce-Novoa's question, "Does Chicano literature have a particular language or idiom", there were several typical responses. Some of the contributors stressed bilingualism and its reflection in "interlingual" usage. This view may be summed up in Abelardo Delgado's statement:

> Chicano literature's main characteristic is that it is a literature that is naturally at ease in the way Chicanos express themselves, and that is a natural bilingualism, with the influence of English naturally prominent, as that is the language in which all Chicanos are educated. . . Let it suffice to repeat that in the total sum of Chicano literature, bilingualistic mix, even more than two languages at times, is a trademark too big to ignore. (Bruce-Novoa 1980, p. 100).

This opinion would subsume that of other writers who find the use of *caló* to be a major feature of Chicano literature, since the knowledge of *caló* assumes some degree of mastery of Spanish. A second opinion, which does not contradict the foregoing, was that Chicano writers have access to such a variety of codes that it would be misleading to establish a single most representative one. The poet Alurista reflects the attitude of several of the contributors when he writes:

> What truly makes Chicano literature so rich and fertile is the fact that we can and do in fact write in Black English and Yankee English, in Mexican Spanish and Chicano Spanish. ... So I really don't think there is a particular language in Chicano literature. We cover this full range in Chicano literature, the full range of colors, the full rainbow. All of the sarape. It is one great sauce and that makes it all the tastier, don't you think? (Bruce-Novoa 1980, p. 272).

A third, more conservative opinion shared by some of the contributors was that Chicano literature does not depend on overt linguistic markers ("dialect", "caló", "pochismos"), since it arises from specific historical/ cultural circumstances. None of the writers deny that these contribute to style, but there appears to be a concern that Chicano literature may become stereotyped, perhaps by its own practitioners, in terms of language. Novelist José Antonio Villarreal. . . whose *Pocho* (1959) is among the first major Chicano works. . . gives a qualified answer:

> As for the question, 'Has this literature we call Chicano literature a particular language or idiom?', the answer must be *yes*, if only because of the cultural overtones within the narrative or the dialog and in some cases, of course, the use of Spanish words as well as Mexican philosophy. Pochismos and caló lend a very specific flavor to the idiom in terms of the culture, but certainly not in any artistic sense.

There is nothing new about the use of dialect. It is traditional in letters. (Bruce-Novoa 1980, p. 41).

Villarreal might well have cited the many Frenchmen, Welshmen, and other outlanders who troop through Shakespeare's theater with their accentedness, their deviant syntax, and their mighty oaths in one language or another. It may be noted that when Henry IV was performed at the University of Texas at Austin in 1982, the Texanized version replaced French with Spanish in the interlingual scenes. Both Anglo-American and Chicano literatures are well within the tradition of the media dialect, whose authenticity is more or less irrelevant to its communicative effects as long as a few salient traits are present to evoke the stereotype.

In using our four descriptors with the C-Texts, we are testing only a limited range of Chicano creative writing. If this approach were to involve quantification, one might set up a null hypothesis to the effect that there is no significant difference between the distributions of these four variables from one text type to the other. If it were possible to reject the null hypothesis, we might then proceed to interpret the actual distributions in Texts A1, A2, C1, and C2. This might indeed be possible given an adequate sample, a proper criterion for text selection, and a more clearly defined set of variables. We consider the present materials merely initial observations which may suggest future research.

Text C1 has samples dating back to 1965 (Muro), 1969 (Barrio), and 1970 (Zeta). Muro's Don Ignacio is a well-read older man who writes articles on bull-fighting; Zeta's Nicolás sells corn in the barrio; Barrio's Manuel is a farm worker. The characters appear more authentic than those of A-texts, and *they all have names*.

The samples here show neither accentedness in the phonological domain nor remarkable morphosyntactic deviation from standard spoken English. The choice of vocabulary and grammatical structure seems appropriate to the context, with the exception of the *I shall* in the Barrio passage. Of the four descriptors used, only code-switching appears well-represented.

Spanish-language material continues to include vocatives like *señora* and *muchachitos*, oaths and interjections with religious content, and names of objects or activities which are part of the Chicano milieu in some regions (*estropajo, Pachangas. . .*). Utterances like *Ay María, madre mía* and *Sí, muchachos?* are not only believable Spanish. . . cf.*diabla bonita* and *Hidalgo,yo!*. . . but in addition they are quite acceptable in context. The dialogues flow smoothly, and there is obviously communication: the sentences are addressed to other Spanish-speakers, not to possibly non-understanding Anglos.

One major link between A- and C-Texts lies in the folksy nature of their content. Whether *barrio* or *rancho*

is the setting, the people who speak occupy certain traditional roles. These roles may lack the stigma attached to
them in early Anglo literature, or the spurious nobility
of a period which Pettit calls one of repentance for earlier degradation of the Me-Chicano. Nevertheless, one may
feel in such writing some of the "Mediterranean schmalz"
associated with, say, Fellini's *Amarcord*. Text C1, in our
opinion, breaks with the imagery of Texts A1 and A2 but re-
tains some of the self-conscious folksiness of A2.

At this point it is interesting to show a similar trend
in motion pictures and their representation of the MeChicano. Pettit points out, in great detail, ways in which
early movies degraded Mexicans and Chicanos to such a degree that they elicited protests from the Mexican govern-
ment. In Pettit's words:

> Whether as villains or buffoons, half-breed sluts or
> 'white' dark ladies, celluloid Mexicans tend to be
> treated as a series of shadow figures. . . By the end
> of the first half-century of Hollywood cinema, the
> artistic image of the Mexican was still one of the
> gullible greaser, capable at best of a primitive and
> unreliable allegiance to white folks--and for that
> very reason to be ridiculed and reviled more than ad-
> mired, respected, and even feared. (Pettit 1980, p.
> 151).

The image was to improve slightly with Brando's *Viva
Zapata*, whose dialogue would most likely fit well into the
characteristics of Text A2: less emphasis on accentedness,
morphosyntactic deviation based mostly on calques, and an
elevated style of spoken English. In *The Wild Bunch*, one
finds both Text A1 MeChicanos (bandidos, renegade revolu-
tionaries, the stereotypical Generalissimo) and A2-style
speakers like the heroic Angel and the wise old village
headman. *Wild Bunch* has clear overtones of what Pettit
calls the Samaritan movie, in which one or a few Anglos,
with limited MeChicano help, invade Mexico to do good work
of some sort;[15] cf. *The Magnificent Seven* and the more
recent *The Border*. As the MeChicano characters acquire
somewhat greater realism than that of shadow figures,
their English evolves into that of A2.

With Text C2 we come to writing that is somewhat more
recent than that of C1. The selections here are from a
novel (Acosta), a short story (Candelaria), and a play
(Valdez) which has been widely staged. Once more, the
characters are all Chicano or Mexican, as in C1 but not
in the A-texts. In the latter, the dialogue takes place
either between a Me-Chicano and an Anglo or is being reported by an Anglo observer. Another trait of C-texts is
that characters are identified by name, and their names
are used frequently.[16]

In common with C1, the C2 samples show no marked
accentedness or morphosyntactic deviation. Their styles

vary from the fairly formal of the Candelaria selection,
through the semi-formal salesman's pitch of *Los Vendidos*,
to the easy conversational flow of the Acosta passage. No
stylistic incongruities are observed. This is not to say
that there is no stylistic variation in these writings,
but that the usage seems contextually appropriate.

The C2 selections share with those of C1 the use of
code-switching. In distinction to the type of code-switching found in A-texts, that of the C-samples is believable;
it blends well into the stream of speech; and it assumes
that the reader has some knowledge of Chicano language and
culture.

Some writers distinguish between *stylistic* code-
switching, which may serve to give emphasis, focus, and
other textual features, and *situational* code-switching
conditioned by participants, topic, setting, and other
extratextual variables.[17] This distinction may be useful
in comparing Texts A and C. Further, interlingual humor
. . . such as the "Old Sobaco, my favorite!" remark. . .
requires the reader to be bilingual/bicultural.

The following overall comparison among the four sub-
sets may be useful:

Texts:	A1	A2	A3	A4
Descriptors				
accentedness	yes	no	no	no
morphosyntax	yes	some	no	no
stylistic inc.	yes	yes	some	no
code-switching:				
stylistic	yes	yes	some	no
situational	no	some	yes	yes

Hollywood remains, as far as the evidence indicates,
at the A-level: portrayal of the MeChicano along lines
established in popular literature. It is still unclear
how far the movies have shifted to the A2, condescending
but non-degrading (?) stage of the Samaritan movie. One
may point to a few recent examples of movies which approach
the C-text level, such as the Cheech-and-Chong series or
pictures like *Boulevard Nights* or *Walk Proud*. The image
remains in any case a negative one.

Television offers even less in this regard, once we
set aside Spanish-language programming. Educational and
public-service television have certainly made contributions, particularly in bilingual education. On the whole,
prime-time representation of Chicano people or themes has
not increased since the disappearance of *Chico and the
Man*. Hispanic-oriented magazines like *Nuestro* and *Caminos*
usually devote some space to Hispanics in the media, including live shows and music.[18] Still, in the field of
general entertainment (comedy and drama) there has been a
decline in participation by Chicanos in either starring
or secondary roles.[19] In cinema, too, major figures like
Quinn and Montalban have phased into non-Hispanic roles.[20]

A recent UNESCO publication points out that while
television may have the power to maintain social stability,
it has failed in its responsibility to a pluralistic public.[21] Another critic urges that the media (particularly
televison) should act as "honest broker" among the many
conflicting groups making up U.S. society.[22] Similar cri-
ticisms may be directed at public school texts which, if
they portray Chicanos at all, continue a long-standing
traditional lack of ethnosensitivity.[23]

In these circumstances, Media Chicano English is to
be found mainly in two printed media: scholarly publications (as object of study) and Chicano literature. The
former may help to give this newly recognized sociolect
recognition and status. The latter may interact with the
many varieties of Chicano usage, in either or both
languages, in contributing to the enrichment of American
English.[24] The overall situation of Chicano English in the
media will be summarized below.

PRINT MEDIA

Newspapers and magazines use Standard English. This
includes Hispanic-oriented, widely circulated ones like
Nuestro, Caminos, and *Latino*.

Scholarly books and periodicals have provided a great
deal of information on Chicano usage. The bibliography
contains a representative sample of recent publications
in (socio)linguistics and education. Some of this material
provides samples of Chicano English, but most scholars
approach this variant as an object of study and analysis.
Chicano speech behavior is but one aspect of a broader
ethnographic interest. There is a limited body of work on
Chicanos and the media.

Literature, particularly prose fiction, is a rich
source of stereotyped speech traits which have come to
be associated with the MeChicano. Anglo-American letters
have cultivated such a literary dialect since the 19th
century, along with various and mostly degrading images
of the Mexican/Chicano. Both linguistic and cultural
stereotypes have to a great extent been perpetuated by
the cinema.

MeChicano English as a creation of the media (mostly
print) has evolved over time. Two of the major trends
discussed above are (1) an emphasis on accentedness defined in terms of a few phonological variables, such as
the height of English /i/, and (2) a downplaying of phonological traits in favor of a reliance on calquing and
code-switching. Obviously, it is in dialogue that a vernacular is most likely to be simulated in writing; much
of that writing is caricature.

Chicano literature, and particularly prose fiction,
tends to be written in English. While its practitioners
state that there is no distinctively Chicano literary

language, some Chicano writing does represent vernacular
usage in dialogue. It would be misleading to identify any
one writer's usage as "Chicano English according to Chicanos", but it is possible to point out two stages comparable to those cited for Anglo-American literature.

These are (1) extensive use of code-switching of the
sort that requires a limited knowledge of Spanish, accompanied by standard but occasionally over-formal English
usage; and (2) a decreased reliance on code-switching
(which nevertheless preserves some importance) and the use
of a fluent, unaccented form of familiar English expressing a culturally Chicano reality.

CINEMA

Hollywood movies have developed an image of the Me-
Chicano and of MeChicano English which resembles that of
traditional popular prose fiction. One major difference
is that while the print media relied on a few stereotypical pronunciations, the cinema has developed a full-
fledged profile of Chicano accentedness (including the
fundamental dimension of intonation and stress).

As the image of the MeChicano has been upgraded from
Steenkeeng Bandido to Noble Savage, and as MeChicano roles
are given to non-Hispanics, there has been a shift away
from accentedness to bookish usage; such as, Brando in
Viva Zapata. Accentedness cannot be discounted, nor can
the more degrading imagery, such as, El Indio Fernández's
role in *Wild Bunch*. In some recent movies, both Hispanic
and non-Hispanic portrayals of MeChicano roles move away
from the heavy accentedness of earlier films. Witness
Rod Steiger's *bandido* in *Fistful of Dynamite*, whose Me-
Chicano accent is even fainter than James Coburn's Irish
brogue, or Anthony Quinn's bandido-cum-guerrilla in *High
Risk* (limited accentedness, extensive code-switching).

The *californio* tradition of well-spoken *caballeros*
and quaint *peones* lives on in George Hamilton's *Zorro,.
the Gay Blade*. On the other hand, in Jack Nicholson's
The Border, many of the MeChicano characters speak only
Spanish while others shift easily into a rather Standard
English. The Anglos speak little or no broken Spanish,
Finally, the Cheech-and-Chong movies tend to rely on an
accentedness more based on prosodies than on consonants
or vowels, while those making use of the low-rider motif
(e.g., *Boulevard Nights*) show limited accentedness,
limited code-switching, and strong reliance on culture
content.

TELEVISION

There has been decreasing representation of Mexicans
or Chicanos in leading roles on popular shows, such as
comedies or dramas. Nothing at this time seems to have
replaced *Chico and the Man*, at least on national TV.

Eric Estrada plays an unaccented Chicano role on *CHIPS*.
Other Hispanic actors are to be found in non-Hispanic leading roles, such as Montalban on *Fantasy Island*. Cartoons
and commercials were once a source of MeChicano English,
and Speedy Gonzalez still rushes about the screen from
time to time, but for the most part the Frito Bandido is
gone.

News and weather reporting by Chicanos is generally
done in network English, which excludes Chicano accentedness; that it does not exclude non-U.S. accents is attested to by the various Commonwealth or mid-Atlantic voices
of CNN. It must be remembered that most television addressed to Hispanics is in *Spanish*, and that educational
programs like *Carrascolendas* are basically Spanish-language
with English normally subordinate.

Movies make up an important portion of television fare,
particularly on cable television. The June 1982 offerings
of HBO/Cinemax, for instance, included Mexican/Chicano-
motif films like *High Risk*, *Fistful of Dynamite*, and
Zorro, the Gay Blade, along with *Welcome to Miami, Cubano*,
a half-hour comedy. This instance of a Cuban-oriented,
English-language show offers the opportunity of studying
how the media treats a non-Chicano variant of Hispanic
English. Such a study would have to consider what images
of Cuban English were established by long-running shows
like *I Love Lucy*, where Desi Arnaz's performances made use
of accentedness, code-switching, and cultural stereotypes.

RADIO

Much of the popularity of Hispanic-oriented radio involves music. Spanish-language radio has long been present in the traditionally Hispanic areas, but there seems
to be a dearth of English-language broadcasting addressed
to Chicanos. More generally, the public service features
of radio are transmitted in network Standard English, as
is the case with television. In both electronic media,
Chicano variants of English are unlikely to be permitted
in this context.

In summary, we find MeChicano English--a variant or
style attributed to Mexicans/Chicanos--evolving in some
sectors of the popular mass media. Radio and television,
if not broadcast in Spanish or in network Standard English,
tend to exclude the Chicano vernacular except for tele-
vised movies. The movies themselves have developed forms
of MeChicano English related to those earlier created by
Anglo-American popular fiction. The written simulation
of Chicano English vernacular--whatever its authenticity
--has evolved, and will probably continue to do so, with
the changing situation of Chicanos in U.S. society.

NOTES

1. Halliday 1978, p. 157, For a general discussion of non-standard
speech as a social issue, see Edwards 1979, Ch. 4 which includes
references to Chicano English. Similarly, Cazden and Dickinson 1981
discusses other non-standard varieties. Lourie and Conklin 1978 discusses a number of speech communities and regional variants of U.S.
English, but the only Hispanic English dealt with in detail is that
of Puerto Ricans in East Harlem (Wolfram in Lourie and Conklin, pp.
141-60).
2. Peñalosa 1980, Ch. 6. Chicano English should be much better
known when Ornstein-Galicia (1983) appears.
3. Phonological studies include: Doriak and Hudson-Edwards 1980,
Sosa 1977, and Penfield 1980; more general ones including discussion
of morphosyntax include: Dubois 1978, Natalicio and Williams 1975,
Ornstein and Dubois 1977, Ornstein 1976, Metcalf 1974, García 1974,
Rodriguez 1976, Webb 1980. For an overview see Metcalf 1979 and reviews by Teschner 1980 and Terrell 1981.
4. Attitude studies include Brennan et al. 1980, Carranza 1978,
Flores 1975, MacIntosh and Ornstein 1974, Macaulay 1977, Thompson
1975, Ryan 1973, Ryan and Carranza 1977, Williams 1973, and Ramirez
1981. Kahane and Kahane 1977 relates standard usage to sociocultural values. More general sociolinguistic treatments include:
Aguirre 1978, Elías-Olivares 1975, and Shuy 1981.
5. For an overall treatment see Carter and Segura 1979, Cazden and
Dickinson 1981, Johnson 1970; applications to teaching include:
Hoffer 1976, Montgomery 1974, Lamberg 1975, Merrill 1976, Riggs
1971, Schon 1978, Santos 1978. Hernández 1969 and Seidman 1967 are
California texts which give detailed comparisons of Chicano usage
(both phonological and morphosyntactic) with that of Standard Oral
English. Another field of increasing interest is intercultural communication (Glenn and Glenn 1981) and its teaching, illustrated by
Asunción Laide 1977, Barkin and Brandt 1979, Carty 1980, Gumperz
and Cook-Gumperz 1981, Gumperz and Hernández-Chávez 1978, and Longstreet 1978.
6. Useful titles include Baron 1981, Cortes 1980, McWilliams 1976,
and Moore 1976. Some stress racism and internal colonialism, such
as Acuna 1981, Machado 1978, and Camarillo 1979 (the California
experience). Community studies include Achor 1978 and Foley et al.
1977, both dealing with Texas communities. Of great interest are
autobiographical treatments of assimilation such as Rodríguez 1982
and Acosta 1972 and 1973. Wolfram's study of the linguistic assimilation of Puerto Ricans is important for content and methodology.
7. Veldman 1980 uses data from the 1976 Survey of Income and Education to show that Hispanics, both men and women, were handi-
capped in job advancement by limited English-speaking ability. See
also U.S. Commission on Civil Rights 1971 regarding public schools
in the Southwest.
8. Gómez et al. 1974 has a section on Mexican-Americans which includes some reference to Chicano Spanish. Thernston 1980 devotes a
larger section to Mexican-Americans than to any other traditional
U.S. ethnos.
9. Bruce-Novoa 1980 provides in his introduction a succinct overview of Chicano literature and its major practitioners from 1959

to 1979. Anthologies include Harth and Baldwin 1974, Cardenas de
Dwyer 1975, Simmen 1981 (which includes both Anglo and Chicano
authors), and Keller and Jiménez 1980. Sociolinguistic criticism includes Córdova 1978, Geuder 1974, and Saldívar 1979.
10. Lewels 1974 deals extensively with the problem of Chicano access
to media, particularly newspapers and television; see Schement et
al. 1977 as an instance of license challenge. Martínez 1969 is one
of the early attacks on racist advertising. Several Chicano advocacy groups are discussed in Texas Chicano Coalition on Mass Media
1977 as well as license challenges. There are studies of Chicanos
as reading or viewing public; Dunn 1977, Meyer and Hexamer 1981,
Pasqua 1975, Soriano 1977, Zaffirini 1978; articles dealing with
public service/educational programming include Tan 1978, Scott and
Allen 1979, Barrera 1976, and Williams and Van Wart 1972. For a more
general overview of the media and the public see Brown et al. 1978;
for non-Hispanic ethnics, the Civil Rights Commission (U.S. CSR 1976)
includes testimony by Prof. Richard Gambino (Gambino 1976) and repre-
sentatives of other south European ethnic groups. UNESCO 1977b illustrates patterns of prejudice in the media (mostly newspapers) of
various English-speaking countries other than the U.S.
11. A companion volume to Pettit 1980 is the earlier Robinson 1963.
Robinson concentrates on literature and uses many of the same authors
as Pettit to illustrate racism directed at Chicanos/Mexicans in
popular fiction. Pettit's book was unfinished at his death. The
short Afterward by Showalter briefly reviews some TV programs (Chico
and the Man, Sesame Street, CHIPS, High Chaparral, etc.). Showalter
concludes (p. 245): "If this book has established anything, it is
the strength of Mexican stereotypes in Anglo-American popular culture and the absence of significant external and internal challenges
to these stereotypes." See also Robinson 1973, Gaviglio 1973, and
Simmons 1973 for a resume of the various myths and legends which
Anglos and Chicanos appear to accept about each other.
12. Peñalosa op cit., p. 125-6 et passim. A survey taken by this
writer among Anglo students at University of Texas at Austin yielded
such examples of what the students considered stilted utterances by
Chicanos as ". . . and you?" for "How about you?", or "I'll go for
you at 8" for the more likely "I'll pick you up at 8", Most of the
examples given appeared to be transparent calques, as here: " . . .
y tu?", "Paso por ti a las 8".
13. Rodríguez, op. cit. p. 11-40. Rodríguez views Chicano language
--particularly Spanish, but at least by implication the familiar
usage in English--as a vernacular, a language of intimacy, which
would be falsified by use as a "public" or literary language. However, as Williams (1968, p. 82) points out, "Communication about
racial and ethnic groups carried out by word of mouth within any
one ingrouping tends to be highly selective, restricted, simplified,
incomplete, and inaccurate. The stereotypic quality is likely to
represent greatest distortion when close contact with persons in
the outgroup is least."
14. Bruce-Novoa, op. cit. Contributors were asked to provide background data, such as education and language proficiency; to relate
Chicano literature to other literatures; and to discuss Chicano
literature as such. The language question fell under the latter
category.

15. Pettit op cit., p. 215 seq. The samaritan film sometimes over-laps with the team movie *(Dirty Dozen, Where Eagles Dare)* to pro-duce films like *The Magnificent Seven*.
16. The issue of Chicano naming practice and attitudes toward proper names merits greater attention than it seems to have received so far. See Peñalosa op cit. p. 125-6, pronunciation of etymologically Spanish place names. Meza 1972 shows a highly favorable attitude of Chicanos toward traditional Hispanic personal names. Rodriguez (op. cit., p. 27) shows a seldom-discussed aspect of assimilation when he says, "The social and political advantages I enjoy as a man result from the day I came to believe that my name is, indeed, Rich-heard Road-ree-guess." Note in the C.2 sample (Valdez's *Los Vendidos*) the sar-castic emphasis on the Anglo pronunciation JIM-enez.
17. Peñalosa op. cit. p. 71 et passim. The clarification of termin-ology that resulted from the distinction between "bilingualism" and "diglossia" is, I believe, an example of what is needed in the realm of "code-switching".
18. *Nuestro* 1981 and *Caminos* 1981. Their bibliographic entries here give a sampling of their coverage of Hispanics in the U.S. media. These magazines are written in Standard English or--not and/or--in Standard Spanish. A similar phenomenon apparently occurs with Chicano radio and TV announcers, weathercasters, etc.: their diction will tend to be standard network English. Peñalosa tells us (p. 184) ". . . Chicano (and other ethnic) announcers now appear on television, but. . . few if any speak other than unaccented English." Comedian Danny Mora (in "The serious business of being funny", *Nuestro*, March 81), "At the radio station, I learned to speak in round, dulcet tones, just like an Anglo." Spanish-language radio is expanding (Gutierrez and Schement 1979) as is Spanish-language television, par-ticularly SIN.
19. Seggar et al. 1981 shows that while most participation of Chicano men and women in major or secondary roles has steadily decreased throughout the seventies, there has been an increase in one category --Hispanic males--but only in non-ethnic or non-Hispanic roles.
20. Lewels 1974 relates the creation in 1969 of *Nosotros*, an or-ganization "established to improve the image of Spanish-speaking people within the entertainment industry." (p. 162) Acosta (1973, p. 168) describes some Chicano media figures in sarcastic terms which combine image and accent: "the ones who hide behind grass skirts, the ones with the mustaches, with the broken accents. . . the Chilie Charlie types, the tontos, the sidekicks of Zorro."
21. "However much it may be contributing to social stability and unity in American society, the medium of commercial television is not contributing much to enhance or enrich the pluralismo of Ameri-can society." (Cawelti 1977, p. 66) "The media system itself is not committed to history or to truth." (Yoder 1981, p. 222, quoting Miller 1977)
22. Williams 1968 (p. 72) states that "it seems reasonable to be-lieve that if there is to be a realistic and viable working con-sensus concerning intergroup relations in this country, the mass media have an essential part to play, at two quite different but crucially related levels, namely, the level of a basic intellectual framework and the level of specific facts, values, beliefs, and symbols."

23. Achor op. cit. p. 95 speaks of the degrading stereotypes in schoolbooks--the Sleepy Mexican with Sombrero. It may be pointed out that the U.S. Civil Rights Commission (1979) has set forth guidelines for ethnically/racially "fair" textbooks and other teaching materials.
24. Fishman 1981 urges an upgrading--with the aid of public funds--of both ethnicity and bilingualism as part of a rational linguistic policy. "Ethnicity and bilingualism need to be retooled so that their 'image' will appear to be as much in line with the public good as is the image of other organized self-interest groups in America." (p. 523) Writing in 1970, Philip Ortego (in Durán and Bernard 1978, p. 441), points to the value of this ongoing scholarly work: "It seems to me that genuine linguistic research in the Southwest can help considerably in reducing language prejudice by pointing out--that the English spoken by Mexican-Americans is as much English as the English spoken by a New Englander or a native of the Bronx."

BIBLIOGRAPHY

Achor, Shirley. 1978. *Mexican-Americans in a Dallas Barrio*. Tucson: Var Press.

Acosta, Oscar Z. 1972. *The Autobiography of a Brown Buffalo*. London: Charisma Books.

_____. 1973. *The Revolt of the Cockroach People*. San Francisco, Ca.: Straight Arrow Books.

Acuña, Rodolfo. 1981. *Occupied America: A History of Chicanos*. New York: Harper and Row.

Aguirre, Adalberto. 1978. "The Sociolinguistic Situation of Bilingual Chicano Adolescents in a California Border Town." (ERIC ED152063)

Arthur, B. et al. 1974. "Evaluative Reactions of College Students to Dialect Differences in the English of Mexican-Americans." *Language and Speech* 17(3): 255-270.

Asunción Laide, Nobleza. 1977. "Intercultural Communication: Teaching Strategies, Resources, and Materials." Paper presented at 63rd Speech Communication Association Meeting, Washington, D.C.

Barrera, Aida. 1976. "Carrascolendas." *Public Telecommunications Review* 4(4): 20-24.

Barkin, Florence and Elizabeth Brandt, eds. 1979. *Speaking, Singing, and Teaching: A Multidisciplinary Approach to Language Variation*. Tempe, Az.: Anthropological Research Papers No. 20.

Barón, Augustine. 1981. *Explorations in Chicano Psychology*. New York: Praeger Publications.

Blansitt, Edward and Richard Teschner, eds. 1980. *A Festschrift for Jacob Ornstein*. Rowley, Mass.: Newbury House.

Brennan, E.M. et al. 1980. "Language Attitudes of Mexican-American Adolescents in Two Midwestern Cities." In Paul Schach, ed., *Languages in Conflict: Linguistic Acculturation on the Great Plains*. Lincoln, Nebraska: University of Nebraska Press, pp. 148-156.

Brown, Charlene. 1978. *The Media and the People*. New York: Holt, Rinehart, and Winston.

Bruce-Novoa, Juan. 1980. *Chicano Authors: Inquiry by Interview*. Austin, Tx.: University of Texas Press.

Camarillo, A. 1979. *Chicanos in a Changing Society*. Cambridge, Mass.: Harvard University Press.

Caminos. 1981. "Cheech and Chong's Nice Dream." May 81, pp. 30-1. "Teatro Chicano/Teatro Latino." Dec. 81, pp. 34-5.

Cárdenas de Dwyer, Carlota, ed. 1975. *Chicano Voices*. Boston: Houghton Mifflin.

Carranza, Miguel. 1978. "Language Attitudes and Other Cultural Attitudes of Mexican-American Adults: Some Sociolinguistic Implications." Ph.D. dissertation. Notre Dame University.

Carter, T. and R. Segura. 1979. *Mexican-Americans in School: A Decade of Change*. New York: College Board Publications.

Carty, Mary. 1980. "Strategies Used by Native Speakers in Native/Non-native Conversations." MA thesis. Northeastern University

Cawelti, John. 1977. "Cultural Pluralism and the Media of the Future: A View from America." In UNESCO, *Ethnicity and the Media*. Paris: UNESCO Press.

Cazden, Courtney and D. Dickinson. 1981. "Language in Education: Standardization vs. Cultural Pluralism." In Charles Ferguson and Shirley Heath, eds. *Language in the USA*. New York: Cambridge University Press, pp. 446-468.

Córdova, Roberto. 1978. *Syntax and Bilingual Chicano Poetry*. Ann Arbor, Michigan: Dissertation Abstracts International A0419-4209.

Cortés, Carlos. 1980. "Mexicans." In S. Thernston, ed., *Harvard Encyclopedia of American Ethnic Groups*. Cambridge, Mass.: Harvard University Press, pp. 697-719.

DiPietro, Robert and Edward Blansitt, eds. 1977. *Third LACUS Forum*. Columbia, SC: Hornbeam Press.

Doriak, Martin and Allan Hudson-Edwards. 1980. "Phonological Variation in Chicano English: Word-final (z)-devoicing." In Edward Blansitt and Richard Teschner, eds., *A Festschrift for Jacob Ornstein*. Rowley, Mass.: Newbury House.

Dubois, Betty Lou. 1978. "A Cloze Study of Verb Usage in Context: Anglos and Chicanos." In Michel Paradis, ed., *Fourth LACUS Forum*. Columbia, SC: Hornbeam Press, pp. 604-610.

Dunn, Edward. 1975. "Mexican-American Media Behavior." *Journal of Broadcasting* 19(1): 3-10.

Durán, L. and H. Bernard, eds. 1973. *Introduction to Chicano Studies: A Reader*. New York: Macmillan.

Durán, Richard, ed. 1981. *Latino Language and Communicative Behavior*. Norwood, NJ: Ablex Publishing Co.

Edwards, John. 1979. *Language and Disadvantage*. New York: Elsevier.

Elías-Olivares, Lucía. 1975. "Language Use in a Chicano Community: A Sociolinguistic Approach." Washington, D.C.: *Working Papers in Sociolinguistics* No. 30.

Ferguson, Charles and Shirley Brice Heath, eds. 1981. *Language in the USA*. New York: Cambridge University Press.

Fishman, Joshua. 1981. "Language Policy: Past, Present, and Future." In Charles Ferguson and Shirley Heath, eds., *Language in the USA*. New York: Cambridge University Press, pp. 516-526.

Flores, Nancy de la Zerda. 1975. "Mexican-Americans' Evaluation of Spoken Spanish and English." *Speech Monographs* 42(2): 91-98.

Foley, Douglas et al. 1977. *From Peones to Politicos: Ethnic Relations in a South Texas Town, 1900 to 1977*. Austin, Tx.: University Texas Center for Mexican-American Studies.

Gambino, Richard. 1976. "The Communications Media and Southern and Eastern European Ethnic Groups." In U.S. Commission on Civil Rights. *Civil Rights Issues of Euro-Ethnic Americans in the United States: Opportunities and Challenges*. Chicago: U.S. Civil Rights Commission, pp. 515-525.

García, Ricardo. 1974. "Toward a Grammar of Chicano English." *English Journal* 63(3): 34-38.

Gaviglio, Glen. 1973. "The Myths of the Mexican-American." In L. Durán and H. Bernard, eds., *Introduction to Chicano Studies: A Reader*. New York: Macmillan, pp. 398-406.

Geuder, Patricia. 1974. "Sociolinguistics and Chicano Literature." Paper presented at meeting of the Rocky Mountain MLA, Laramie, Wyoming (ERIC ED082585).

Glenn, E. and C. Glenn. 1981. *Man and Mankind: Conflict and Communication Between Cultures*. Norwood, NJ: Ablex Publishing Co.

Gómez, R. et al, eds. 1974. *The Social Reality of Ethnic America*. Lexington, Mass.: D.C. Heath.

González, Gustavo. 1983. "The Range of Chicano English." In Jacob Ornstein-Galicia, ed., *Form and Function in Chicano English*. Rowley, Mass.: Newbury House.

Gumperz, John and Jenny Cook-Gumperz. 1981. "Ethnic Differences in Communicative Style." In Charles Ferguson and Shirley Brice Heath, eds. *Language in the USA*. New York: Cambridge University Press, pp. 430-445.

Gumperz, John and Eduardo Hernández-Chávez. 1978. "Bilingualism, Bidialectalism, and Classroom Interaction." In M. Lourie and N. Conklin, eds., *A Pluralistic Nation: The Language Issue in the United States*.

Gutiérrez, F. and J.R. Schement. 1979. *Spanish-language Radio in the Southwestern United States*. Austin, Tx.: University of Texas Center for Mexican-American Studies.

Halliday, M.A.K. 1978. *Language as a Social Semiotic*. London: University Park Press.

Harth, D. and L. Baldwin, eds. 1974. *Voices of Aztlan: Chicano Literature of Today*. New York: New American Library.

Hernández, Luis. 1969. *Standard Oral English: Seventh Grade*. Los Angeles, Cal.: Division of Secondary Education.

Hoffer, Bates. 1976. "Toward Implicational Scales for Use in Chicano English Composition." *Papers in Southwest English I*. San Antonio, Tx.

Johnson, H.S. and M. Hernández. 1970. *Educating the Mexican-American*. Valley Forge, Pa.: Judson Press.

Kahane, H. and R. Kahane. 1975. "Virtues and Vices in the American Language: A History of Attitudes." *TESOL Quarterly* 11(2): 185-202.

Keller, Gary and F. Jiménez, eds. 1980. *Hispanics in the United States: An Anthology of Creative Literature*. Ypsilanti, Mich.: Bilingual Review Press.

Lamberg, W. et al. 1975. "Training in Identifying Oral Reading Departures from Text Which Can Be Explained as Spanish-English Phonological Differences." *Bilingual Review* 1-2: 65-75.

Lewels, Francisco. 1974. *The Uses of the Media by the Chicano Movement*. New York: Praeger Publishers.

Longstreet, Wilma. 1978. *Aspects of Ethnicity: Understanding Differences in Pluralistic Classrooms*. New York: Teachers College.

Lourie, M. and N. Conklin. 1978. *A Pluralistic Nation: The Language Issue in the United States*.

Macaulay, Ronald. 1977. "Attitudes Toward Language and Their Importance for Children's Language Learning." California State Univ., Los Angeles: *Bilingual Education Paper Series*, 1(5).

Machado, M.A. Jr. 1978. *Listen, Chicano! An Informal History of the Mexican-American*. Chicago: Nelson Hall.

MacIntosh, R. and Jacob Ornstein. 1974. "A Brief Sampling of West Texas Teacher Attitudes Toward Southwest Spanish and English Varieties." *Hispania* 57(4): 920-926.

Martínez, T. 1969. "Advertising and Racism." *El Grito* 3: 3-13.

McWilliams, Carey. 1978. *North from Mexico*. New York: Greenwood Press.

Merrill, Celia. 1976. "Contrastive Analysis and Chicano Compositions." Paper presented at Conference on College English and the Mexican American, Jan. 77.

Metcalf, Allan. 1974. "The Study (or Non-Study) of Chicano English." *International Journal of Sociological Linguistics* 2: 53-58.

Metcalf, Allan. 1979. *Chicano English*. Washington, D.C.: Center for Applied Linguistics.

Meyer, T.P. and A. Hexamer. 1981. "Perceived Truth and Trust in Television Advertising Among Mexican-American Adolescents." *Journal of Broadcasting* 25(2): 139-147.

Meza, Ruth. 1972. *Ethnic Stereotypes: A Semantic Differential Analysis*. MA thesis, University of Texas at El Paso.

Miller, Randall. 1978. *Ethnic Images in American Film and Television*. Philadelphia, Pa.: Balch Institute.

Montgomery, Linda. 1974. "A Carnaval of Bilingual Learning." *American Education* 10(7): 34-37.

Moore, Joan. 1976. *Mexican-Americans*. Englewood Cliffs, NJ: Prentice Hall.

Murguía, Edward. 1975. *Assimilation, Colonialism, and the Mexican-American People*. Austin, Tx.: University of Texas Center for Mexican-American Studies.

Natalicio, Diana and Frederick Williams. 1975. "What Characteristics Can Experts Reliably Evaluate in the Speech of Black and Mexican-American Children." *TESOL Quarterly* 6(2): 165-171.

Nuestro. 1981. "The Serious Business of Being Funny." pp. 35-39. "Tierra Hits Paydirt." pp. 41-44.

Ornstein, Jacob. 1976. "Mexican American English: Prolegomena to a Neglected Regional Variety." In Robert DiPietro and Edward Blansitt, eds., *Third LACUS Forum*. Columbia, SC: Hornbeam Press,

_____ and Betty Lou Dubois. 1977. "Mexican-American English." In Robert DiPietro and Edward Blansitt, eds., *Third LACUS Forum*. Columbia, SC: Hornbeam Press, pp. 95-107.

Ortego, Philip. 1973. "Some Cultural Implications of a Mexican-American Border Dialect of American English." In L. Durán and H. Bernard, eds., *Introduction to Chicano Studies: Reader*. New York: Macmillan, pp. 435-441.

Paradis, Michel, ed. 1978. *Fourth LACUS Forum*. Columbia, SC: Hornbeam Press.

Pasqua, Tom. 1975. "Newspaper Readers' News Values: An Exploratory Comparison of Chicanos and Anglos," *Aztlan* 6(3): 347-361.

Peñalosa, Fernando. 1981. *Chicano Sociolinguistics: A Brief Introduction*. Rowley, Mass.: Newbury House.

Penfield, Joyce. 1980. "Prosody in Mexican-American English: Parameters of Intonation." (BEBA BE006303)

Pettit, Arthur. 1980. *Images of the Mexican-American in Fiction and Film*. College Station, Tx: Texas A & M.

Ramírez, Arnulfo. 1981. "Language Attitudes and the Speech of Spanish-English Bilingual Pupils." In L. Durán and H. Bernard, eds., *Introduction to Chicano Studies: Reader*. New York: Macmillan, pp. 217-235.

Riggs, Virginia. 1971. "Action Research in Oral English for the Linguistically Different." MA thesis, University of Texas at Austin.

Robinson, Cecil. 1963. *With the Ears of Strangers*. Tucson, Az.: University of Arizona Press.

_____. 1973. "A Kaleidoscope of Images: Mexicans and Chicanos as Reflected in American Literature." In Paul Turner, ed., *Bilingualism in the Southwest*. Tucson: University of Arizona Press, pp. 107-129.

Rodrigues, Raymond. 1976. "A Statistical Study of the English Syntax of Bilingual Mexican-American and Monolingual Anglo-American students." *Bilingual Review* 3(3): 205-212.

Rodriguez, Richard. 1982. *Hunger of Memory: The Education of Richard Rodriguez*. Boston: David Godine.

Ryan, Ellen B. 1973. "Subjective Attitudes Toward Accented Speech." In Roger Shuy and R. Fasold, eds., *Language Attitudes: Current Trends and Prospects*. Washington, D.C.: Georgetown University Press, pp. 60-73.

_____ and Miguel Carranza. 1977. "Attitudes Toward Accented English," *Atisbos Journal of Chicano Research*, Winter 27-34.

Saldívar, Ramón. 1979. "A Dialectic of Difference: Toward a Theory of the Chicano Novel." Los Angeles, Cal.: *MELUS* 6(3): 73-92.

Santos, Richard. 1978. *Mexican-American Cultural Contributions, Module V: The Language of the Tejano*. Austin, Tx.: Bilingual Bicultural Teacher Training Program..

Seggar, J.F. et al. 1981. "Television's Portrayal of Minorities and Women in Drama and Comedy Drama, 1971-80." *Journal of Broadcasting* 25(3): 277-288.

Schach, Paul, ed. 1980. *Languages in Conflict: Linguistic Acculturation on the Great Plains*. Lincoln, Nebraska: University of Nebraska Press.

Schement, Jorge et al. 1977. "The Anatomy of a License Challenge." *Journal of Communication* 27(1): 89-94.

Schon, Isabel. 1978. *Bicultural Heritage: Themes for the Exploration of Mexican and Mexican-American Culture in Books for Children and Adolescents*. Metuchen, NJ: Scarecrow Press.

Scott, R. and C. Allen. 1979. "Cancion de la Raza: An ETV Soap Opera." *Television Quarterly* 8(4): 24-37.

Seidman, Dolores. 1967. *Standard Oral English, Tenth Grade: Instructional Guide D*. Los Angeles, Cal.: Division of Secondary Education.

Shuy, Roger. 1981. "Variability and the Public Image of Languages." *TESOL Quarterly* 15(3): 315-326.

Shuy, Roger and R. Fasold, eds. 1973. *Language Attitudes: Current Trends and Prospects*. Washington, D.C.: Georgetown University Press.

Simmen, Edward, ed. 1971. *The Chicano: From Caricature to Self-Portrait*. New York: New American Library.

Simmons, Ozzie. 1973. "The Mutual Images and Expectations of Anglo Americans and Mexican Americans." In L. Durán and H. Bernard, eds., *Introduction to Chicano Studies: A Reader*. New York: Macmillan, pp. 387-397.

Sommers, Joseph. 1974. "Critical Approaches to Chicano Literature,"
    Bilingual Review/Revista Bilingüe 4(1-2): 92-98.

Soriano, Michael. 1977. "Minority Activism and Media Access: An
    Analysis of Community Participation in Policy, Programming, and
    Production," Ph.D. dissertation, Stanford University

Sosa, Francisco. 1977. "The Phonic Consistency of Barrio English,"
    In Robert DiPietro and Edward Blansitt, eds., *Third LACUS Forum*.
    Columbia, SC: Hornbeam Press, pp. 120-127.

Tan, Alexis. 1978. "Evaluation of Newspapers and Television by Blacks
    and Mexican-Americans." *Journalism Quarterly* 55(4): 673-681.

Terrell, T.D. 1981. "Review of Metcalf (1979)," *Modern Language
    Journal* 65(3): 327-328.

Teschner, Richard V. 1980. "Review of Metcalf (1979)," *Canadian
    Modern Language Review* 37(1): 115-116.

Texas Chicano Coalition on Mass Media. 1977. *Reporte* 1(1).

Thernston, S, ed. 1980. *Harvard Encyclopedia of American Ethnic
    Groups*. Cambridge, Mass.: Harvard University Press.

Thompson, Roger. 1975. "Mexican-American English: Social Correlates
    of Regional Pronunciation." *American Speech* 50(1-2): 18-24.

Turner, Paul, ed. 1973. *Bilingualism in the Southwest*. Tucson: Uni-
    versity of Arizona Press.

UNESCO. 1977a. *Cultural Trends V*. Paris: UNESCO Press.

UNESCO. 1977b. *Ethnicity and the Media*. Paris: UNESCO Press.

U.S. Commission on Civil Rights. 1971. *Mexican-American Education
    Study: Isolation of Mexican-Americans in the Public Schools of
    the Southwest*. Washington, D.C.: GPO.

U.S. Commission on Civil Rights. 1976. *Civil Rights Issues of Euro-
    Ethnic Americans in the United States: Opportunities and
    Challenges*. Chicago: U.S. Civil Rights Commission.

U.S. Commission on Civil Rights. 1979. *Fair Textbooks: A Resource
    Guide*. Washington, D.C.: U.S. Commission on Civil Rights.

Veltman, Calvin. 1980. *The Role of Language Characteristics in the
    Socioeconomic Attainment Process of Hispanic Origin Men and
    Women*. Washington, D.C.: Government Printing Office.

Wald, Benji. 1983. "The Status of Chicano English as a Dialect of
    American English," In Jacob Ornstein-Galicia, ed., *Form and
    Function in Chicano English*. Rowley, Mass.: Newbury House.

Webb, John T. 1980. "Pidgins (and creoles?) on the U.S.-Mexican Border." In Edward Blansitt and Richard Teschner, eds., *A Festschrift for Jacob Ornstein*. Rowley, Mass.: Newbury House, pp. 326-331.

Williams, Frederick. 1973. "Some Research Notes on Dialect Attitudes." In Roger Shuy and R. Fasold, eds., *Language Attitudes: Current Trends and Prospects*. Washington, D.C.: Georgetown Univ. Press, pp. 113-128.

_____ and G. Van Wart. 1972. "On the Relationship of Language Dominance and the Effects of Viewing Carrascolendas." Austin, Tx.: Center for Communications Research.

Williams, Robin. 1968. "Implications for the Mass Media of Research on Intergroup Relations and Race," In Frederick Yu, ed., *Behavioral Sciences and the Mass Media*. New York: Russell Sage Foundation.

Wolfram, Walt. 1973. *Sociolinguistic Aspects of Assimilation: Puerto Rican English in New York City*. Arlington, Va.: Center for Applied Linguistics.

Yoder, J. 1981. "Review of Miller (1978)," *Journal of Broadcasting* 25(2): 221-223.

Yu, Frederick, ed. 1968. *Behavioral Sciences and the Mass Media*. New York: Russell Sage Foundation.

Zaffirini, Judith. 1978. "A Social Categories Perspective on Mass Media Habits and Attitudes of Mexican-American College Students," Ph.D. dissertation, University of Texas at Austin.

APPENDIX A

TEXT A.1

O.Henry:

"I no hurt-y you, Señorita," he said.
"You bet you won't," answered the Queen. . .
"Not hurt-y you--no. But maybeso take one beso--one li'l kees,
you call him."
"Vamoose, quick," she ordered preemptorily. "You coon!" The red
of insult burned through the Mexican's dark skin.
"Hidalgo, Yo!" he shot between his fangs. "I am not neg-r-ro!
Diabla bonita, for that you shall pay me!"

                    "An Afternoon Miracle"
                    (Robinson 1971, p. 170)

Walter Noble Burns:

"Billee the Keed. Ah, you have heard of heem? He was one gran'
boy, señor. All Mexican pepul his friend. You nevair hear a Mexican
say one word against Billee the Keed. Everybody love that boy. He
was so kind-hearted, so generous, so brave. And so 'andsome. Nombre
de Dios! Every leetle señorita was crazy about heem. . . Poor
Billee the Keed! He was a good boy--muy valiente, muy caballero."

                    "The Saga of Billy the Kid"
                    (Pettit 1980, p. 162)

Eugene Manlove Rhodes:

"Thees redhead, he pass this way, pasó por aquí. . . and he
mek here good and not weeked. But, before that--I am not God!"

                    "Pasó por aquí"
                    (Pettit 1980, p. 164)

TEXT A.1: ANALYSIS

Accentedness

1. raising of English /i/ to /iy/: *kees, leetle, heem*. . .
2. consonant cluster reduction: *hurt-y* (presumably VCC# to
   VC-CV#), *gran'*
3. diphthong reduction: *mek*
4. schwa-fronting: *nevair*
5. loss of initial /h/: *'andsome*
6. trilled /r/: *neg-r-ro*

Morphosyntactic deviations

1. deletion of third person singular marker: *he pass, everybody
   love*

2. deletion of past tense marker: *he mek* (i.e., made)
3. subject pronoun deletion: *maybeso take* (i.e., I take)
4. masculine object pronoun for neuter: *l'il kees, you call him*
5. subject pronoun reiteration: *thees redhead, he pass*
6. copula deletion: *all Mexican pepul his friend*
7. failure to invert auxiliary in questions: *you have heard?*
8. negation with *no*: *I no hurt-y you*
9. present for future *will*: *I not hurt-y you, I take one beso*
10. adverb placement: *he mek here good*

Code-switching

1. phrase-level items, untranslated: *muy caballero. señor, señorita* (both as common noun and as vocative)
2. oaths and interjections: *diabla bonita, nombre de Dios*
3. sentences: *muy caballero, muy valiente, Hidalgo, yo!*
4. Spanish followed by translation: *one beso--one li'l kees; he pass this way, pasó por aquí*

Stylistic incongruity

1. failure to contract: *I am not neg-r-ro. I am not God. You have heard of heem?*
2. *shall* for (contracted) *will*: *for that you shall pay me*
3. bookish vocabulary, given the context: *weeked* (wicked), *so kind-hearted*

TEXT A.2

Charles Lummis:

"Válgame Diós," groaned Cristóbal, after they had gone a few miles. "But it is very long without to drink. For the love of the Virgin, cuñado, give a little to me!"

"But how! But that thou not rememberest our compromise," asked the virtuous Tránsito.

"It is truth, compadre, that we compromised not to give us one drop. But of the to sell was nothing said. See! That I have cinco centavos! Sell me a drinklet to me." "Sta bueno!" said Tránsito.

"A New Mexico David"
(Robinson 1971, p. 217)

John Steinbeck:

Mama nodded. "Yes, thou art a man, my poor little Pepé. Thou art a man. I have seen it coming on thee. I have watched you throwing a knife into the post, and I have been afraid." . . . "Come! We must get you ready. Go. Awaken Emilio and Rosy. Go quickly."

Emilio put his head in the door. "'Qui 'st 'l caballo, Mama."

"Flight"
(Simmen 1971, p. 145)

J. Frank Dobie:

"Excuse me, patrón. I am but of the gente uninstructed. I
never looked inside a dictionary. . . I only know that according
to nature this man, that man, says, 'I am bound to pluck this
flower no matter how many thorns prick my hand.' And then, the
flower plucked, he is like the buck that sheds his horns. . . You
know best patron. There is no blame for nature. As our fathers
said, 'A pair of chiches (breasts) pulls stronger than a yoke of
oxen'. . . Remember the dicho, 'All meat is to be eaten, all women
sampled.' Come, my friend. Molest your mind no further on this
matter."

"The Mexico I like"
(Robinson 1971, p. 245)

TEXT A.2: ANALYSIS

Accentedness: no written indication

Morphosyntactic deviations:

1. complementation with preposition plus *to*: *without to drink,
   of the to sell*
2. reiteration of indirect object: *sell-me a drinklet to me*
3. postposed adjective: *the gente uninstructed*
4. subject-verb inversion: *but of the to sell was nothing said*
5. non-reflexive pronoun *us* for reciprocal *each other: we compromised not to give us one drop*

Code-switching

1. phrase-level, untranslated: *cinco centavos, gente, patrón,
   cuñado, compadre, dicho, Mama*
2. oaths and interjections: *válgame Dios*
3. sentences: *'qui 'st' 'l caballo, sta bueno*
4. Spanish followed by translation: *chiches* (breasts)

Stylistic incongruity

1. (false-cognate) calques: *compromise* (compromiso), *we have
   compromised* (nos hemos comprometido), *but how* (pero   como
   . . .?), *it is truth* (es verdad)
2. archaic pronouns (representing *tu*): *that thous rememberest,
   thou art a man, on thee*
3. failure to contract: *it is very long, I am bound, he is
   like the buck, I have seen it*
4. bookish vocabulary, given the context: *drinklet, awaken,
   go quickly, we must get you ready*
5. nominative absolute construction: *and then, the flower
   plucked, he. . .*

APPENDIX B

TEXT C.1

Amado Muro:

   After the Pachangas were over, Don Ignacio always started for
the back door of the cafe, ostensibly to wash himself down with és-
tropajo. But the clamorous cries of the children and the shouts of
the men and women massed on the balconies of the adjacent tene-
ments never failed to bring him back. "The ballad, Don Nacho,"
the crowd yelled. "The ballad of Niño de la Palma." "Ay María,
madre mía," Don Ignacio complained every Sunday. "Muchachitos, it's
hot as three o'clock in Acapulco, and I swear by our sainted Guada-
lupana, the Señora of all the world and the Mother of the Mexicans,
that I've got to dress for the bullfight."

"Sunday in Little Chihuahua"
(Harth and Baldwin 1974, p. 21)

"Zeta" (Oscar Z. Acosta):

   The old man continued to sharpen the knife. "Sí, muchachos?
Qué es?" The brown boy looked at his own mud-caked feet. "Well,
Nicolás Bordona, he said. . . he said we could have the, some
plums." "Oh, sí, muchachos." The old man hesitated, for he was
unaccustomed to dealing with children. "Take them, there they
are."

"Perla is a Pig"
(Harth & Baldwin 1974, p. 117)

Raymond Barrio:

   "Pretty good fat corn, mi vida, my life!" Manuel planted a
big kiss on Lupe's attractive neck, then guzzled down the other
half of his glass of red vino. "I shall make you a necklace of
beautiful green esmeraldas, greener than your eyes, you watch,
you witch, my chula, my precious wife, you wait and see!"

"The Plum Plum Pickers"
(Barrio 1969, p. 87)

TEXT C.1: ANALYSIS

Accentedness: no written indication

Morphosyntactic deviation: no written indication

Code-switching:

1. phrase-level, untranslated: *pachangas, estropajo, muchachitos, señora, esmeraldas, chula*
2. oaths and interjections: *ay María, madre mía*
3. sentences: *oh sí, muchachos. ¿Qué es? Sí, muchachos?*

4. Spanish followed by translation: *mi vida, my life!*

Stylistic incongruity

1. *shall* for *will:*   *I shall make you a necklace*

TEXT C.2

Oscar Zeta Acosta:

He laughs. "Hey, ese, don't you read the papers?. . . I'm
supposed to be the leader of you guys. . . Of course I support
you." "How about the Chicano Liberation Front?" "Who is that?"
Corky says. "Hey, aint'choo heard about. . ." a kid with a beanie
begins to ask. Gilbert slaps him with a brown beret, laughing.
"Don't be so tapado, ese. . . this vato is cool."

The Revolt of the Cockroach People
(Acosta 1973, p. 213)

Nash Candelaria:

"I have come for only a moment, Señor Rivera," Carlos said,
"to say adiós. The war is no longer a rumor. It has been declared.
There has been fighting at the mouth of the Rio Grande at Matamoros.
Both the regular troops and the militia have been put on alert. I
will not be able to visit you and your family again until after
we turn back the invaders." The merchandise slipped through Señor
Riviera's hands, and his mouth fell open. He turned his anxious
gaze on Carlos. "War? I did not believe it would come to that.
God! What can we do against the Americans? All will be lost."

"Only a Yankee"
(Keller and Jiménez 1980, p. 16)

Luis Valdez:

SANCHO: Yes, señorita, this model represents the apex of
American engineering! He is bilingual, college educated, ambitious!
Say the word "acculturate" and he accelerates. He is intelligent,
well-mannered, clean--did I say clean? . . . Smell. SECRETARY
(smells): Old Sobaco, my favorite. SANCHO: Eric? (to secretary)
we call him Eric García (to Eric) I want you to mee Miss JIM-enez,
Eric. MEXICAN-AMERICAN: Miss JIM-enez, I am delighted to make your
acquaintance. (he kisses her hand).

"Los Vendidos"
(Harth and Baldwin 1974, p. 217)

TEXT C.2: ANALYSIS

Accentedness: not indicated in writing

Morphosyntactic deviation: not indicated in writing

Code-switching:

    1. vocatives: *Señor Rivera, ese, señorita*
    2. phrase-level, untranslated: *tapado, adiós, Sobaco*

Stylistic incongruity: not indicated in writing in the Acosta and
    Valdez samples. Uncontracted auxiliaries in Candelaria sample
    are not incongruous with the overall stylistic level of the
    passage:

      *the war is no longer a rumor; all is lost; I did not believe
      it would come to that, etc.*

16

ASPECTS OF PROSE STYLE IN THREE CHICANO NOVELS: IN THREE CHICANO NOVELS: *Pocho, Bless Me, Última,* AND *The Road to Tamazunchale*

Willard Gingerich
Department of English
The University of Texas at El Paso

Chicano English is not English spoken with a Spanish accent - though in some regions that may be one of its characteristics, albeit the least significant one. Nor is it a dialect of invented and specialized words, distinct speech rhythms and syntax, generated from a fundamentally English speech pool, as is Black English. The English learned and spoken by the sons and daughters of Spanish-speaking immigrants, most but not all of Mexican origin, throughout the American West and Southwest, is often neither English nor Spanish but something other, a *tertium quid* which leans first to one, then to the other of its source languages, never fully one or the other. Bilingualism in the Southwest usually means not the calculated mastery of two separate and distinct languages but rather the inventive and often precarious spanning of an officially disparaged, linguistic free-fire zone between them. Nowhere is the hazard and creative challenge of this linguistic situation more apparent than in the attempts of Chicano poets and fiction writers to evolve effective and authentic styles of literary expression, within or against the mainstream stylistic traditions of Mexico and/or the U.S.

In an acute assessment of the parameters of Chicano literary "space" within Anglo culture published in the midpoint of the last decade, Juan Bruce-Novoa says the following about the linguistic resources of the Chicano writer:

> As for our language, it . . . is neither Spanish
> or English, not bilingual. We do not go from
> one to the other, nor do we keep them separate.
> The two are in dynamic tension creating a new,
> interlingual "language." Ricardo Sanchez calls
> it the tertiary principle. I prefer the term
> interlingual, because as Ricardo himself has
> demonstrated, the two languages fragment into
> types of Spanish and English, and what the Chicano
> speaks is the product of many fragments. Using
> the same principle . . . Chicanismo is the sum
> total of all our modes of expression and no one
> alone. (Bruce-Novoa, 1975, p. 28)

This interlingual tension among fragments, Bruce-Novoa
asserts, is precisely the image and appropriate medium
of the Chicano writer's cultural position.

> We are neither [Mexican nor North American]
> as we are not Mexican-American. I propose
> that we are the space (not the hyphen) between
> the two, the intercultural nothing of that
> space. We are continually expanding that
> space, pushing the two out and apart as we
> build our own separate reality, while at the
> same time creating strong bonds of interlocking
> tension that hold the two in relationship.
> (ibid., p. 27)

This sense of being between-ness, of an identity and
experience which must be asserted first as a no-thing,
as neither this nor that but a newness, was not easily
or readily arrived at in Chicano fiction, and its
implications are still being explored. Bruce-Novoa's
formulation makes the role of language style in Chicano
experience evident: it is both the key to and the
mystery of that experience, for by understanding the
meaning and dimensions of the language(s) he speaks he
will understand the space of existence he occupies and,
therefore, who he is. In a real sense, the much-touted
search for identity in Chicano literature is the metaphor
of a search for an authentic interlingual writing style
(not vice versa), and only those writers who have
seriously undertaken the second search have been given
serious consideration, by Chicano readers, as guides in
the first.

   What these considerations suggest is that the
analysis of language style in Chicano literature, though
at first glance it might appear a marginal and pedantic
exercise, could provide the royal road into a given
writer's deepest beliefs, convictions, intuitions, and
fears about his or her existential space as Chicano and
as human, thrown toward death in a life of particularly
focused and restrained choices; could provide, in short,

the clearest window to his or her unique vision of
Chicanismo.

The study of literary style is always in some degree
the analysis of three factors: choice, deviation from
the norm, and personal or representative expression in a
range of language use which both participates in and
transcends the commonality of use. Style is a specifically literary, as opposed to linguistic, phenomenon in
that it identifies the expression of a superior particu-
larity rather than a universality of utterance. While a
literary work must always rise against the background of
a common speech (Chaucer's "dialect spoken in and within
50 miles of London"), the study of its style is the study
of precisely that rising, its patterns of expressive
deviation which reflect the precise choices of its
composer. Style is *parole* rather than *langue*. The view
and challenge of style analysis, once linguistic patterns
have been identified and described, is to explain in
terms of the work's overall aesthetic economy, its unity
of form, performance, and intent, why those choices were
necessary and what they reveal. In his much reprinted
"Prolegomena to the Analysis of Prose Style," Richard
Ohmann argues, convincingly, that stylistic choice no
longer makes sense to us as selection among a variety of
cosmetic alternatives for saying the same thing. This
does not mean style is an obviated or meaningless concept; on the contrary, Wittgenstein, Whorf, and other
modern semanticists (considerably reinforced now by the
ephebes of Heidegger and their philosophical hermeneutics)
suggest a complex of interdependence among language,
thought, fact, and even cosmology (and being itself in
Heidegger's messianic formulations) which grants the act
of linguistic discrimination an almost sacred aura:
style as the untouchable, untranslatable perfection of
saying, of exactly the right words in exactly the right
order. But all stylistic choice, Ohmann points out, must
take place within the constraints of a language community
and can be attributed reliably to authorial intent (or
textual performance) only when it parts from or sur-
passes those constraints through the patterns of the
writer's "epistemic choices."

> What is relevant to the study of style is the
> fact that any language persuades its speakers
> to see the universe in certain set ways, to the
> exclusion of other ways. It thereby limits the
> possibilities of choice for any writer, and the
> student of style must be careful not to ascribe
> to an individual the epistemic bias of his
> language. A writer cannot escape the boundaries
> set by his tongue, except by creating new words,
> by uprooting normal syntax or by building metaphors,
> each of which is a new ontological discovery.
> Yet, even short of these radical linguistic

activities, an infinite number of meaningful
choices remain to be made by the writer. . . .
Any . . . pattern of expression, when repeated
with unusual frequency, is the sign of a habit of
meaning, and thus of a persistent way of sorting
out the phenomena of experience. And even single
occurrences of linguistic oddities, especially in
crucial places, can point out what might be
called temporary epistemologies.

Here, then, is one way in which the term
"style" is meaningful, one kind of *choice* which
really exists for the author. (Ohmann, 1959,
p. 43)

Certainly, it would be difficult to imagine a body of
literary texts which more immediately, graphically, and
explicitly demonstrates the epistemic function of the
writer's stylistic choices than Chicano literature. For
the bilingual writer, escaping the boundaries of English
and Spanish is a daily necessity (as it is in some
degree, however small, for all of us who live in the
Southwest) of his or her experience, and neologisms,
uprooted syntax, and metaphor-building are the indispensable tools of the bilingual writer's profession -
under the guises of code-switching, word borrowing, and
oral interpretation.

If, then, we examine the prose styles of several
Chicano novels, narratives composed by authors of Chicano
background and treating characters and events from the
same culture, what do we find? It is my purpose to
demonstrate, by means of brief discussions of select
fictional scenes, that stylistic analysis may be a
particularly profitable and penetrating mode of critical
reading for exposure of the rich linguistic and aesthetic
resonances in which a novel like *The Road to Tamazunchale*
and a poem like "El Louie" abound, so obvious to even
the minimally bilingual and so invisible to the vastly
monolingual North American public. Specifically, I
propose that even a cursory review of the English used
by Chicano writers over the past two decades reveals
(1) the evolution of a growing awareness of "epistemic
choice" in language resources actually available in the
process of composition; (2) that the struggle for an
adequate literary language, one which does not falsely
delimit the image of Chicano experience within the
epistemological framework of Anglo-American language, is
at the heart of the unique genius which Chicano literature demonstrates; and (3) that just as Bruce-Novoa's
description of the Chicano writer's idiom as a dynamic
interlingual tension between fragments of English and
Spanish is the image of "the intercultural nothing" of
Chicano existence - a nothing, Bruce-Novoa points out,
pregnant with infinite and simultaneous possibility - so
stylistic awareness and analysis of that idiom's

interlingual features is our window to the being which
that no-thing becomes.

Ohmann asserts that beyond the questions of
epistemic choice which stylistic analysis seeks to
describe, it must also take account of the habitual
qualities of feeling, of emotion, as these generate the
unique expressive and persuasive tone of the essay,
novel, story, etc. No question for the Chicano author
is more implicitly fraught with emotional tension, and
bristling with an array of word choices that are at
bottom epistemological, than the question of his or her
use of English as a creative medium. In order to sell
in North America, books must be written in English; how
does one represent honestly, authentically, and fully a
Spanish or bilingual experience only in the alien language of the dominant social and economic class? What
compromises are inevitable and what stylistic strategies
can be employed to minimize or outwit those compromises?
How does one manipulate the matrix language (English) to
express the experience of the core language (Spanish),
especially considering that the latter is itself often a
dialect (caló, "border" Spanish, regional dialect, etc.)
deeply buried within the matrices of Mexican and
Castilian Spanish.

In the opening scene of José Antonio Villarreal's
Pocho (1959) the father of protagonist Richard Rubio,
Juan Rubio, shoots a Spaniard in a Cd. Juárez bar over
a bar girl. The purpose of this scene and of nearly all
of Chapter One is to define the image of revolutionary
machismo which Juan Rubio personifies and which functions
always in the background of Richard's childhood and
struggle to maturity. The scene takes place in Mexico,
and it is obvious that all the principals must be
speaking Spanish in the "original" event of which this
written account presumes to be the artistic "imitation."
Only one phrase occurs in Spanish, "*¿Qué quieres?*," but
a number of expressions are clearly phrased as
translations from an imaginary Spanish original. An
especially common pattern is an adjective followed by
the indefinite pronoun "one" to translate a variety of
Spanish nouns and pronouns for which there is no one-
word equivalent in English: "He is a bad one!"; "This
one stays with me"; "Can you not hear, deaf one?"
Somewhat speculatively we could reconstruct the
nonexistent originals as: "*¡Es malo!*"; "*Esta se queda
conmigo*"; "*¿No me oyes, sorda?*" Only the first of these
might naturally occur in normal English speech; the
other two would almost certainly come out as "She stays
with me" and "Are you deaf?" or "What are you, deaf?"
Then, as the insults precede the bullets, these phrases
occur: "'The peón has larger balls than the city-bred
gauchupín'" and "'Son of the great mother whore!'" which
we might reconstruct as "*El peón tiene los huevos más*

grandes que el gauchupín del barrio" or "*El peón es más huevon que el gauchupín del barrio*" and as "*¡Hijo de la gran puta madre!*" But Villarreal has drawn his epistemological line, performed a code switch, at the words *peón* and *gauchupín* which might have easily been rendered as "peasant" and "Spaniard" - at the expense, of course, of all the rich cultural nuances of pride and disdain so essential to those words. Not depending on the audience, Villarreal later makes those attitudes explicit in the conversation between Rubio and General Fuentes. Another device is the literal rendition of idiomatic Spanish phrases or metaphoric expressions. "I have -- years," for the Spanish "Tengo -- años," is used often in place of the normal English "I am -- years old." When Richard is born his father tells his sisters, "Your mother has given light," a literal rendition of the metaphoric *dar luz*.

Such examples could be multiplied. None are particularly original; the latter device especially was used by Hemingway in *For Whom the Bell Tolls* to lend an air of exotic rusticity to his characterizations of the Spanish guerrillas, especially of the gypsy woman, Pilar. To the bilingual reader all of the stylistic devices I've mentioned are immediately obvious. What may not be so obvious is the way in which Villarreal's epistemic choice to resolve the matrix/core language dilemma with this strategy of a translation illusion implicates him in a network of aesthetic choices which reach into nearly every structural element of the novel. Take the narrator's stance. *Pocho* is told in the third person, a *Bildungsroman* in which the protagonist enjoys the complete and unrestrained sympathy of the narrator. In electing to tell Richard's story to an English audience - an Anglo audience - Villarreal must assume a vast ignorance about the context, values, history, symbols, and emotional habits of Richard's Chicano culture, all of which must be explained if Richard is to be understood and taken to heart by that audience. Consequently the need for the long-winded, discursive narrator who rambles on in summaries and digressions about Richard's father's values, Mexican catholicism, the history of the pachuco. Given the epistemic choice, however, with which the novel begins, it is difficult to see what other narrative option Villarreal could have had; how could a first person narrator have supplied all this explanation about himself without swallowing the book utterly?

But even this translating narrator (both linguistically and culturally) chokes at certain inviolable limits. The choice *not* to use English in certain expressions, that is, to break the translation illusion and switch codes, is perhaps a more obviously epistemological choice in that it identifies a limit to

the resources of English for the Chicano artist. *Peón*
and *gauchupín* from the above scene are ready examples.
The play of insult around the word *peón* between Juan
Rubio and the Spaniard leads into the direct affront of
the word *gauchupín*: "You need not associate with
peones," says the Spaniard to the bar girl seated with
Juan Rubio. "The peón has larger balls than the city-
bred gauchupín," Rubio replies. The Spaniard's casual
disdain is transformed through the same word into Rubio's
grotesque arrogance. Perhaps "redneck" could provide
something of a cultural analogue - but not a
translation - in American English. Behind these words
is the consciousness that *peones* made the Revolution,
part of which was the occasional unrestrained massacre
of Spaniards. These things, Villarreal chose to believe,
cannot be translated and must be learned, even by Anglo
readers, in the original.

Richard's father, in fact, becomes for the narrator
of *Pocho* the living symbol of Mexican Spanish and his
decline from an almost superhuman revolutionary patriot
to a paunchy, bitter, exploited farm worker runs directly
parallel to Richard's growing ambition to become an
artist, a writer, one who masters the alien tongue of a
yet unconquered identity.

> "Silence!" roared Juan Rubio. "We will not
> speak the dog language in my house!" They
> were at the supper table.
> "But this is America, Father," said
> Richard. "If we live in this country, we must
> live like Americans."
> "And next you will tell me that those are
> not tortillas you are eating but bread, and
> those are not beans but *hahm an' ecks*."
> "No, but I mean that you must remember
> that we are not in Mexico. In Mexico --"
> "*Hahm an' ecks*," his father interrupted.
> (Villarreal, 1959, p.133)

Juan Rubio knows that "bread" cannot say "tortilla" and
"ham and eggs" cannot become "huevos con jamón"; the
cuisine of the culture lives in its words. Rubio knows
the "correct" name for things, but it is a defeated
knowledge, a knowledge to which "America" is somehow
opposed. Again the conversation is presented as a
translation from Spanish; Juan Rubio says "and" in one
sentence and "an'" in another when he is actually
speaking the "dog language." This scene, and in some
ways the entire novel, is an exploration of the tragic
irony and ambivalence implicit in Rubio's first
sentence. "We will not speak the dog language," he says
in the vocabulary, syntax, and grammar of the dog
language itself. It is, of course, the narrator's
irony and ambivalence, not Juan Rubio's. By no accident

is *Pocho* a *bildungsroman* of the young artist, as are a
number of other early Chicano fictional works, nor are
they less resonantly symbolic of the Chicano struggle
for being so. The struggle with the irony and
expressive ambivalence of Juan Rubio's roaring declara-
tion is the struggle for Chicano identity itself; the
struggle for a language *is* a struggle for exact, dis-
criminating, and authentic identity, and in that
struggle the writer finds him- or herself willy-nilly in
the vanguard. Many will no longer find Richard Rubio's
answer viable (nor likewise Villarreal's aesthetic
strategy of the translation illusion and its attendant
network of stylistic and epistemic choices) but the
novel is an honest and integral effort to account for
its own style and being.

By the time Rudolfo Anaya's *Bless Me, Ultima*
appeared in 1972 a sufficient public for artistic production had developed within and around the Chicano
community itself to support enterprises such as Tonatiuh
International which published the novel. No longer did
Chicano authors presume they had first and foremost to
address an alien, monolingual audience. The tone of
explanation almost totally disappears and the expressive
purpose comes clearly to dominate the shape of stylistic
devices. The translation illusion strategy is still
fundamental, but it is less obvious in the English style
and can usually be detected only in contextual details
of plot and characterization. "All of the older people
spoke only in Spanish, and I myself understood only
Spanish. It was only after one went to school that one
learned English," the narrator informs us in the first
chapter. We can presume, therefore, that every scene
in which adults predominate is "originally" in Spanish.
Except in school, of course: "'¡A la veca!' 'What does
that mean?' Miss Violet asked. 'It means okay!'"
(Anaya, 1972, p. 145). Or "'Gosh, okay, let's go!'"
exclaim the protagonist's older sisters on the morning
of his first day of school. "'Ay! What good does an
education do them,' my father filled his coffee cup,
'they only learn to speak like Indians. Gosh, okay,
what kind of words are those?'" (ibid., p. 50) Without
such specific indications there would be almost no
textual clue that a generational language shift is
occurring within this culture; none of *Pocho*'s direct
translation devices are found in the English style of
Bless Me, Ultima. The only stylistic pattern that
hints at a Spanish original is a certain vague
formality of address between adults and especially from
children to adults: "'Your son lives, old man.' Ultima
said. She undid her rolled sleeves and buttoned them.
My grandfather bowed his head. 'May I send the word to
those who wait?' he asked" (ibid., p. 96). In only one
case, the conversations between Cico and Antonio

concerning the golden carp, does a similar tone occur
between children:

> "There are many gods," Cico whispered. "Gods
> of beauty and magic, gods of the garden, gods
> in our own backyards -- but we go off to foreign
> countries to find new ones, we reach to the stars
> to find new ones --"
>   "Why don't we tell others of the golden
> carp?" I asked.
>   "They would kill him," Cico whispered. "The
> god of the church is a jealous god, he cannot live
> in peace with other gods. He would instruct his
> priests to kill the golden carp --" (ibid., p. 227)

These are not phrases, however, that can be easily
reconstructed in some hypothetical but precise Spanish;
in Cico's case we cannot at all be sure the rather
stilted parallel syntax and glorified diction is actually
meant to reflect any Spanish original; there is no
compelling reason to believe Anaya intends anything more
than the direct imitation of preadolescent speech. In
other words, the stylistic limits between the fictional
transcription of direct speech and the illusion of
translation from a Spanish original become blurred in
Bless Me, Ultima. The translating narrator recedes
before a presentational one; explanation fades into
expression. What does make awareness of a Spanish original inescapable in numerous conversations is the direct
transcription (without translation) of Spanish words and
sometimes entire sentences. The formal "*buenos días le
de Dios*" salutation is used repeatedly, and in the
presentation of Ultima to Antonio's family no less than
seven phrases or full sentences (out of fourteen verbal
exchanges) are rendered in untranslated Spanish. The use
of Spanish words and phrases is a frequent device
scattered throughout the novel; a count of fifteen pages
chosen at random reveals the following frequency per
page, not counting proper names or repeated words: 6,3,
1,2,5,0,4,3,1,0,3,3,0,4,0. A closer analysis of such
expressions in two scenes, one in which the narrator
clearly functions as translator and one in which he does
not, will clarify Anaya's use of this stylistic feature.
    In Chapter 12 (all chapter numbers are given in
Spanish) a lynch mob led by Tenorio Trementina comes
after Ultima, whom Trementina accuses of having killed
his daughter by witchcraft. It is a scene deeply imbued
in every sense with the law, custom, emotion, and
expectations of the pre-Anglo New Mexican Hispanic rural
culture; given what the narrator has told us of the
language habits of this community, it is reasonable to
assume that dialogue in this scene would "originally"
have been as free of English as any passage in the book.
The narrator, in other words, must be at one of his

translation peaks. In the space of five and one-half
pages the following Spanish words, phrases, or sentences
occur once each: *¿Quién es?*; *¡La mujer que no ha pecado
es bruja, le juro a Dios!*; *¡Chinga tu madre!*; *¿Qué pasa
aquí?*; *jodido*; *mira*; while *sí* occurs four times, *bruja*
three times, and *curandera* and *cabrón* twice each for a
total of seventeen separate narrative choices to not
translate the "original" Spanish expressions of the
scene's characters. If we examine a scene of roughly
equal length from one of the school episodes where
English is presumably dominant (that is, where the translating narrator keeps his lowest profile) we find the
following. The hilarious and ill-fated Third Grade
Christmas play in Chapter *Catorce* occurs in English; if
the narrator's earlier comments about his school language
are not sufficient to demonstrate that, this little
phonetic device drives home the point: "'No play, shit!'
Abel moaned. Miss Violet came in. 'What did you say,
Abel?' 'No play, shucks,' Abel said." In six and one-
half pages the boys say *mierda*, *puto*, *jodido*, *qué* once
each, *a la veca* twice, and *cabron* and *chingada* four times
apiece, or a total of fourteen Spanish expressions in
this scene - only three less than the fully Spanish lynch
mob scene. Clearly Anaya does not distribute his Spanish
expressions only through the scenes where the original
event is imagined to have occurred in Spanish. The
differences are that in the lynch mob scene, only three
of those expressions could be classified as profane
expletives or insults while in the Christmas play scene
only one is not a profanity, *qué*. And only in the
Spanish-original scene do complete sentences in Spanish
occur.

Beyond and around these uses of Spanish in dialogue,
Anaya frequently employs another device which echoes
Villarreal's uses of *peón* and *gauchupín*: certain richly
culture-bound terms are never translated. The *Llano
estacado* which endures so vividly in the memories of
Antonio's father and of all the Márez clan is never
called the Staked Plains as it became when Texas moved
into eastern New Mexico in the 19th century; *llano* and
llaneros persists throughout the novel, likewise *vaquero*
in place of "cowboy." *Curandera* is the frequent title
for Ultima, and *compadre* and *vatos* are found here and
there. *Gabacha*, deprecatory term for "Anglo girl,"
occurs once. None are translated or specifically
explicated anywhere in the story. Anaya's final and
unique stylistic use of Spanish is in the symbolism of
the names Luna and Márez (from *mares*, seas) which the
narrator continually juggles as the conflicting names of
warring destinies.

What these various stylistic devices add up to in
Bless Me, Ultima is an aggressively bilingual mode of

presentation. Though the book is in English, a reader
with no knowledge of Spanish would be literally unable
to read the emotional intensity of the confrontation
between Antonio's father and the lynch mob or the
exuberant profanity of the boys in the Christmas play.
In essence, Anaya's narrative voice insists, you can't
know this community, can't assimilate this fictional
image, unless you are familiar with a certain number of
its linguistic habits. The author's authentic expressive purpose takes priority over any desire to explain
the background, power, or nuances of those habits. By
refusing to assume his major audience must be monolingual North Americans, Anaya broadens the range of
epistemic choices available to his expressive style -
though the strictly English resources of *Bless Me, Ultima*
are clearly inferior, in my judgment, to those of *Pocho*.
By insisting on *llano* instead of "plain," *curandera*
instead of "herbalist," *ristas* instead of "strings of
chili," *Buenos dias le de Dios* instead of "A good day to
you," *compadre* instead of "godfather," and *por dios*,
cabron, mierda, a la veca, puto, and *chingada* instead of
their equally rude Anglo Saxon analogues, Anaya is
adding to his fictional image the "temporary epistemologies" that each of these words contains.

   The first person narrator of *Bless Me, Ultima* is a
man of indeterminate age who recounts events of some two-
and-a-third years of his childhood between the ages of
six and eight or nine, the period of his acquaintance
with Ultima. This narrator is characterized in the
vaguest of terms and never clearly materializes; one must
presume, in the absence of evidence to the contrary, that
he is a figure of the artisan's consciousness attempting
to account for its own origins. But, consistent with
the stylistic tendency described above to express rather
than explain Chicano reality, this narrator speaks of
the events and characters of this moment in his life
through a style which I could only call nostalgic "rhap-
sody." Its chief characteristics are the frequent and
often abrupt use of value descriptors - "good,"
"beautiful," "free," "evil," "clean," "lovely"; and a
diction of exaggeration almost entirely free of any
ironic undercutting, sometimes reflecting exaggerated
violence:

> "Ay maldecido!" Tenorio grunted and *hurled
> himself* at Narciso. The two came together
> again, *like two rams locking horns*, and the
> bartender and the other two men had to pull
> *with all their strength* to pry them loose.
> (Anaya, 1972, p. 153)

sometimes reflecting the excessive vitality of the
children:

> Bones climbed up a stage rope and perched on a
> beam near the ceiling. He refused to come down
> and be in the play. "Booooooooo-enz!" Miss
> Violet called, "come down!" Bones *snapped down*
> *at her like a cornered dog.* "The play is for
> sissies!" he shouted. *Horse threw a chunk of a*
> *two-by-four at him* and almost clobbered him.
> The board fell and hit the Kid and *knocked him*
> *out cold.* It was funny because *although he*
> *turned white and was out, his legs kept going*
> . . . . (ibid., p. 145)

sometimes reflecting the influence of Ultima in the
emotions of young Antonio:

> Huddled *in the kitchen* we bowed our heads.
> There was no sound. "En el nombre del Padre,
> del Hijo, y el Espiritu Santo--" I felt
> Ultima's hand on my head and at the same time
> *I felt a great force, like a whirlwind, swirl*
> *about me.* I looked up in fright, thinking the
> wind would knock me off my knees. Ultima's
> *bright eyes held me still.* (ibid., p. 51)

and often reflecting the romantic sentiment of the
narrator's memories:

> "Ah, there is no freedom like the freedom of
> the llano!" my father said and breathed in the
> fresh clean air. "And there is no beauty like
> this earth," Ultima said. They looked at each
> other and smiled, and I realized that from
> these two people I had learned to love the
> magical beauty of the wide, free earth.
> (ibid., p. 217)

Another rhapsodic quality is the heavily symbolic and
ritualistic dream descriptions revolving around the
"blood" of the Lunas and Marez's, a language which for
all its symbolism nevertheless lacks specificity of
image and detail:

> It is blasphemy to scatter a man's blood on
> unholy ground, the farmers chanted. The new
> son must fulfill his mother's dream. He must
> come to El Puerto and rule over the Lunas of
> the valley. The blood of the Lunas is strong
> in him. He is a Márez, the vaqueros shouted.
> His forefathers were conquistadores, men as
> restless as the seas they sailed and as free
> as the land they conquered. His is his father's
> blood. (ibid., p. 6)

A similarly ritualistic language emerges in the episodes
of the golden carp. Finally, the language of a messianic mysticism which gathers around the image of
Ultima gives the nostalgic style its central focus:

And that is what Ultima tried to teach me, that
the tragic consequences of life can be overcome
by the magic strength that resides in the human
heart. (ibid., p. 237)

Her hand touched my forehead and her last words
were, "I bless you in the name of all that is
good and strong and beautiful, Antonio. Always
have the strength to live. Love life, and if
despair enters your heart, look for me in the
evenings when the wind is gentle and owls sing
in the hills, I shall be with you--" (ibid.,
p. 247)

All of these stylistic qualities - blurring the
limits of the narrator's translator role by code-
switching and scattering Spanish phrases homogeneously
throughout; using untranslated culture-bound Spanish
terms and symbolic names; a vaguely conceived adult
narrator who makes frequent use of heavily polarized
value descriptors; an irony-free diction of exaggeration
reflecting violence, childish vitality, and the sentiment of memory; dreamily imprecise but heavily symbolic
dream descriptions; and a language of messianic optimism
focused on the figure of Ultima - combine to produce a
fictional experience which is simultaneously expressive
and escapist. All conflict in *Bless Me, Ultima* is within
the Chicano culture itself, with two highly significant
but backgrounded exceptions: the seizure of the *llano*
by the Anglo intruders, and the distant World War from
which the older brothers return. For all the bravado
of their vaquero and conquistador heritage the Márez
clan has tragically lost its birthright, the open ranges
of Eastern New Mexico, to an alien power and is impotent
either to recover it or redirect their masculine energies
into other activities. Gabriel Márez is reduced to
repairing the westward roads of other men. The rage,
frustration, and restlessness which is Márez's legacy to
his oldest sons is romantically transferred by the
narrator to a Poesque curse of the "blood"; its true
source is the historic aggression of the dominating
Anglo culture, though the narrator summons all the
defenses of his imagination against the awareness of that
fact. The deepest, most secret, conflict in *Bless Me,
Ultima* is between the power of Ultima and the dis-
possessing power of the invaders who have emasculated the
Márez men, a conflict for which the much foregrounded
Luna-Márez disputes are only a diversionary tactic,
hence the rather wooden and insubstantial tone of these
disputes. The domestic drama of Antonio's parents is
a ritual displacement of which the now-adult narrator
has become dimly and unwillingly aware. Ultima (promise
of a potential ultimatum to the usurpers) is the fantasy
image of compensatory power through which the narrator
hopes to escape the destiny of frustration which has

fallen on his older brothers. Here is the motive and
source of the rhapsodic, nostalgic style I have described above: in his mythical retelling of the story
of Ultima, the narrator literally seeks a personal
"magic" which will either empower him to take up the
burden of the historical injustice for which he must
eventually demand redress or will grant him a peace
from that burden such as she gave to the wandering souls
of the three Comanches who had been dispossessed of
the *Llano* by the grandfather of Tellez, three souls who
are, as Antonio's dream insists, the three dark figures
of his brothers, "driven to wander by the wild sea-blood
in their veins" (ibid., p. 225). The power Ultima
wields is not a real power of the real world but an
image of promise, an image of spiritual power which the
adult Antonio sees as a promise of his salvation from
the historical injustice which has embittered his
father and seems destined to consume his brothers.

    The Road to Tamazunchale (1975) marks a more
accomplished and self-assured stage in the evolution of
Chicano prose style. Set in the East Los Angeles barrio
during contemporary times, this exquisitely crafted
little novel follows an old Chicano encyclopedia salesman, Fausto Tejada, through the last vertiginous,
desperate, and glorious week of his life. There is no
alter ego of the narrator, no voice elaborating an
image of its own origins as in *Pocho* and *Bless Me,
Ultima*. In *Tamazunchale* we find a fluency, control,
forthrightness, and transparency of style which renders
both narrator and novel credible to a degree we cannot
feel in either *Pocho* or *Bless Me, Ultima*. Credible
because this story projects an expressive image of a man
and a culture which is at once more sensory than that of
Pocho and more "real" than that of *Bless Me, Ultima*, in
spite of the incredible and wildly unrealistic turns of
its plot.

    In *Tamazunchale* the translation illusion strategy
almost entirely disappears. There is no direct comment
and only the flimsiest of stylistic evidence to suggest
that the narrator ever functions as translator of any
Spanish-original conversation. With *Tamazunchale* the
image of a lost language which the narrator presumes
his audience cannot hear or understand has been
abandoned. With the evolution of language awareness and
control (not assimilation – *Tamazunchale* is not an
assimilationist novel), the narrator's sense of
inaccessible original experience, the authentic image
of his cultural reality which he feels must be "translated," is gone. A tone of adequacy and self-contained
wholeness characterize this style. If we examine
briefly Chapter Seven, the "wetback" episode in which
Fausto plays a minor part and which stands as an
especially autonomous event in the novel, we notice the

following. First, though the gathering of barrio
residents around the body of the young *mojado* which the
children find in the riverbed and their subsequent
dealings with him are scenes as deeply imbued with the
narrator's sense of Chicano values as is the lynch mob
scene in *Bless Me, Ultima*, we cannot with any certainty
say, as we can in both *Pocho* and *Bless Me, Ultima*, that
the narrator requires us to imagine a scene transpiring
"originally" in some other linguistic form than that in
which he has rendered it. There are no literal translation devices which call attention to some idiomatic
Spanish expression, as in *Pocho*. The children and even
the adults speak in common, colloquial English phrases:
"'I'm telling!' the other boy said, backing away"
(Arias, 1975, p. 57). "'No,' Tiburcio said. 'Leave
him alone, he's been through enough. Next you'll want
to take off his clothes'" (ibid., p. 58). "'How can
you tell?' Smaldino asked" (ibid., p. 59). (This last
question is an especially telling note on the cultural
ambience as it occurs in response to Fausto's assertion
that the dead young man is a "wetback." As other
commentaries make clear, the image *Tamazunchale*'s narrator spins is of an emphatically Chicano community at some
distance from Mexican "roots" and the realities of
Mexican migrants.) Untranslated Spanish phrases (code-
switches), however, do occur with only slightly less
frequency than in *Bless Me, Ultima*. In this six-page
chapter, *qué, mojado, mija (mi hija), vato, tío, no te
apures, está bién Señora,* and *chaparrito y con una gorrita*
each occur once while the title *Señora* is used three
times. A count of such expressions on 15 pages chosen
at random gives 0,0,4,1,0,3,1,1,2,1,3,0,3 – not counting
proper names.

Most revealing of Arias's particular stylistics of
code-switching and his sense of bilingual epistemic
options is his use of "wetback"/*mojado* and his description of the naming of the corpse. The narrator of
Tamazunchale does not fix on certain key words which he
always renders in Spanish, as Anaya does with *llano* and
curandera; the epistemology of Arias's code-switching is
more varied, subtle, and at first glance even haphazard.
Chapters Seven through Eleven (pp. 57-90) all have
wetbacks/*mojados* in primary roles; from the incident of
the dead young man the story moves on to a wild scheme
(which may all be a feverish fantasy) in which old
Fausto brings hundreds of undocumented workers across
the border at Tijuana disguised as drunken U.S. sailors,
marches them north to Los Angeles where the barrio residents prepare a huge picnic to feed them and then
improvise a stage happening at the Los Feliz Theater for
the diversion of the visitors; called "The Road to
Tamazunchale," the play shows an imaginary busload of
people on their way to the semi-legendary village of

Tamazunchale which seems to be death, but only for those
who "pretend" to be dead: "Once we're there, we're free,
we can be everything and everyone. If you want, you can
even be nothing" (ibid., p. 90). At the close actors
and audience, including the horde of Mexican guests, all
march up a stage ramp into the sky, "and eventually all
were lost, diminished, gone between the horizon and the
stars."

    In these chapters the word "wetback" occurs three
times (pp. 59, 70, 71), "*mojado(s)*" eleven times (pp.
59, 63, 66, 67, 72, 81, 82, 83, 84, 86, 90), and
"illegals" once (p. 69). "Wetback" occurs only in the
first two of these five chapters, and only in the
descriptions of the narrative voice, never in direct
conversation among barrio residents: "Fausto turned to
the young wetback" (p. 70); "The signal was given, and
the army of wetbacks rose and started off toward Los
Angeles (p. 71); "Fausto, winking at his niece,
immediately grasped the situation. David was a wetback"
(p. 59). Only in the latter case (actually the first use
of the word in the novel) does the narrator say "wetback"
when reporting a thought process of one of his characters.
Twelve lines later on the same page the word "*mojado*"
occurs for the first time: "'You think I don't know a
mojado when I see one?'" and the semantic link is subtly
joined for the monolingual, non-Chicano audience (who
would not have understood *mojado* otherwise) without
alienating the bilingual audience whose hackles might
well rise in response to the offensive and disparaging
connotations of the Anglo word. From pp. 72 to 90 only
mojado is used, whether in conversation ("'Eva, a few
mojados isn't the world.'"), in describing a character's
thoughts ("The problem of the mojados called for something drastic, but Fausto had no idea where or how to
find a solution."), or in the descriptive voice of the
narrator alone ("Filled and belching, the mojados
wandered back to the river."). Clearly, Arias's pattern
of code-switching in the uses of "wetback"/*mojado* is
calculated to lead the reader through a transition into
bilingualism if he or she is monolingual, and to avoid
offense if he or she already knows. It is a strategy as
much artistic and educational as epistemic and provides
a concrete instance of Arias's comprehensive image of
audience which insistently reaches beyond the alien,
monolingual audience to which *Pocho* seeks to explain
Richard Rubio, and beyond the narrow Chicano audience
which Antonio Márez strives to enchant out of its
condition of social marginality and loss; Arias wants
both. This image of a universal audience governs his
epistemic choice to first project a linguistic distance
between the narrator's use of "wetback" and the
characters' use of "*mojado*" which is then collapsed as
the narrative voice shifts also to the exclusive use of

"*mojado*," the only word that adequately denotes the
unique and ambivalent balance of identity and dis-
association with which this Chicano reality views the
recent, undocumented immigrant. The shift is a calculated, efficient figure of the reader's perspective which
is forced by this stylistic use of code-switching to move
from the Anglo, outsider's view ("wetback") to the
internal, Chicano perspective of Fausto, Tiburcio, Mrs.
Rentería, and the children ("*mojado*") as the narrative
progresses.

In Chapter Seven, after the children report their
discovery of the dead youth in the riverbed, this little
scene occurs:

> "David is mine!" Mrs. Rentería shouted
> for all to hear.
> "David?" Tiburcio asked. "Since when is
> his name David? He looks to me more like a
> . . ." Tiburcio looked at the man's face.
> ". . . a Luis."
> "No, señor!" another voice cried, "Roberto."
> "Que Roberto--Robert!"
> "Antonio."
> "Henry."
> "Lupe!"
> Alex, Ronnie, Armando, Trini, Miguel . . .
> Everyone had someone.
> Meanwhile Mrs. Rentería left her neighbors
> who one by one turned away to debate the issue.
> . . . When the others returned no one noticed
> the change, for David appeared as breathtaking
> dressed as he did naked. "You're right,"
> Tiburcio announced, "his name is David . . . but
> you still can't have him." (Arias, 1975, p. 59)

The reader already knew the outcome of this little
naming ritual, since in the first sentence of the
chapter the reader is told, "Mrs. Noriega's grandchildren
discovered David in the dry riverbed" (ibid., p. 57).
He is destined, the narrator seems to suggest, to this
Anglo-Jewish name, even though he "looks like a Luis."
Mrs. Rentería wants a David and even a corpse will
do - especially a corpse will do because there is no
David from the South such as she imagines. This poor,
dead illegal is no more David than he is alive. The
irony of his naming is another resonance of the various
ironies of which the chapter is constructed. "They all
agreed it was death by drowning. That the river was
dry occurred only to the children, but they remained
quiet. . . " (ibid., p. 58). So dry, in fact, that when
the barrio residents return him to the riverbed after
a three-day "honeymoon" with Mrs. Rentería, this
"wetback" has to be soaked down with several pitchers
of water brought from the house. He is "restored to

his former self" by an ancient ritual, but remains dead.
The name David, which the narrator mentions was also the
name of a small boy who really had drowned in the
riverbed years before when an unexpected cloudburst had
filled it, serves everyone's needs but his own.

The ironies of this chapter are variations of
Tamazunchale's most significant and characteristic
stylistic feature, the breakdown of traditional realist
and modernist narrative devices for separating "illusion"
and "reality" in fictional structure. Here is Arias's
deepest yet perhaps least obvious influence from the
Spanish. Despite his apparent commitment to English as
a creative medium, he is in this regard the most "Latin"
of Chicano authors; his artistic apprenticeship has been
as much with Borges, Quiroga, d'Assis, Juarroz, Donoso,
Benedetti, Garcia Marquez, Rulfo, and Fuentes as with
Hemingway, Joyce, Faulkner, Lawrence, Mailer, Updike,
or Bellow. It is from these Latin masters that
Tamazunchale takes its post-Modern techniques and
effects: a central character - Marcelino, the Inca
alpaca-herder - who originates as the sound of a flute
in Fausto's mind, then appears with a herd of alpaca on
the LA Freeway (he'd gotten lost in the Andes), but is
not actually seen by anyone else in the story until
Chapter Six when he appears in Fausto's bathtub and is
thereafter one more "person" in the barrio family; a
continual blending of "actual" and dream events in the
life of the protagonist (Fausto's trip to Peru, his
racing trip to Mexico, his smuggling operation, and the
whole Los Feliz Theater show); fantastic events depicted
in "realistic" detail (the little cloud which blows all
about the barrio dropping snow here and there); and
dead characters who act alive (Fausto's wife Eva and
Fausto himself in the transcendental picnic of
Chapter Thirteen when people become foxes, chrysanthemums,
a dog's howl, a rustle of wind, and cars prance like
horses). As though to confirm this influx of Latin
American narrative style which numerous critics have
observed in *Tamazunchale*, Arias has referred to a taco
vender he once observed in Michoacan as a model of
artistic performance. Describing how this "Señor
Chivo" heckled, teased, and challenged his customers,
Arias notes that his "jiving, cabuleando . . . style of
expressing language and experience, this exchange of
assaults and retreats, glimpses of truth and untruth,
this game-playing with reality" offers the image of a
truly epistemic alternative to the crisp, reductive,
journalistic prose style so common in American English:
"I'm annoyed when someone says they can explain or
understand another person completely, as if they were
writing *Time* or *Newsweek* epithets: 'Juan Valera, the
balding, 40-year-old misogynist from Tijuana.' Poor
guy. He's now relegated to the 'known' world of facts.

No mystery, no complexity, no questions. We can drop him
and go on to the next item" (Arias, 1976). Having worked
as a reporter with the *Buenos Aires Herald*, as a stringer
whose exclusives have appeared in *The New York Times* and
whose commentaries (most recently on the Falklands/
Malvinas war) continue to appear in *The Los Angeles Times*,
Arias's acquaintance with English journalistic style, the
proving ground of so many American novelists, is intimate,
thorough, and professional. He teaches journalism. But
the shape-shifting, double-jointed realities of Chicano
experience cannot be encompassed, in his opinion, by
that realistic, straightforward, and essentially naive
prose style. The mysteries, complexities, and questions
of a Fausto Tejada require the shape-shifting narrative
techniques which can at present only be learned in
Spanish. Surely some part of the critical excitement
with which this little novel was received by the Chicano
journals is the realization that the interlingual space
which its style defines, the "intercultural nothing"
which it ascribes to Chicano reality is something considerably more than a river zone between Mexico and the
U.S.; it is a space which can reach as far as the Andes
and as deep as *Don Quixote*, taking Hollywood in stride
between them.

There are three passages of "advice" passed between
characters at crucial moments in each of the three novels
under discussion, three messages which provide a sum-
marizing view of the stylistic intent and accomplishment
of these three works. After a climactic, violent family
scene in Chapter Ten of *Pocho*, Juan Rubio gives his son
a parting blessing; both father and son are recovering
from the trauma of their first physical confrontation,
and Richard has now told Rubio for the first time of
his aspiration to be a writer.

> "Do you want that more than anything?"
> "Yes, my father. More than anything,
> and forgive me if I put that before you and
> my mother."
> "There is nothing to forgive," said
> Juan Rubio. "Only, never let anything stand
> in your way of it, be it women, money,
> or -- what people talk about today -- position.
> Only that, promise me -- that you will be
> true to yourself, unto what you honestly
> believe is right. And, if it does not stand
> in your way, do not ever forget that you are
> Mexican." It was Juan Rubio who was now
> crying.
> "I could never forget that!" said
> Richard. (Villarreal, 1959, p. 169)

Pocho is a Mexican-American novel and its style par-
takes only of polarities - Spanish or English, Mexican

or American. Since Richard is not, cannot be, Mexican,
he must become an "American" writer, a master of Anglo
English who keeps his Spanish at a distance and incorpo-
rates it into that English only through clearly identifiable stylistic devices in which a tendency toward literal
translation rather than code-switching predominates to
the point of echoing that classic English platitude of
Shakespeare's Polonius, "To thine own self be true."
Again, the irony of that advice in the mouth of Juan
Rubio is a figure of the tragic irony of polarities in
which the narrator sees Richard trapped. ". . . and
forgive me if I put that before you and my mother"; since
as we have seen in the symbolic economy of the novel the
father is intimately bound to the power and priority of
Mexican Spanish as an epistemological system, it is *only*
by putting "that" - the professional domination of Anglo
English - before his father that Richard has any hope of
success. From these authorial determinations, epistemic
choices, the style of *Pocho* has its genesis.

I have already called attention to the final words
of Ultima to Antonio in *Bless Me, Ultima*, the blessing
from which the novel takes its title:

> I bless you in the name of all that is good
> and strong and beautiful, Antonio. Always
> have the strength to live. Love life, and
> if despair enters your heart, look for me
> in the evenings when the wind is gentle and
> owls sing in the hills, I shall be with you.
> (Anaya, 1972, p. 247)

The romantic sentimentality of this prose style - light
years distant from the verbal brutalities of *An American
Dream* or *Executioner's Song*, from the despairing
jocularity of *Giles Goatboy*, or the adolescent meta-
physics of *Slaughterhouse Five* - can be taken seriously
only if its focus and image of audience are held in
mind, only if we remember the social background of loss
and marginality and despair against which Ultima speaks
and against which the "blessing" of her book rises up.
That is, in speaking strictly to a Chicano audience
whose historical and psychological needs are adjudged to
be distinct and separate from those of the dominant
language class, Anaya can generate a deviational prose
style calculated to serve those needs. The nostalgic,
rhapsodic English style in which the voice of the
dying Ultima is cast focuses her advice on that segment
of the Chicano audience (of which young Antonio is the
embryonic symbol) which is actively searching for its
most fundamental images of cultural integrity and power.
It is a voice neither credible nor comprehensible to
the monolingual Anglo reader. Withdrawn into a
gestational isolation, the voice of *Bless Me, Ultima*
proclaims a romantic detachment from the dominating

Anglo styles, as its narrative enacts a corresponding
detachment from the dominant cultural mores, scientific
values, medical arts, and reality principles of the
matrix language.

Finally, in the magical tragedy of *The Road to
Tamazunchale* a new voice of confidence, promise, and
assurance speaks through its protective layers of
shape-shifting and disguise. Within the play "The Road
to Tamazunchale" in Chapter Eleven (of the novel *The
Road to Tamazunchale*) the following dialogue occurs
on stage between two actors, an "old man," who is
"probably Robert, Smaldino's eldest son," with his face
patterned by black crayon wrinkles, and a little girl in
pigtails:

> "Mijita . . . everyone should go to
> Tamazunchale."
> "What's it like?"
> "Like any other place. Oh, a few things
> are different . . . if you want them to be."
> "What do you mean?"
> "Well, if you see a bird, you can talk to
> it and it'll talk back. If you want something,
> it's yours. If you want to be an apple, think
> about it and you might be hanging from a tree
> or you might be held in someone's hand, maybe
> your own."
> "Could I be a flower?"
> "You can be the sun."
> "How 'bout the moon?"
> "You can be the stars. . . ."
> "What if I want to be me again?"
> "Mijita, you can be a song of a million
> sounds, or you can be a little girl listening
> to one sound."   (Arias, 1975, p. 89)

The old man (who is not really an old man), the girl
perceives, is speaking of death (which is not really
death): "Tio, are we going to die?" she asks, planting
the communal first person plural pronoun squarely
against the one reality which ought to cut through every
layer of dramatic, narrative, fictional, and personal
illusion; yes, mijita, the reader responds to that small
voice, "we" are going to die, book, paper, print,
author and, perhaps lastly, reader. But Arias's old
man confounds that priority, that "natural" response,
with an assertion as baffling as it is certain.

> "No one dies in Tamazunchale."
> "No one?"
> "Well, some people do, but they're only
> pretending."
> "Like in the movies?"
> "Not exactly. They do die, they're even
> buried and people cry, and some of the men

become very drunk. . . ."
                . . .
        "Then what happens to the dead people?"
        "They usually see how stupid it is to
die, so they come out of the earth and do
something else."
        "Do we have to die if we don't want to?"
        "Not unless you're curious. That's what
happens to most people. They have to try it
once." (ibid., pp. 89-90)

Are we going to die? "No one dies in Tamazunchale"
(Tamazunchale: the play, the novel, the liberated
fictive imagination, the mystery which human imagination
itself is only the figure of). Do we have to die if we
don't want to? "Not unless you're curious." With
these questions Chicano fiction addresses a "we" for
which the labels "Anglo" and "Chicano" become just that,
useless labels. This is decidedly *not* to say, as one
reviewer has, that *The Road to Tamazunchale* "transcends
Chicano experience." Precisely the contrary. I
believe the fictional voice which speaks in this imaginary drama could only have come from the interlingual
space of Chicano experience. Its tone of familiar
commerce with the dead - reflected in the easy presence
of Fausto's dead wife Eva, in the David episode, in
Marcelino (who seems like a visible spirit), and cul-
minating in the supra-rational certainties of this
dialogue and the vision of Fausto's wake in the final
chapter - owes more to the memories of the Mexican Day
of the Dead festival (November 2) and its magnificent
ofrendas of candies and sweet breads, to the vivid
intercession of a multitude of *santos* in daily affairs,
to the skeletal cartoons of Posada, and the poem "Muerte
sin fin" of Jose Gorostiza than to anything in the North
American Gothic derived from Edgar Allen Poe. On the
other hand, *Tamazunchale*'s conquest of despair, its tone
of assurance beyond everything, so evident in the above
dialogue, echoes directly that sublime Anglo-American
prophecy of Walt Whitman: "To die is different from
what anyone supposed, and luckier" ("Song of Myself,"
I.130). Only in that distinctly interlingual Chicano
space, of but not in both Mexican and North American
linguistic and folk traditions, could a fictional voice
in the 1970s find the stylistic grace with which to
avoid, to sidestep capably and convincingly the flat
realistic "yes" we must feel looming in the little
girl's primeval questions: Are we all going to die?
Do we have to die if we don't want to? And that,
raising yet another faithful and *fidedigna* illusion in
the face of death's dominion, is what the art of
narration has always been for.

REFERENCES

Anaya, Rudolfo A. 1972. *Bless Me, Ultima*. Berkeley, Calif.:
Tonatiuh International.

Arias, Ron. 1975. *The Road to Tamazunchale* Reno, Nev.: *West
Coast Poetry Review*.

_____. 1976. "El Señor del Chivo." *Journal of Ethnic
Studies*, 3 (4): 58-60.

Babb, Howard S., ed. 1972. *Essays in Stylistic Analysis*. New
York: Harcourt Brace Jovanovich.

Bruce-Novoa, Juan. 1975. "The Space of Chicano Literature."
De Colores, I (4): 22-42.

Córdova, Roberto H. 1977. "Syntax and Bilingual Chicano Poetry."
Ph.D. dissertation, University of Colorado, Boulder.

de la Fuente, Patricia, et al., eds. 1982. *riverSedge* IV (2),
"Chicano Collection."

Empringham, Toni, ed. 1981. *Fiesta in Aztlan: Anthology of
Chicano Poetry*. Santa Barbara, Calif.: Capra Press.

Grajeda, Rafael. 1980. "The Pachuco in Chicano Poetry: The
Process of Legend-Creation." *Revista Chicano-Riqueña*,
VIII (4): 45-59.

Jiménez, Francisco, ed. 1979. *The Identification and Analysis
of Chicano Literature*. New York: Bilingual Press/Editorial
Bilingüe.

Keller, Gary D. "The Literary Stratagems Available to the Bilingual
Chicano Writer." In Jiménez, ed., *The Identification and
Analysis of Chicano Literature*. New York: Bilingual Press/
Editorial Bilingue, pp. 263-316.

Ohmann, Richard M. 1959. "Prolegomena to the Analysis of Prose
Style." In Babb, ed., *Essays in Stylistic Analysis*. New
York: Harcourt Brace Jovanovich, pp. 35-49.

Sommers, Joseph, and Tomas Ybarra-Frausto, eds. 1979. *Modern
Chicano Writers*. Englewood Cliffs, N.J.: Prentice-Hall.

Villarreal, José Antonio. 1959. *Pocho*. Garden City, N.Y.:
Doubleday.

SECTION V:
A BRIEF ANNOTATED
BIBLIOGRAPHY
ON CHICANO ENGLISH

A BRIEF ANNOTATED BIBLIOGRAPHY
ON CHICANO ENGLISH

Allan Metcalf
MacMurray College
Jacksonville, Illinois

In the past two decades much has been published on the English spoken by Chicanos, but the mass of publication is more like an iceberg than a mountain; it is not readily apparent, and is sometimes difficult to find. Little of it appears in the standard journals: hardly anything in Orbis or American Speech, for example, and nothing in Language. Instead, the researcher will become accustomed to typewriter-prepared pages in irregular journals, collections and monographs put out by universities and research institutes in the Southwest. This does not seem to be the result of a conspiracy by mainstream linguists, but rather the consequence of eagerness for information about Chicanos and their language at those universities and institutes; those who study Chicano English sometimes find that the opportunities for immediate publication of their research results are greater than their production of new results, even without taking time to offer articles to standard journals.

Another consequence of ready publication, and a great benefit to the researcher, is the number of works that turn out to be reviews of previous research. Brennan and Brennan (1981a), for example, review not only their previous work but also that of Ryan and Carranza. Amastae (1981), for another example, presents the same data as in McQuade (1980). Reading a number of such recapitulations will give the researcher a good sense of progress to date, although Jacob Ornstein's caution of a decade ago (1974, p. 30) remains valid: "The extreme difficulty of keeping abreast of the literature on sociolinguistics and bilingualism at present should not be underestimated."

The following list is of necessity selective. It emphasizes recent publications, which in turn will provide references to earlier studies.

BIBLIOGRAPHIES

Bills, Garland D., Jerry R. Craddock, and Richard V. Teschner. 1977. "Current Research on the Language(s) of U.S. Hispanos." Hispania, 60, 347-358. A bare-bones continuation of Teschner et al. (below), giving 253 items published between January 1974 and January 1977, but without classification or annotation, and omitting another 100 items "relating only in part to U.S. Hispanic language."

Teschner, Richard V., Garland D. Bills, and Jerry R. Craddock. 1975. Spanish and English of United States Hispanos: A Critical, Annotated, Linguistic Bibliography. Arlington, Va.: Center for Applied Linguistics. The 675 items include more than 40 dealing primarily with the English of Chicanos, and many others of peripheral relevance. Most are annotated in detail. The bibliography aims to be complete through 1974. An essential reference.

COLLECTIONS

Many of the individual studies (see following section) appear in special volumes dedicated to particular themes. Only studies of direct relevance to Chicano English will be mentioned here, but the other papers in a collection often provide useful background.

Barkin, Florence, and Elizabeth Brandt, eds. 1980. Speaking, Singing and Teaching: A Multidisciplinary Approach to Language Variation. Proceedings of the Eighth Annual Southwestern Areal Language and Linguistics Workshop. Tempe, Arizona: Arizona State University, Anthropological Research Papers 20. (McQuade, 1980)

Berry, J.W., and W.J. Lonner, eds. 1975. Applied
    Cross-Cultural Psychology: Selected Papers from the
    Second International Conference for Cross Cultural
    Psychology. Amsterdam: Swets and Zeitlinger.
    (Ryan, Carranza, and Moffie, 1975)

Bills, Garland D. 1974. Southwest Areal Linguistics. San
    Diego, California: San Diego State University,
    School of Education, Institute for Cultural
    Pluralism. (Metcalf 1974, Ornstein 1974, Thompson
    1974)

Blansitt, Edward L., Jr., and Richard V. Teschner, eds.
    1980. A Festschrift for Jacob Ornstein: Studies in
    General Linguistics and Sociolingistics. Rowley,
    Mass.: Newbury House. (Doviak and Hudson-Edwards,
    1980)

Bowen, J. Donald, and Jacob Ornstein, eds. 1976. Studies
    in Southwest Spanish. Rowley, Mass.: Newbury House.
    (Cohen, 1976)

Cronnell, Bruce, ed. 1981. The Writing Needs of
    Linguistically Different Students. Proceedings of a
    conference held June 25-26, 1981. Los Alamitos,
    Calif.: SWRL Educational Research and Development.
    (Amastae, 1981; García, 1981)

DiPietro, Robert, and Edward Blansitt, Jr., eds. 1977.
    The Third LACUS Forum 1976. Columbia, S.C.: Hornbeam
    Press. (Ornstein and Dubois, 1977)

Dubois, Betty Lou, and Isabel Crouch, eds. 1976. The
    Sociology of the Language of American Women. Papers
    in Southwest English 4. San Antonio, Tex.: Trinity
    University. (Hartford, 1976)

Dubois, Betty Lou, and Bates Hoffer, eds. 1975. Papers in
    Southwest English I: Research Techniques and
    Prospects. San Antonio, Tex.: Trinity University.
    (Hoffer, 1975)

Durán, Richard P., ed. 1981. Latino Language and
    Communicative Behavior. Advances in Discourse
    Processes 6. Norwood, N.J.: ABLEX Publishing Corp.
    (McClure, 1981; Ramirez, 1981)

Fishman, Joshua A., and Gary D. Keller, eds. 1982.
    Bilingual Education for Hispanic Students in the
    United States. New York: Teachers College Press,
    Columbia University. (Elías-Olivares and Valdés,
    1982)

Gilbert, Glenn G., ed. 1970. Texas Studies in
    Bilingualism: Spanish, French, German, Czech,
    Polish, Sorbian, and Norwegian in the Southwest.
    Studia linguistica germanica 3. Berlin: de Gruyter.
    (Sawyer, 1970)

Gilbert, Glenn, ed. 1978. Problems in Educational
    Sociolinguistics. Berlin: de Gruyter. (Hoffer,
    1978)

Giles, H., ed. 1977. Language, Ethnicity, and Intergroup
    Relations. London: Academic Press. (Ryan and
    Carranza, 1977b)

Hernández-Chávez, Eduardo, Andrew D. Cohen, and Anthony F.
    Beltramo, eds. 1975. El Lenguaje de los Chicanos:
    Regional and Social Characteristics Used by Mexican
    Americans. Arlington, Va.: Center for Applied
    Linguistics. (Barker, 1974; Cohen, 1975a; Gonalez,
    1975; Lance, 1975; Sawyer, 1970)

Hoffer, Bates, and Betty Lou Dubois, eds. 1977. Southwest
    Areal Linguistics Then and Now. Papers in Southwest
    English 7. San Antonio, Tex.: Trinity University
    Press.

Hoffer, Bates, and Jacob Ornstein, eds. 1974.
    Sociolinguistics in the Southwest. San Antonio,
    Tex.: Trinity University Press.

Key, Harold, Gloria McCullough, and Janet Sawyer, eds.
    1978. SWALLOW VI: Proceedings of the Sixth
    Southwest Areal Linguistics Workshop: The Bilingual
    in a Pluralistic Society. Long Beach, Calif.:
    California State University, Long Beach. (Sanchez,
    1978)

Lozano, Anthony, ed. 1978. Proceedings of the Southwest
    Areal Language and Linguistics Workshop (SWALLOW)
    VII: Bilingual and Biliterate Perspectives.
    Boulder: University of Colorado. (McQuade, 1978)

Ornstein-Galicia, Jacob, and Robert St. Clair, eds. 1979.
    Bilingualism and Bilingual Education: New Readings
    and Insights. Papers in Southwest English 8. San
    Antonio, Tex.: Trinity University. (Jacobson, 1979;
    Ornstein-Galicia and Goodman, 1979)

Perren, G.E., and J.L.M. Trim, eds. 1971. Applications of
    Linguistics: Selected Papers of the Second
    International Congress of Applied Linguistics.
    Cambridge: Cambridge University Press. (Ornstein,
    1971)

Raffler-Engel, Walburga von, ed. 1975. Child Language.
    Special issue of Word. New York: International
    Linguistic Association. (Ornstein, Valdes-Fallis,
    and Dubois, 1976)

Redden, James E., ed. 1978. Proceedings of the Second
    International Conference on Frontiers in Language
    Proficiency and Dominance Testing. Occasional Papers
    on Linguistics 3. Department of Linguistics, Southern
    Illinois University at Carbondale. (Peña and Bernal,
    1978)

Shuy, Roger W., and Ralph W. Fasold, eds. 1973. Language
    Attitudes: Current Trends and Prospects.
    Washington, D.C.: Georgetown University Press.
    (Ryan, 1973)

Spolsky, Bernard, ed. 1972. The Language Education of
    Minority Children: Selected Readings. Rowley,
    Mass.: Newbury House. (Lance, 1970)

Willcott, Paul, and Jacob Ornstein, eds. 1977. College
    English and the Mexican American. Papers in
    Southwest English 5. San Antonio, Tex.: Trinity
    University. (Gonzalez, 1977a; Ryan and Carranza,
    1977a)

INDIVIDUAL STUDIES

Amastae, Jon. 1981. "The Writing Needs of Hispanic
    Students." In Cronnell, 1981, pp. 99-127. A study of
    Hispanic students' writing at Pan American University
    found relatively few errors, and those of the sort
    Anglo students make; Spanish interference does not
    seem a major source of error. The students, however,
    showed a low degree of syntactic elaboration, thereby
    risking less error. Sentence-combining seemed an
    appropriate focus of instruction. (See McQuade,
    1980.)

Arthur, Bradford, Dorothee Farrar, and George Bradford.
    1974. "Evaluative Reactions of College Students to
    Dialect Differences in the English of Mexican
    Americans." Language and Speech, 17: 255-276.

Barker, George C. 1974. "Social Functions of Language in a
    Mexican-American Community." Acta Americana, 5:
    185-202. Reprinted in Hernández-Chavez, Cohen, and
    Beltramo, 1975, pp. 170-182. A study of 100
    individuals of Mexican descent in Tucson found four
    types of linguistic behavior patterns correlated with
    types of social experience. Some bilinguals who wish
    to improve their relations with Anglos will deny that
    they speak Spanish.

Bills, Garland D. 1977. "Vernacular Chicano English:
    Dialect or Interference?" Journal of the Linguistic
    Association of the Southwest, 2 (2): 30-36. Examples
    of VCE features not predictable from contrastive
    analysis of English and Spanish provide evidence for
    considering it a dialect in its own right.

Brennan, Eileen M., and John S. Brennan. 1981a.
    "Measurements of Accent and Attitude toward
    Mexican-American Speech." Journal of Psycholinguistic
    Research, 10: 487-501. Gives the complete
    Accentedness Index of 18 phonological variables.

Brennan, Eileen M., and John Stephen Brennan. 1981b.
    "Accent Scaling and Language Attitudes: Reactions to
    Mexican-American English Speech." Language and
    Speech, 24: 207-221. Both Anglos and Mexican-
    Americans showed similar correlations among accent
    estimation scores, Accentedness Index (see Brennan
    and Brennan, 1981a), and status ratings. Reviews
    previous studies by Ryan and Carranza.

Chesterfield, Ray A., and Ray S. Pérez. 1981. Language
    Acquisition Among Hispanic Preschoolers in Bilingual
    Settings." The Bilingual Review/La revista bilingüe,
    8: 20-27. Testing 247 four-year-old Hispanic children
    in Head Start programs, the authors were surprised to
    find bilingualism "a much rarer event than is
    generally believed"; only 29 were bilingual. They
    performed as well as the others.

Cohen, Andrew D. 1975a. "Assessing Language Maintenance in
    Spanish-Speaking Communities in the Southwest." In
    Hernández-Chavez, Cohen, and Beltramo, 1975,
    pp. 202-219.

Cohen, Andrew D. 1975b. "Mexican-American Evaluational
    Judgments about Language Varieties." Linguistics,
    136: 33-51.

Cohen, Andrew D. 1975c. A Sociolinguistic Approach to
    Bilingual Education: Experiments in the American
    Southwest. Rowley, Mass.: Newbury House.

Cohen, Andrew D. 1976. "The English and Spanish Grammar of
    Chicano Primary School Students." In Bowen and
    Ornstein, 1976, pp. 125-164. (Chapter 8 of Cohen,
    1975c.) A 1970 study of grammatical errors or
    deviations in the speech of Redwood City, California,
    Chicano students, 45 in bilngual classes, 45 in a
    "comparison" group; detailed explanation and full
    listing of types of errors.

Doviak, Martin J., and Allison Hudson-Edwards. 1980.
    "Phonological Variation in Chicano English:

Word-Final (Z)-Devoicing." In Blansitt and Teschner, 1980, pp. 82-96. Reports on fourth-graders in Albuquerque. One-third of the 3,000 examples of word-final (z) were pronounced [s]; a variable rule with a hierarchy of six phonological constraints accounts for most of the devoicing, with a following voiceless segment the greatest influence.

Dubois, Betty Lou. 1974. "Written English Communicative Competence of UTEP Chicanos: A Preliminary Report." System, 2: 49-56. Defines Chicano; gives a detailed list of errors in punctuation, spelling, grammar, and usage by Chicano college students. The errors are similar to those made by Anglo students.

Dubois, Betty Lou, and Guadalupe Valdés. 1980. "Mexican-American Child Bilingualism: Double Deficit?" Bilingual Review/La revista bilingüe,7: 1-7. Knocks over nine "straw man" postulates which have led others to the false conclusion that bilingual means a double deficit for the Chicano child learning language.

Elías-Olivares, Lucía. 1976. Language Use in a Chicano Community: A Sociolinguistic Approach. Working Papers in Sociolinguistics 30. Austin, Tex.: Southwest Educational Development Lab. In the East Austin Chicano community, speakers have access to English and four varieties of Spanish.

Elías-Olivares, Lucía, and Guadalupe Valdés. 1982. "Language Diversity in Chicano Speech Communities: Implications for Language Teaching." In Fishman and Keller, 1982, pp. 151-166. Reviews the continuum of the Chicano speech community repertoire and discusses appropriate and inappropriate approaches for teaching Spanish to Chicano bilinguals.

Flores, N. de la Zerda, and Robert Hopper. 1975. "Mexican-Americans' Evaluations of Spoken Spanish and English." Speech Monographs, 42 (2): 91-98.

Galvan, Jose L., James A. Pierce, and Gary Underwood. 1975. "Relationships between Teacher Attitudes and Differences in the English of Bilinguals." In Proceedings of Southwest Areal Linguistics Workshop IV. San Diego: Institute of Cultural Pluralism, San Diego State University.

García, Eugene E., Lento Maez, and Gustavo Gonzalez. 1981. A National Study of Spanish/English Bilingualism in Young Hispanic Children of the United States. Bilngual Education Paper Series, Vol. 4, No. 12. Los Angeles: National Dissemination and

Assessment Center, California State University, Los
Angeles. As part of a survey for Educational Testing
Service's CIRCO, 300 bilingual four-to-six-year-olds
were tested in Spanish, 300 in English. The
proportion of language switching differed by region.

García, Maryellen. 1981. "Spanish-English Bilingualism in
the Southwest." In Cronnell, 1981, pp. 45-62. Gives
examples of first, second, and third generation
Mexican-Americans' English and Spanish.

Godinez, Manuel, Jr., and Mona Lindau-Webb. 1980.
"Reliable Phonetic Differences between Dialects:
Chicano and General Californian English." Paper
presented at the summer meeting of the American
Dialect Society, July 1980. Phonetics Laboratory,
University of California, Los Angeles. Spectrograms
of initial stop consonants showed significant
differences in the English of three groups of male
eleventh-graders: four Chicano monolinguals, four
Chicano bilinguals, and four Anglo monolinguals. The
bilinguals also used significantly different
voiceless stops for their English and Spanish. It is
clear that Chicano English is not simply a matter of
interference from Spanish.

Godinez, Manuel, Jr., and Ian Maddieson. 1980. "Vocalic
Differences between Chicano and General Californian
English?" Paper presented at the meeting of the
Linguistic Association of the Southwest, October
1980. Phonetics Laboratory, University of California,
Los Angeles. Spectrograms showed significant
differences in vowel quality in the English of three
groups of male eleventh graders: 15 Chicano
monolinguals, 15 Chicano bilinguals, and 15 Anglo
monolinguals. There was no significant difference
among groups in vowel duration.

González, Gustavo. 1974. "Potential Negative Interference
from a First Language: Spanish." In A
Sociolinguistic Analysis of the Armed Services
Vocational Aptitude Battery. Arlington, Va.: Center
for Applied Linguistics, pp. 59-71. Lists errors
made by Spanish-speakers learning English. Most
serious are semantic errors involving cognates.

González, Gustavo. 1975. "The Acquisition of Grammatical
Structures by Mexican-American Children." In
Hernández-Chavez, Cohen, and Beltramo, 1975,
pp. 220-237. Stages in the acquisition of Spanish
grammar from ages two through five.

González, Gustavo. 1976. "Some Characteristics of the
English Used by Migrant Spanish-Speaking Children in

Texas." Aztlan, 7 (1): 27-49. A study in 1968 of the speech of 30 elementary school children in McAllen, Texas. All were fluent in Spanish; all but four knew English, too, in most cases fluently. Details errors in grammar and choice of words, and discusses Spanish influence as source for some of the errors.

González, Gustavo. 1977a. "Persistent English Language Difficulties in the Speech of Chicano College Students." In Willcott and Ornstein, 1977.

González, Gustavo. 1977b. "Teaching Bilingual Children." In Bilingual Education: Current Perspectives, Vol. 2, Linguistics. Arlington, Va.: Center for Applied Linguistics.

Hartford, Beverly S. 1976. "Phonological Differences in the English of Adolescent Chicanas and Chicanos." In Dubois and Crouch, 1976, pp. 73-80. Studies adolescents in Gary, Indiana, whose mothers "had minimal English." Despite the absence of maternal linguistic examples, the females used prestige forms significantly more often than the males.

Hartford, Beverly S. 1978. "Phonological Differences in the English of Adolescent Female and Male Mexican-Americans." International Journal of the Sociology of Language, 17: 55-64.

Herrick, Earl M. 1977. "Spanish Interference in the English Written in South Texas High Schools." In Hoffer and Dubois, 1977, pp. 162-169. Lists typical deviations from Standard written English in writing by bilingual high school students. There were some differences from city to city and social class to social class, but no overall patterns.

Hoffer, Bates. 1975. "Towards Implicational Scales for Use in Chicano English Composition." In Dubois and Hoffer, 1975, pp. 59-71. Lists grammatical errors associated with different levels of English writing ability of students at Trinity University, San Antonio, Texas. Students often avoid the more complicated constructions. In speech, "intonation is the last interference problem to be overcome."

Hoffer, Bates. 1978. "The Acquisition of English Syntax by Mexican Americans: Grades 1-6." In Gilbert, 1978, pp. 63-71.

Jacobson, Rodolfo. 1979. "Semantic Compounding in the Speech of Mexican-American Bilinguals: A Re-examination of the Compound-Coordinate Distinction." In Ornstein-Galicia and St. Clair,

1979, pp. 145-181. Tests of upper division and graduate students, Mexican-American and Anglo, at the University of Texas at San Antonio, in word association and "deceptive cognates" showed bilingual Mexican-Americans much closer to Anglo norms than to Mexican ones.

Lance, Donald M. 1969. A Brief Study of Spanish-English Bilingualism. Final Report. Research Project ORR-Liberal Arts-15504, Texas A&M University, College Station.

Lance, Donald M. 1970. "The Codes of the Spanish-English Bilingual." TESOL Quarterly, 4: 343-351. Reprinted in Spolsky, 1970. Summarizes Lance, 1969.

Lance, Donald M. 1975. "Spanish-English Code Switching." In Hernández-Chavez, Cohen, and Beltramo, 1975, pp. 138-153. (Part of Lance, 1969.) Detailed examples and analysis of code-switching from interviews with three generations of a bilingual family in Bryan, Texas.

McClure, Erica. 1981. "Formal and Functional Aspects of the Code-switched Discourse of Bilingual Children." In Durán, 1981, pp. 69-94. Summarizes issues in and previous studies of Spanish-English code-switching. Discusses conditions of language choice for children in Head Start and kindergarten through fourth grade. Children used Spanish for commands and to comfort younger ones when hurt.

McQuade, Judy. 1978. "On Errors and Elaboration in Freshman Themes." In Lozano, 1978, pp. 122-131.

McQuade, Judy A. 1980. "Factors Affecting the Composition Performance of PAU Students." In Barkin and Brandt, 1980, pp. 227-234. Reports on a study of 155 bilingual freshman English students at Pan American University. Their syntax showed low complexity; no strong foreign language interference was evident, nor was there a related grouping of errors associated with bilinguals only. (See Amastae, 1981.)

Metcalf, Allan A. 1972. "Mexican-American English in Southern California." Western Review (Silver City, N.M.), 9 (1) (Spring): 13-21.

Metcalf, Allan A. 1974. "The Study (Or, Non-Study) of California Chicano English." In Bills, 1974, pp. 97-106.

Metcalf, Allan A. 1979. Chicano English. Language in Education: Theory and Practice 21. Arlington, Va.:

Center for Applied Linguistics. Reviews previous
studies; attempts to characterize Chicano English in
its common features and diversity; draws
implications for teachers. A review by Joyce
Penfield (Okezie) and Jack Ornstein-Galicia in
English World-Wide, 2 (1), pp. 117-121 (1981) fills
in lacunae.

Ornstein, Jacob. 1971. "Language Varieties along the
    U.S./ Mexican Border." In Perren and Trim, 1971.

Ornstein, Jacob. 1974. "The Sociolinguistic Studies on
    Southwest Bilingualism: A Status Report." In Bills,
    1974, pp. 11-33. Describes surveys and studies of
    students at the University of Texas at El Paso,
    collected under the SSSB program. Lists 14
    phonological and grammatical variants each for both
    the Spanish and the English of bilinguals in the
    area. Shows signficant interrelationships among
    sociocultural factors and language performance. By
    the time Chicanos reach college, their command of
    English is not a handicap.

Ornstein, Jacob, and Betty Lou Dubois. 1977.
    "Mexican-American English: Prolegomena to a
    Neglected Regional Variety." In DiPietro and
    Blansitt, 1977, pp. 95-107.

Ornstein-Galicia, Jacob, and Paul W. Goodman. 1979.
    "Correlating Socio-educational and Linguistic
    Variables among Chicano College Bilinguals: A
    Research Study." In Ornstein-Galicia and St. Clair,
    1979, pp. 323-352. A sample of 30 Mexican-American
    students at the University of Texas at El Paso
    performed better in English than in Spanish. English
    performance correlated significantly both with
    Spanish performance and with grade point average.
    Reports on Anglo and Chicano attitudes toward the
    language they use and hear.

Ornstein, Jacob, Guadalupe Valdes-Fallis, and Betty Lou
    Dubois. 1976. "Bilingual Child Language Acquisition
    along the U.S.-Mexican Border: The El Paso-Ciudad
    Juarez-Las Cruces Triangle." In Raffler-Engel, 1975,
    pp. 386-404. Reviews previous studies, noting that
    border pidgin has not been studied at all. Gives
    plans for investigating the complicated language
    acquisition situation. Includes a typology of
    model-sources from which children learn language;
    describes language used in various social
    circumstances.

Peña, Albar A., and Ernest M. Bernal, Jr. 1978.
    "Malpractices in Language Assessment for Hispanic

    Children." In Redden, 1978, pp. 102-108. Reviews
    mistaken assumptions about Hispanic children and
    misapplied tests; the CIRCO test for four-to-six-
    year-olds is a happy exception.

Peñalosa, Fernando. 1980. Chicano Sociolinguistics: A
    Brief Introduction. Rowley, Mass.: Newbury House. A
    review of the field, with discussions of previous
    studies.

Peñalosa, Fernando. 1981. Introduction to the Sociology
    of Language. Rowley, Mass.: Newbury House.

Penfield, Joyce. 1980. "Chicano English: Interference
    and/or Community Norms. Where Do We Go From Here?"
    Paper presented at the meeting of the Linguistic
    Society, December 1980.

Politzer, Robert. 1973. "Judging Personality from Speech:
    A Pilot Study of Effects of Bilingual Education on
    Attitudes toward Ethnic Groups." R & D Memo 106.
    Center for Research and Development in Teaching,
    Stanford University, Stanford, California.

Politzer, Robert L., and Arnulfo Ramirez. 1973a. "Judging
    Personality from Speech: A Pilot Study of the
    Attitudes toward Ethnic Groups of Students in
    Monolingual Schools." R & D Memo 107. Center for
    Research and Development in Teaching, Stanford
    University, Stanford, California.

Politzer, Robert L., and Arnulfo G. Ramirez. 1973b. "An
    Error Analysis of the Spoken English of
    Mexican-American Pupils in a Bilingual School and a
    Monolingual School." Language Learning, 23: 39-62.
    The children (120, kindergarten through third grade,
    Redwood City, Calif.) from both schools performed
    about the same; their deviations from Standard
    English are discussed in detail.

Ramirez, Arnulfo G. 1981. "Language Attitudes and the
    Speech of Spanish-English Bilingual Pupils." In
    Durán, 1981, pp. 217-235. Teachers had negative
    attitudes to code-switching and positive attitudes to
    Standard English; inservice workshops, contrary to
    expectations, actually lowered attitudes to
    code-switching. Appendix has text of the CERAS
    Bilingual Attitude Measure.

Ramirez, Arnulfo, Eduardo Arce-Torres, and Robert
    Politzer. 1978. "Language Attitudes and the
    Achievement of Bilingual Pupils in English Language
    Arts." Bilingual Review/La revista bilingüe, 5 (3):
    190-206.

Register, Norma A. 1977. "Some Sound Patterns of Chicano
    English." Journal of the Linguistic Association of
    the Southwest, 2 (3-4): 111-122. Reports on the
    speech of 14 adult bilinguals in southern Arizona:
    -ing is often [in], for example. Relates
    pronunciation variants to characteristics of local
    Spanish as heard on AM radio as well as elicited from
    informants.

Ryan, Ellen Bouchard. 1973. "Subjective Reactions toward
    Accented Speech." In Shuy and Fasold, 1973,
    pp. 60-73.

Ryan, Ellen B., and Miguel Carranza. 1975. "Evaluative
    Reactions of Adolescents toward Speakers of Standard
    English and Mexican-American Accented English."
    Journal of Personality and Social Psychology, 31:
    855-863.

Ryan, Ellen B., and Miguel Carranza. 1977a. "Attitudes
    toward Accented English." In Willcott and Ornstein,
    1977.

Ryan, E. Bouchard, and M.A. Carranza. 1977b. "Ingroup and
    Outgroup Reactions to Mexican-American Language
    Varieties." In Giles, 1977, pp. 59-82. A review of
    previous studies, which consistently find a negative
    attitude toward Mexican-American accented English.
    There are a few exceptions; for example, Mexican-
    born high school students in a Midwestern city
    favored higher accentedness. Also reviews
    methodology of studies.

Ryan, Ellen Bouchard, and Miguel A. Carranza. 1980. "A
    Methodological Approach to the Study of Evaluative
    Reactions of Adolescents toward Speakers of Different
    Language Varieties." The Bilingual Review/La Revista
    Bilingüe, 7 (1): 19-23. Briefly summarizes previous
    studies. Chicanos in a Chicago high school did not
    prefer accented English; and the greater the accent,
    the less favorable the impression.

Ryan, Ellen B., Miguel Carranza, and R.W. Moffie. 1975.
    "Mexican-American Reactions to Accented English." In
    Berry and Lonner, 1975, pp. 174-178.

Ryan, Ellen Bouchard, Miguel A. Carranza, and Robert W.
    Moffie. 1977. "Reactions toward Varying Degrees of
    Accentedness in the Speech of Spanish-English
    Bilinguals." Language and Speech, 20: 267-273.

Sánchez, Rosaura. 1978. "Bilingualism in the Southwest."
    In Key, McCullough, and Sawyer, 1978.

Sawyer, Janet. 1970. "Spanish-English Bilingualism in San Antonio, Texas." In Gilbert, 1970, pp. 18-41. Also in Hernández-Chavez, Cohen, and Beltramo, 1975, pp. 77-98. Argues that the English of these Mexican-Americans is not a dialect, but "an imperfect state in the mastery of English." For one of the many replies to this argument, see Bills, 1977.

Teschner, Richard V. 1981. "Historical-psychological Investigations as Complements to Sociolinguistic Studies in Relational Bilingualism: Two Mexican-American Cases." Bilingual Review/La revista bilingüe, 8 (1): 42-55. Anecotal case histories of two male bilingual students at the University of Texas at El Paso explain why one of the two speaks English with Anglo pronunciations, the other with Chicano pronunciations.

Thompson, Roger M. 1974. "The 1970 U.S. Census and Mexican American Language Loyalty: A Case Study." In Bills, 1974, pp. 65-78. Despite apparent testimony to stable bilingualism in Austin, Texas, in the 1970 Census, a survey attending to the variable of childhood residence suggests that English is supplanting Spanish.

Thompson, Roger M. 1975. "Mexican-American English: Social Correlates of Regional Pronunciation." American Speech, 50 (1-2): 18-24. Mexican-American men interviewed in Austin were fairly evenly divided among speakers of Standard English, Regional English, and Standard but Spanish-influenced English; very few had both Regional English (fronting of diphthong /ay/) and Spanish-influenced English (devoicing of word-final [z]).

Valdés-Fallis, Guadalupe. 1978. Code Switching and the Classroom Teacher. Language in Education: Theory and Practice 4. Arlington, Va.: Center for Applied Linguistics.

Wald, Benji. 1979. "Limitations on the Variable Rule Applied to Bilingual Phonology: The Unmerging of the Voiceless Palatal Phonemes in the English of Mexican-Americans in the Los Angeles Area." Paper presented at NWAVE 9; in press. A study of working-class adults shows overlap but differentiation of [š] and [č] in East Los Angeles. Detailed discussion of the nature of the variable rule.

Williams, Frederick, Robert Hopper, and Diana S. Natalicio. 1977. The Sounds of Children. Englewood Cliffs, N.J.: Prentice-Hall. With accompanying

recordings. For non-experts; avoids technical
terminology. Gives many examples of children's
speech, including that of the native, Spanish-
speaking child. Suggested activities. Many photos.
Usefully non-intimidating for beginners.

DISSERTATIONS

Brekke, George. 1973. "Evaluational Reactions of
     Adolescent and Pre-Adolescent Mexican-American and
     Anglo-American Students to Selected Samples of Spoken
     English." Ph.D. University of Minnesota at
     Minneapolis St. Paul.

Brennan, Eileen Mary Muench. 1977. "Mexican-American
     Accented English: Phonological Analysis, Accent
     Scaling, and Evaluative Reactions." Ph.D. University
     of Notre Dame, Notre Dame, Indiana. DAI, 38 (3):
     1434B.

Carranza, Michael Anthony. 1977. "Language Attitudes and
     Other Cultural Attitudes of Mexican-American Adults:
     Some Sociolinguistic Implications." Ph.D. University
     of Notre Dame, Notre Dame, Indiana. DAI, 38 (3):
     1693A.

Carter, Ruth Barrera. 1976. "A Study of Attitudes:
     Mexican-American and Anglo-American Elementary
     Teachers' Judgments of Mexican-American Bilingual
     Children's Speech." Ed.D. University of Houston,
     Houston, Texas. DAI, 37 (8): 4941A.

Cohen, Andrew David. 1973. "Innovative Education for La
     Raza: A Sociolinguistic Assessment of a Bilingual
     Education Program in California." Ph.D. Stanford
     University, Stanford, California. DAI, 33 (12):
     6582-6583A.

De la Zerda, Nancy. "Employment Interviewers' Reactions
     to Mexican-American Speech." Ph.D. University of
     Texas at Austin.

Elias-Olivares, Lucia Ernestina. 1976. "Ways of Speaking
     in a Chicano Community: A Sociolinguistic
     Approach." Ph.D. University of Texas at Austin.
     DAI, 37 (5): 2829A.

Hartford, Beverly Ann Slattery. 1975. "The English of
     Mexican-American Adolescents in Gary, Indiana: A
     Sociolinguistic Description." Ph.D. University of
     Texas at Austin. DAI, 36 (5): 2778A.

Hernández-Chavez, Eduardo. 1977. "The Acquisition of
    Grammatical Structures by a Mexican-American Child
    Learning English." Ph.D. University of California,
    Berkeley. DAI, 38 (11): 6689A.

Mahoney, Mary. 1967. "Spanish and English Usage by
    Mexican-American Families in Two South Texas
    Counties." M.A. Texas A&M University, College
    Station.

Merino, Barbara Jean. 1976. "Language Acquisition in
    Bilingual Children: Aspects of Syntactic Development
    in English and Spanish by Chicano Children in Grades
    K-4." Ph.D. Stanford University, Stanford,
    California. DAI, 37 (10): 6319A.

Natalicio, Eleanor Diana Siedhoff. 1969. "Formation of
    the Plural in English: A Study of Native Speakers of
    English and Native Speakers of Spanish." Ph.D.
    University of Texas at Austin. DAI, 30 (7): 2993A.

Overall, Patricia Montiel. 1978. "An Assessment of the
    Communicative Competence in English of
    Spanish-speaking Children in the Fourth and Sixth
    Grades." Ph.D. Stanford University, Stanford,
    California. DAI, 39 (6): 3428A.

Ramirez, Arnulfo Gonzalez. 1974. "The Spoken English of
    Spanish-speaking Pupils in a Bilingual and
    Monolingual School Setting: An Analysis of Syntactic
    Development." Ph.D. Stanford University, Stanford,
    California. DAI, 35 (6): 3401-3402A.

Rodrigues, Raymond J. 1974. "A Comparison of the Written
    and Oral English Syntax of Mexican-American Bilingual
    and Anglo-American Monolingual Fourth and Ninth Grade
    Students (Las Vegas, New Mexico)." Ph.D. University
    of New Mexico, Albuquerque. DAI, 35 (9): 6123-6124A.

Sánchez, Rosaura Arteaga. 1974. "A Generative Study of
    Two Spanish Dialects." Ph.D. University of Texas at
    Austin. DAI, 35 (5): 2971A.

Sawyer, Janet Beck Moseley. 1957. "A Dialect Study of San
    Antonio, Texas: A Bilingual Community." Ph.D.
    University of Texas at Austin. DA, 18 (2): 586.

Thompson, Roger Mark. 1971. "Language Loyalty in Austin,
    Texas: A Study of a Bilingual Neighborhood." Ph.D.
    University of Texas, Austin. DAI, 32 (11): 6408A.

Tipton, Robert Lee. 1974. "Sociological Correlates of
    English Proficiency." Ph.D. University of Texas at
    Austin. DAI, 35 (1): 436A.

Valadez-Love, Concepción Monreal. 1976. "The Acquisition
      of English Syntax by Spanish-English Bilingual
      Children." Ph.D. Stanford University, Stanford,
      California. DAI, 37 (10): 6452A.